Controlling Institutions

How is the United States able to control the IMF with only 17 per cent of the votes? How are the rules of the global economy made? This book shows how a combination of formal and informal rules explain how international organizations really work. Randall W. Stone argues that formal rules apply in ordinary times, while informal power allows leading states to exert control when the stakes are high. International organizations are therefore best understood as equilibrium outcomes that balance the power and interests of the leading state and the member countries. Presenting a new model of institutional design and comparing the IMF, WTO and EU, Stone argues that institutional variations reflect the distribution of power and interests. He shows that US interests influence the size, terms and enforcement of IMF programs, and new data, archival documents and interviews reveal the shortcomings of IMF programs in Mexico, Russia, Korea, Indonesia and Argentina.

RANDALL W. STONE is Professor of Political Science at the University of Rochester. He is the author of *Lending Credibility: The International Monetary Fund and the Post-Communist Transition* (2002) and *Satellites and Commissars: Strategy and Conflict in the Politics of Soviet-Bloc Trade* (1996). His articles have appeared in the *American Political Science Review*, *International Organization*, *International Studies Quarterly*, *Journal of Conflict Resolution*, *Review of International Organizations* and *Global Environmental Politics*.

Controlling Institutions

International Organizations and the Global Economy

RANDALL W. STONE

CAMBRIDGE UNIVERSITY PRESS
Cambridge, New York, Melbourne, Madrid, Cape Town, Singapore,
São Paulo, Delhi, Dubai, Tokyo, Mexico City

Cambridge University Press
The Edinburgh Building, Cambridge CB2 8RU, UK

Published in the United States of America by Cambridge University Press, New York

www.cambridge.org
Information on this title: www.cambridge.org/9780521183062

First published 2011

Printed in the United Kingdom at the University Press, Cambridge

A catalogue record for this publication is available from the British Library

ISBN 978-1-107-00540-2 Hardback
ISBN 978-0-521-18306-2 Paperback

To Norma and Robert Koenig

Contents

List of figures

List of tables

Preface

As I write these words, the international economy is emerging from its most serious crisis since the Second World War. The Great Recession began in the US housing market, but quickly spread through the global network of financial institutions to affect every country in the world, most much more severely than the United States. The crisis has underscored weaknesses that had become apparent earlier in the institutions that govern the global economy – the International Monetary Fund (IMF, or the Fund), the World Trade Organization (WTO) and the European Union (EU); each of these institutions suffers from a severe crisis of legitimacy and effectiveness. Sweeping changes have been proposed in the architecture of international governance, and significant reforms have been introduced in the IMF and the EU. Meanwhile, politics continues: many states are seeking unilateral or bilateral rather than multilateral policy solutions, and the existing international governance mechanisms appear to be inconsistent with the changing distribution of global power.

The IMF responded to the impact of the crisis in some of the peripheral countries, including Belarus, Hungary, Iceland, Latvia, Pakistan, Romania, Ukraine, and finally Greece, but its resources were woefully inadequate to address the problems in the core countries. As the crisis deepened, the IMF's leading members tripled the size of its available resources, but it was apparent that states and their central banks remained the major players in international finance. The EU was challenged by the depth of the financial crisis in its poorer members, which seemed to threaten the stability of the euro zone and called for coordinated responses that were slow to emerge. As a result, a renewed debate arose about changing EU governance mechanisms. It remains to be seen what the effects of the crisis will be on the trade regime, where the WTO has developed into a robust legal regime for adjudicating disputes, but has been unable to advance an agenda of liberalizing trade and investment rules since the close of the Uruguay Round. Each of these institutions is profoundly affected by shifts in the distribution of global economic power, each is struggling to establish its legitimacy, and each is continuously reforming itself.

This project began as a study of the governance mechanisms of the IMF, but as the principles behind IMF governance emerged, it became clear that the argument applied broadly to international organizations of all sorts. In 2007, the Independent Evaluation Office of the IMF asked me to write an evaluation of IMF governance during financial crises of systemic importance to the world economy. As a temporary insider, I was granted access to reams of fascinating documents and was given a guided tour through the corridors of power at the Fund.[1] Perhaps most importantly, I had the opportunity to interact on a daily basis with Fund personnel and test my hypotheses against the accumulated experience of numerous careers in the IMF. As the author of a previous book and several articles on the IMF, I thought of myself as a bit of an expert on the subject, but I soon learned that many of my preconceived notions were erroneous. In particular, I had long been aware that the United States exercised a great deal of influence in the IMF, but I had never really asked the question, how is it that a country with (now almost) 17 percent of the votes can exert so much control? Once I learned the answer, I felt that I had to write this book; and along the way, I discovered that the answer shed a lot of light on other institutions, including ones that are deliberately designed to be quite different from the IMF. I framed my emerging understanding in the form of a formal model that is broadly applicable to international organizations, and indeed to many other sorts of organizations. The project gradually developed into a book about international organizations that treats the IMF as a focal case rather than a book about the IMF and financial crises.

Some readers (including one anonymous reviewer) may be suspicious of the claim that a single model of informal governance can explain essential features of the politics of diverse international organizations. I suspect, and indeed hope, that the reviewer has struck upon a question that will arise whenever the book is discussed. Most critics will concede the empirical analysis and description of the IMF case, which inspired the model, but may question the claims that the logic of informal governance works in similar ways in diverse institutional settings, and that the model illuminates the reasons for institutions for different issue areas to be structured in different ways. Had I wanted to write an uncontroversial book, I could have done so by scaling back my claims to the least common denominator that would evoke general agreement. However, I would miss the opportunity to draw what I think is the essential insight from the model, which is that institutional design is largely determined by the

[1] As a condition of this access, I was required to maintain the anonymity of my interview subjects. I apologize for the consequent lack of transparency in the footnotes.

balance of power and interests – in a precise way that the model delineates – rather than by technocratic efficiency.

More broadly, the book contradicts the conventional wisdom among students of international organizations that these institutions are efficient by design and designed to minimize transaction costs.[2] This view reflects a strong intellectual tradition in the economics of organization,[3] and a very influential strain of research in international relations variously described as institutionalism, neoliberalism, or neofunctionalism.[4] I argue that institutional design is mainly a matter of balancing power and interests rather than of minimizing costs. While realists in international relations have long suspected as much, they have never had anything very precise or rigorous to say on the subject.

The last part of the book conducts a detailed empirical study of IMF lending using new data and a series of case studies focusing on financial crises in Mexico (1995), Indonesia (1997), Korea (1997), Russia (1998) and Argentina (2001). Readers may be surprised to find how decisively the United States controls the size of IMF loans, the conditions attached to them and their enforcement. This is an important empirical claim of this book, which will surprise some experts on the IMF. There is a substantial literature that has focused on US manipulation of the IMF, but it is generally believed that the G-7 countries share control of the Fund broadly, and it came as a surprise to me to discover the degree of US dominance of important lending decisions as I investigated the individual cases. This, in turn, was confirmed by statistical analysis with a global sample. My analysis could not always reject the hypothesis that other G-5 countries affected the size, terms and enforcement of IMF programs, but generally did so. When other G-5 countries had an effect, it was generally much weaker than the effect of US influence. Whenever a strong comparative test was possible because the measures of US influence and G-5 influence were not highly correlated, the results supported the hypothesis of US influence and rejected the hypothesis of G-5 influence. I published some of the first systematic evidence that the IMF was manipulated by countries other than the United States in an article about Africa in 2004, but revisiting those results, I found that French influence over the terms of IMF programs appears to be limited strictly to Africa, parts of which have been ceded by the United States as a *de facto* French sphere of influence.

Along the way, I have accumulated a large number of intellectual debts. Many of the people I mention here will disagree with some of the arguments I advance, and none of them are responsible for my interpretation of my

[2] Koremenos *et al.* 2001; Hawkins *et al.* 2006.
[3] Williamson 1985; Milgrom and Roberts 1992.
[4] Keohane 1984; Milner and Moravcsik 2009.

findings or for any mistakes I may have made. However, they have improved the final product immensely with their comments, criticism, and occasional opposition. It was an extraordinary opportunity to work closely with the staff of the IEO, and particularly with Ruben Lamdany. I am grateful to former and current IMF officials for their cooperation in providing interviews and access to documents, to the IEO for its support and valuable input from its staff, and to Borislava Mircheva and Roxana Pedraglio for valuable research assistance. In addition, Leonardo Martinez-Diaz, Ruben Lamdany, Thomas Bernes, Nils Bjorksten, Mariano Cortes, Iqbal Zaidi and Borislava Mircheva provided valuable comments and numerous critical insights. The IEO operates within narrow parameters as a unit of the IMF, and in the end it was decided that my paper was too sensitive for them to publish.[5] However, I have immense respect for the people who try to evaluate the IMF from the inside, and I believe their research has led to numerous important findings.

I have been privileged to be able to present my findings over the last two years at some of the top political science departments in the United States, and I wish to thank the faculty and students at Princeton, Harvard, Yale, UCSD, Duke, Tufts, and Rochester for their penetrating questions and comments. I presented this work at the Conference on the Political Economy of International Organizations, the International Political Economy Society, and the Political Economy of International Finance, and at conferences at Beijing University and Jagiellonian University in Kraków, and I thank the audience members for their probing questions and valuable suggestions. Special thanks go to Graham Bird, Lawrence Broz, Clifford Carruba, Mark Copelovitch, Gary Cox, Christina Davis, Axel Dreher, Jeffrey Dunhoff, Simon Hug, Judith Kelley, Robert Keohane, Mareike Kleine, David Lake, Helen Milner, Timothy McKeown, Ashoka Mody, Andrew Moravcsik, Layna Mosley, Thomas Oatley, Eric Reinhardt, Kenneth Scheve, Christina Schneider, Beth Simmons, Branislav Slantchev, James Vreeland, Thomas Willett and several anonymous reviewers. I have received copious suggestions on selected chapters from Deniz Aksoy, Christina Davis, Jeffrey Dunhoff, Alexandra Hennessey, Simon Hug, Bob Keohane, Mareike Kleine and Christina Schneider. Above all, I thank my graduate and undergraduate students at the University of Rochester, who have forced me to hone my arguments. Several of them have served as research assistants at various stages, including Jeffrey Arnold, Youngchae Lee, Jeffrey Marshall and Martin Steinwand. I thank Jeffrey Marshall in addition for typesetting the book in LaTeX. Surjya Ray designed the cover, and I thank CBC for permission to use the photograph. The cover depicts a protest in Thessaloniki, Greece, on May 2,

[5] A summary of the findings was published in Stone 2009a, and is available at www.ieo-imf.org/eval/complete/pdf/05212008/BP08_14.pdf.

2010, after the Greek government announced the policy conditions attached to the agreement by the IMF and euro zone members to extend 110 billion euros in loans. The slogan on the central banner translates as "Down with the Junta of PASOK [the initials of the governing socialist party] – EU – IMF," leaving little doubt about how the protestors felt about multilateral institutions.

I wish to thank the publishers of some of my articles for allowing me to draw on them for short passages from my 2004 *APSR* article, my 2008 *IO* article, my 2008 *RIO* article, and my chapter in Milner and Moravcsik.[6] One table and one figure are adapted from the 2008 *IO* article. All of the data analysis is new for the book. My discussion of the Russia case in Chapter 8 draws heavily on my previous Princeton University Press book, *Lending Credibility* (2002), but all the other cases are based on new research.

[6] Stone 2009b.

List of abbreviations

APD	Asia and Pacific Department, IMF
CAFTA	Central American Free Trade Area
CAP	Common Agricultural Policy
CDU	Christian Democratic Union (German)
CFF	Compensatory Financing Facility
EC	European Community
ECB	European Central Bank
EcoFin	Council of Economic and Finance Ministers
ED	Executive Director, IMF
EEC	European Economic Community
EFF	Extended Fund Facility, IMF
EMS	European Monetary System
EMU	Economic and Monetary Union
ESAF	Extended Structural Adjustment Facility, IMF
EU	European Union
G-7	Group of Seven
G-10	Group of Ten
G-20	Group of Twenty
GATT	General Agreement on Tariffs and Trade
IBRD	International Bank for Reconstruction and Development
IEO	Independent Evaluation Office, IMF
IMF	International Monetary Fund
IMFC	International Monetary and Financial Committee
MFN	Most Favored Nation status
MTS	Medium Term Strategy
NAFTA	North American Free Trade Area
OECD	Organization for Economic Cooperation and Development
PDR	Policy Development and Review Department, IMF

PRGF	Poverty Reduction and Growth Facility, IMF
PTA	Preferential Trade Agreement
QMV	Qualified Majority Voting
SAF	Structural Adjustment Facility, IMF
SBA	Stand-By Arrangement, IMF
SEA	Single European Act of 1986
SPD	Social Democratic Party of Germany
SPE	Subgame Perfect Equilibrium
UN	United Nations
UNSC	United Nations Security Council
WHD	Western Hemisphere Department, IMF
WTO	World Trade Organization

1

Introduction: international organization and US power

Government is gradually replacing anarchy in the international system, and international governance is largely accomplished by means of international organizations. International organizations have proliferated, have expanded in membership, have acquired new legal enforcement powers, and have extended their reach into the details of domestic political economy in their member states. A few, including the International Monetary Fund (IMF, or the Fund), command significant resources and wield considerable authority. International organizations are emerging as important actors in their own right, but they also remain potent power resources for influential states. The informal power that a leading state can exert through international organizations plays an important role in US foreign policy.

By the beginning of the twenty-first century, international organizations had become an essential instrument of effective statecraft even for the most powerful state in the system, and for most other states under most circumstances, they were the only forums in which anything could be accomplished. International organizations are useful, to powerful and weak states alike, because they can extend credibility and legitimacy to efforts that would otherwise lack credibility and legitimacy. This often makes the difference that makes multilateral cooperation feasible; and the challenges posed by an increasingly interdependent global economy typically demand coordinated responses.

The legitimacy and independence of international organizations are always provisional, because they exist in a system of states, and states enjoy very unequal power resources. In order to assure the participation of the most powerful states, international institutions have developed informal procedures that accommodate their interests. States with attractive outside options cannot commit to abide by disadvantageous rules when their preferences are intense. However, when powerful states abuse their informal prerogatives, they undermine the legitimacy and usefulness of international organizations. Any characterization of the role of an international organization in the system, therefore, is a snapshot of a dynamic process, as its informal internal procedures and its external legitimacy and functions change in response to state strategies. In the post-Cold War world, most shocks to the system originated in the foreign policy interests of the leading state, the United States; but even this is changing as the distribution of power shifts.

International organizations are compelled to navigate the treacherous vortex created by US power. If they stray too far from the current, they become irrelevant to US policy, and may find themselves adrift; yet if they are captured by the US policy preoccupations of the moment, they risk losing their legitimacy. An example of the first tendency is the United Nations Security Council, which the United States has marginalized when it failed to support US policies in the former Yugoslavia and Iraq. An example of the latter is the IMF, which has become so tilted towards US preferences that it has lost much of its legitimacy in the developing world. Organizations of which the United States is not a member, such as the European Union (EU), face similar dilemmas with respect to their own most powerful members, as Germany and France have repeatedly demonstrated. However, in the absence of a single dominant member, informal governance is more broadly shared and negotiated among a handful of major players.[1]

The existence of power politics, the frequency of informal manipulation and the possibility of forum shopping by powerful states put important limits on the autonomy of international organizations. Far from marginalizing international organizations, however, these practices highlight their significance as instruments of state power. Even in the field of international security, where states guard their freedom of action most jealously, international organizations play a key mediating role. Despite its global military reach, the United States finds that the use of force is less costly and more effective when employed in conjunction with an international organization. In international trade, the United States has attractive outside options and can often exert more leverage through bilateral bargaining than through the World Trade Organization (WTO); yet the WTO can also serve as an effective fulcrum. Indeed, US influence inside and outside the WTO often complement each other. In international finance, the United States remains the most important player because it issues the global reserve currency, but the integration of global capital markets makes multilateral coordination necessary to manage contagion during financial crises. Furthermore, constitutional barriers generally prevent the United States from reacting to financial crises that originate beyond its borders with the speed or resources

[1] Moravcsik 1998.

that the IMF is able to muster.[2] In each case, international organizations are deeply influenced by US power, but US power also rests in large part upon the ability to influence international organizations.

For all other states in the international system, the choices are starker. Only American elites seriously question the significance of international organizations, because only the United States is able to exercise attractive unilateral options. In some cases, members of the EU are able to exercise an effective threat of exit from another organization by acting as a group; but they are able to do so only because their commitment to the EU is so strong. For European, Japanese, Chinese, Russian and Brazilian elites, the geography of the international system is defined by the opportunities and constraints created by international institutions. Most foreign policy objectives can only be achieved by working through international organizations, and this is increasingly true of domestic policy objectives as well.[3] As these countries become increasingly integrated into the world economy, and the world economy places increasing burdens on the global environment, the number of fundamental national interests that can only be achieved through international organizations expands. These states have only limited informal influence within international organizations, but their membership and formal privileges in international organizations represent significant elements of their national power.

International organizations loom still larger in the calculations of poor countries with weak states, which are most vulnerable to internal conflict and most exposed to the vicissitudes of global markets. In these countries, international organizations are often important players in domestic politics. They can cause governments to fall, or prop them up; they can create irresistible pressure to carry out policy reforms; they can forge or shatter political coalitions.[4] Leaders of these countries find that the only way to exert effective leverage over international organizations is to appeal to the leading states in the system – usually, to the United States – to exert informal influence on their behalf. This intervention tends to undermine the credibility and autonomy of the interna-

2 In the aftermath of the 1995 Mexican peso crisis, Congress imposed limitations on the use of the Treasury's Exchange Stabilization Fund, which had been used as a line of credit for Mexico. In 2008 and 2009 the United States helped to contain the spread of the global financial crisis by lending freely, particularly to Europe and to South Korea, but this was done by the Federal Reserve through exchange swaps, and the Federal Reserve is legally independent of presidential control.

3 Even apparent exceptions seem to reinforce this generalization. The Russian clash with Georgia in August 2008 demonstrated a willingness to use force unilaterally and showcased the rebounding capabilities of the Russian military, but came at a cost that earlier Russian leaders would have been unwilling to pay in terms of isolation from Europe and hardening of NATO. In recognition of this isolation, Russia suspended its long-standing application to join the WTO, which it had made numerous political concessions to advance.

4 Pop-Eleches 2009.

tional organization involved, which may weaken its legitimacy *vis-à-vis* third parties.[5] It also comes at a cost to the client state, because the United States extracts political concessions in return for its intervention, and these concessions may reduce the legitimacy of the organization in the eyes of the client state's population.

The shifting architecture of international governance

At the time of writing, the United States remains the unchallenged leader of the international financial system, but the most severe weaknesses in its financial system and external accounts since the Great Depression and the largest fiscal deficits as a share of output since the Second World War threaten to erode this dominance in the future. Meanwhile, the United States has come to share hegemony in international trade, first with Europe, and subsequently more broadly with a coalition that includes major developing countries. The EU has consolidated its internal authority and expanded its membership, but the positions of its strongest members have slipped in the hierarchy of world power and in relation to other European countries. Substantial weight in the world economy and in international relations has shifted to the largest countries in the developing world, including China, India and Brazil. Both the formal and the informal mechanisms of international organizations are shifting to accommodate these new realities. This book looks backwards to explain the functioning of international organizations, but as soon as the pattern comes into focus, the landscape begins to change.

The international financial institutions are a rapidly moving target. A patchwork of institutions covers various aspects of the financial landscape, including the IMF, with primary lender-of-last-resort responsibilities; the World Bank and various regional multilateral development banks that share responsibility for promoting economic development and related objectives; and the Bank for International Settlements, Organization for Economic Cooperation and Development and a network of standard-setting agencies that perform regulatory functions. This schematic description is simplified, as the various agencies share many of their functions, coordinate with each other, duplicate efforts, and continuously reinvent themselves.

The IMF and the World Bank have evolved gradually for most of their history, although the pace of change has accelerated in response to recent events. The original division of labor between balance of payments support

[5] Steinwand and Stone 2008; Stone 2002, 2004, 2008.

and economic development has become blurred. As the club of net creditors has expanded and demand for financing has increased in the developing world more rapidly than the supply, the policy conditionality required by the IMF and the World Bank has escalated and become more comprehensive. Meanwhile, the net creditors constrained the growth of IMF resources so that they steadily declined as a share of world economic activity, which made co-financing of crisis programs by the Bank essential.[6] In response to the global financial crisis, however, they reversed this trend and approved a tripling of IMF resources in 2009, drawing the necessary financing mainly from the United States, Europe, Japan and China, and dramatically shifting the proportions of financing to the organization. The expansion did not increase IMF quotas, which are analogous to equity shares and are accompanied by voting rights, but instead expanded the Fund's lines of credit with major shareholders. At the time of writing, the implications of this change for the distribution of formal voting rights has not yet been determined, and how changes in formal authority will affect the informal governance of the Fund remains to be seen. However, it is clear that both formal and informal governance of the IMF will respond to the redistribution of economic resources that has been driven by rapid growth in the developing world.

The world trading system has experienced even more dramatic shifts. Established as an informal negotiating forum with no enforcement powers, the General Agreement on Tariffs and Trade was transformed at the conclusion of the Uruguay Round by the creation of the World Trade Organization (WTO) in 1995, accompanied by an expansive set of new rules covering trade in goods and services, intellectual property rights, and foreign investments. The story of how this came about is an interesting study in the use of informal power by the United States and the EU. The result is a formalized system of international trade litigation, the creation of a rapidly growing body of case law, and the emergence of judicial activism. The complexity of the legal landscape has increased dramatically, and the use of litigation to resolve trade disputes has rapidly expanded. Since the end of the Uruguay Round, however, there has been no further progress on trade treaties. An increasingly assertive group of developing countries, led by Brazil, India and China, has resisted efforts by the advanced industrial countries to assert an agenda of further liberalization, and has insisted on substantial progress in reforming trade in agriculture as a precondition for further progress on other fronts. Meanwhile, the industrialized countries have blocked progress on agriculture, which has led to stalemate in the Doha Trade Round. The center of gravity in international trade negotia-

[6] Gould 2006; Stone 2009c.

tions has moved from the WTO to a rapidly growing network of bilateral and regional trade and investment treaties, as countries with attractive outside options have sought alternative ways to exert leverage over their trading partners.

Parallel to the formal international organizations is a shifting set of groupings of privileged countries, which often set the agenda for the international organizations. Between the early 1970s and the end of the 1990s, the preeminent grouping was the G-7, consisting of the United States, Britain, France, Germany, Japan, Italy and Canada. While the G-7 summits of heads of state were often inconclusive, the informal negotiations that took place continuously at lower levels provided guidance to the IMF and defined the parameters for multilateral trade negotiations. The G-7 included countries that issued all of the major currencies, controlled the majority of IMF shares, and conducted the majority of world trade, so when they reached consensus they could generally rely on their ability to bring about a similar consensus in other international forums. Membership in the elite group was a valuable prerogative, which gave countries of middle rank a seat at the table that their closest rivals envied, but influence was by no means equally shared. The United States exercised substantial control over the agenda and enjoyed deference to its proposals, so that consensus operated differently than unanimity voting. For the marginal members of the club, Italy and Canada, admission came at the behest of France and the United States, respectively, and their diplomacy reflected their interest in assuring that the major players continued to regard the G-7 as a valuable instrument.[7] The leading power could gain leverage by forum shopping, or threatening to shift discussions from the G-7 to the G-5, G-10, or G-20.

The G-7 was substantially marginalized in the second George W. Bush administration, and many of the roles it played were replaced by the G-20. This represented an acknowledgment of a sea change in the distribution of world power, but it is significant that the United States was able to accomplish the transition rather effortlessly. Membership in the G-7 had always been valuable primarily because it was a club of the closest US colleagues, so the US announcement that it would henceforth negotiate with a wider grouping was irresistible. At the same time, the transition acknowledged a decline in US influence. US influence within international organizations rests on consensus among the major players, and as the share of world resources controlled by the major US allies declined relative to that of the largest countries in the developing world, the interests of the key players became more heterogeneous. The G-20 will not be as pliable as the G-7. For some purposes, as in IMF lending, G-7 finance ministers and their deputies continue to exert a controlling interest.

[7] Bayne and Putnam 1984.

However, it is significant that it was the G-20 rather than the G-7 that took the lead in coordinating international responses to the 2008 financial crisis. The expansion of IMF financing in 2009 was driven by the United States, but was adopted as a concrete goal by the G-20 summit in April.

Roadmap

This is a book about how international organizations really function, through a combination of formal and informal rules. The book's empirical core is based on extensive qualitative work in the IMF archives and interviews with IMF staff and executive directors, as well as quantitative work using the IMF's records of conditionality. The argument applies broadly to other international organizations, because informal governance is ubiquitous, but it applies with important variations. The terms of informal governance are negotiated differently in different contexts, and depend upon the distribution of issue-specific power and interests. The informal practices of institutions differ from their formal rules, and the varieties of governance respond to shifts in the distribution of power.

Chapter 2 outlines the book's main argument and explains how the mechanisms of informal governance relate to broad debates in political science about international power and legitimacy, on the one hand, and to the particular issues of delegation to international organizations and institutional design, on the other. The formal model developed in Chapter 3 defines the terms of the argument precisely and derives implications from it for institutional design, delegation, performance, and legitimacy.

Chapter 4 describes the formal and informal governance arrangements of the IMF, emphasizing the institutional features – a weak Executive Board and delegation to a strong management – that preserve a back channel that allows the United States to control the organization. Chapter 5 makes a similar qualitative analysis of the WTO, and Chapter 6 presents the case of the EU, illustrating the model's ability to shed light on the logic of institutional design. The model focuses on the use of exit options by powerful countries and informal influence outside formal channels, which are common features across the three institutions, although the balance of formal and informal governance varies substantially. The comparative statics of the model indicate that the degree of long-term conflict of interest among the members of an institution and the number of leading powers in its issue domain account for the variation in delegation across institutions and across issue areas within each institution.

While the three chapters in Part Two illustrate the logic of the theory qualitatively, Part Three turns to rigorous hypothesis testing and focuses on the IMF.

The three chapters that follow trace the course of an IMF program through its product cycle, from decisions about the amount of access allowed to IMF resources, to negotiations over conditionality, and on to enforcement of conditionality when programs go off track. The testable implications of the model are that US informal influence over the Fund should be observable when the United States pushes for exceptions to rules, that these exceptions should only be made for important countries, and that they should be made when the borrowing country has an urgent need for IMF financing. These claims are tested statistically using the Monitoring of Agreements Database (MONA), which contains the IMF's records of conditionality, including which conditions were implemented, modified or waived, and when programs were suspended. The mechanisms involved are illustrated with reference to five major financial crises: Mexico (1994–95), Indonesia (1997), South Korea (1997), Russia (1998) and Argentina (2001).

The concluding chapter returns to broad themes of legitimacy and change in international organizations. The model suggested that power and legitimacy interact in precise ways, and traces out the implications of two kinds of change: change in US structural power, and change in the range of temptations the United States faces to intervene. As American structural power declines, the United States is compelled to act with greater restraint in order to maintain the legitimacy of international organizations, and the role of formal governance in shaping the policies of these organizations should become more important. However, if the temptations that the United States faces to exploit its remaining informal influence rise as US structural power declines, the legitimacy of international organizations is likely to be jeopardized. There is striking evidence that this has occurred already in the IMF and the WTO.

PART ONE

THEORY

2

A theory of international organization

The relationship between power and legitimacy has been a central concern in the study of international politics since the time of Thucydides, which has reflected an appreciation that international order has both normative and material foundations. However, the concepts of power and legitimacy have generally been loosely defined, which has prevented the elaboration of fully-specified theories and slowed the development of cumulative knowledge. The first stage of the argument of this book is to develop precise definitions of legitimacy and power which can be used as the building blocks of a formal model. This chapter presents the general argument: power and legitimacy are related in a particular way, which relies on organizations that combine elements of formal and informal governance. In the following chapter, the argument is rendered in the form of a formal game-theoretic model. The argument applies to international organizations, to political systems, to corporate governance – in short, to all forms of organized political interaction. The conception of power that I offer in terms of outside options, however, is particularly potent in partially institutionalized settings, such as the anarchical international system or incompletely consolidated democracies.[1]

The building blocks of the model of informal governance are: (1) the existence of parallel formal and informal modes of governance; (2) legitimacy defined in terms of voluntary participation; and (3) contingent delegation.

Formal and informal governance

Formal rules facilitate social interactions, whether these interactions occur through markets, within hierarchically organized business firms, in political

1 Hirschman 1970.

systems, or in international relations. Rules help to resolve conflicts, assign property rights, and coordinate expectations. When rules persist, this is generally because they embody equilibrium expectations and facilitate mutually beneficial forms of exchange or cooperation; and although particular agents may be disadvantaged by the substantive content of the rules, the existence of rules rather than anarchy provides public benefits.[2] When the content of the rules becomes perceived as too disadvantageous to agents that have attractive outside options, however, the rules become illegitimate, and the predictable consequences are exit, war, or revolution.

Rules may be precise or imprecise. Imprecision provides advantages in some circumstances, as for example when the costs of compliance are uncertain and the credibility of enforcement is in question.[3] Nevertheless, the precision made possible by formal rules serves important social functions. Formal rules clarify, delineate, and adjudicate. Hard law is preferable in many instances to convention because it reduces uncertainty.[4] The existence of formal rules narrows the range of possible bargaining solutions, provides focal points to coordinate expectations, and reduces transaction costs.[5] The General Agreement on Tariffs and Trade (GATT) provides an example of the effectiveness of rules in reducing the incidence of conflict. Even before the creation of the WTO in 1995 introduced binding enforcement mechanisms, the Dispute Resolution Procedure under the GATT facilitated a remarkably high degree of compliance because the ability to resolve disputes through adjudication was valuable to the participants.[6] In a similarly anarchical environment, the need to resolve disputes and interpret contracts created a demand for "law merchants" in medieval times, which ultimately contributed to the consolidation of central authority in the state.[7]

The interpretation of rules and laws can be problematic, and is certainly very political, but constitutional arrangements generally provide mechanisms for determining who is empowered to make authoritative interpretations. In addition, the development of precedent and case law over time helps to reduce the uncertainty about how principles will be interpreted in the future, which makes it possible for agents to make deals even when many of the possible contingencies cannot be spelled out in any feasible contract. Norms, culture, and shared understandings facilitate cooperation in settings where contracts are incomplete. Norms allow agents who are empowered to adjudicate disputes to

[2] Calvert 2001.
[3] Downs *et al.* 1996.
[4] Abbott and Snidal 2000.
[5] Schelling 1960; Coase 1960.
[6] Reinhardt 2001.
[7] North and Weingast 1989.

credibly commit themselves to following general principles, which makes their decisions more predictable and less opportunistic.[8] All such informal understandings, however, are underpinned by formal rules about which actors are empowered to make authoritative interpretations.

Formal rules are an indispensable element of social organization. Nevertheless, all organizations operate at variance with their formal rules to some degree. A central argument of this book is that political institutions operate according to two sharply divergent sets of rules that can be invoked under different circumstances: formal rules and informal rules. Formal rules represent standard operating procedures – voting rules, property rights, a status quo distribution of costs and benefits – that prevail when the extraordinary procedures are not invoked. Formal rules may specify the conditions under which they may be suspended, as for example in constitutions with emergency powers clauses, or this may be a matter of informal understanding. In consolidated democratic systems, suspension of constitutional rules may be so rare as to be almost unthinkable. What happens off the equilibrium path, however, is an important feature of a democratic equilibrium.[9] The possibility of suspending formal rules allows powerful actors to safeguard their core interests. What is true of political institutions in general is central to the functioning of international organizations in particular. The existence of two parallel sets of rules allows international organizations to achieve a balance between the interests of powerful and weak states. The formal rules specify voting rights and legitimate procedures that embody a broad consensus of the membership, while the informal rules allow exceptional access for powerful states to set the agenda and control particular outcomes.

During ordinary times, an international organization produces predictable policies that reflect the distribution of formal voting rights among its members, and it enjoys discretion within its zone of delegation. However, the leading state – the "G1," as the United States is often called within the international financial institutions – may intervene and assume temporary control when urgent strategic objectives override its interest in the organization's long-term goals. Informal governance practices allow it to retain decisive influence in the organization while shedding most of the formal levers of power. Informal procedures may take a variety of forms. A leading state, like a large minority shareholder in a publicly held corporation, enjoys organizational advantages when it participates in decision making within international organizations: superior information, better access to the key agents, and greater cooperation with its requests. In addition, it can count on deference to its interests on the

[8] Kreps 1990.

[9] Przeworski 1991.

part of other states, which prefer to practice diffuse reciprocity rather than antagonize a leading power. If likely to lose a vote, furthermore, the leading state can generally shift the context to a more favorable forum, such as bilateral negotiations or a meeting of a small group of important countries, and present the results of prior coordination as a consensus decision. The precise modalities vary from institution to institution, but they share the common features that exerting informal influence is costly, and that the informal practices by which leading powers influence outcomes are impractical, if not impossible, for other countries to mimic.

There is a tension between formal and informal rules, but they also depend upon one another. International organizations are equilibrium outcomes that balance the power and interests of the leading state and the member countries, and institutional design – both its formal and its informal elements – is endogenous to this interaction. Although they can control particular outcomes, leading states generally prefer to avoid paying the costs necessary to do so, and they make concessions when they submit to international norms and legalized procedures. They anticipate that rulings will not always go in their favor, and they accept outcomes that are not as favorable as they might have negotiated on an ad hoc basis, because this makes multilateral cooperation attractive to less powerful states that might otherwise refuse to participate.

In order for weak and powerful agents to reach a mutually beneficial understanding in which the powerful give up formal power in return for informal power, it must be the case that the basis exists for an inter-temporal exchange. Powerful states, by definition, have attractive outside options, and therefore cannot commit to complying with rules when they must pay substantial costs in order to do so. Therefore, the informal rules must give them the option to exercise control when their interests are intense. Weaker states, however, are able to commit to rules, because their outside options are unattractive. Furthermore, they are willing to tolerate a degree of informal influence in return for receiving a larger share of formal power, because the participation of important states makes an international institution more valuable to all of the participants. This exchange is possible if interests are not too diametrically opposed in ordinary times, and if the shocks to the preferences of the powerful and weak countries are not too highly correlated. As long as the powerful country's interests are not too deeply wounded by ceding a share of formal power, and the weak country's interests are not too strongly affected by the cases that the powerful country regards as highly important, an institution that incorporates informal governance can be Pareto improving. This requires that there be some agreement about the general interests that the organization promotes, and that the states that are favored by the biases that are built into the organization's procedures do not have such strongly divergent interests that they negate the expected benefits.

In the case of the IMF, this exchange is facilitated because the United States and the other industrialized countries have broadly similar long-term financial interests. The major shareholders have a common interest in promoting prudent macroeconomic management, market-oriented economic reforms, and trade openness. However, the shareholders also have fluctuating short-term strategic interests in particular countries, and for the system leader these interests can be sufficiently intense to override its economic policy preferences. In order to make delegation and consensual decision making tolerable for the United States, therefore, the other leading states acquiesce in an arrangement that allows the United States to assume temporary control of the organization when its core interests are affected.

Informal mechanisms to support great-power manipulation of international institutions do not have to be explicitly designed; powerful states will always find a way to control outcomes of interest to them, if they are not explicitly prevented. Institutional design choices can make manipulation more or less costly, however. For example, institutions that are transparent are more costly to manipulate because the manipulation immediately becomes public knowledge, and may provoke indignant responses from other states or from the public. Similarly, decision-making procedures that allow for majority voting and debate are harder to manipulate than procedures that delegate decision making to agents. The designers of institutions, therefore, have important choices to make, and they generally do not opt for transparency or majority voting. These design choices are tacit concessions to powerful countries, which will not consent to delegate important functions to institutions that they cannot control. The most transparent and democratic of international institutions, such as the UN General Assembly and the European Parliament, are generally given very weak powers. The designers of the United Nations explicitly built in a veto in the Security Council to protect the interests of the great powers in the most important matters. There is substantial evidence, however, that informal influence is decisive within the Security Council as well.[10] Other institutions such as the international financial institutions and multilateral development banks make manipulation possible by shrouding their operations in secrecy, delegating authority to management, and weakening the oversight capabilities of their boards of directors. As I describe in Chapter 4, the IMF has a governance structure and operational procedures that give it substantial autonomy from most of its shareholders, while also minimizing the costs and publicity

[10] Voeten 2001; Kuziemko and Werker 2006.

when the United States chooses to exercise influence. The implication of this analysis is that autonomy, exceptional access and lack of transparency are not accidental; these are endogenous institutional features that reflect the balance of power and interests.

Legitimacy as voluntary participation

International organizations are useful to weak and powerful states alike only to the extent that they enjoy international legitimacy. An organization that elicited no voluntary cooperation from its members would be useless as an instrument. Powerful states could compel compliance only to the extent that they could do so using their own resources, in which case the institution would provide no benefits. In order for international institutions to serve anyone's interests, therefore, they must enjoy some minimal legitimacy, because they must elicit voluntary participation. The puzzle for a power-politics interpretation of international institutions is explaining why weak states consent to participate. Why should weak states participate in an arrangement skewed towards the interests of the strong, and why should secondary powers tolerate an arrangement that disproportionately favors the leader of the system?

The theory of the state has struggled with the same problem. Political order is impossible without some minimal consent of the governed. Indeed, legitimacy is part of a standard definition of the state still widely used in political science – the "monopoly of the legitimate use of force."[11] If states are categorically different from armed factions or criminal organizations, it is because they exercise a claim to represent legal authority within a particular territory. Coercion can substitute for legitimacy to some degree, but repression is costly and relies upon the willingness of some class of citizens to participate in the repression. The Communist police states of Eastern Europe relied on the external threat of Soviet intervention rather than domestic legitimacy, and they immediately collapsed when the external threat was removed in 1989. Even in extreme cases such as this, however, the functioning of society relied on a substantial amount of voluntary cooperation. There were, of course, strong incentives to cooperate. Professionals who refused to join the Communist Party limited the progress they could make in their careers. Dissidents faced severe repression, and those who fled abroad risked reprisals against their family members. However, the ordinary functioning of the state and the economy, even of a centrally planned command economy, required a substantial portion of the citizenry to

[11] Weber 1946 (1919).

voluntarily comply with laws, and enforce them, even when they were not being monitored. The East European economies did not function very well under Communism, and relied on massive subsidies from the Soviet Union, but the cost would have been too high for the Soviet Union to bear for four decades had the Communist regimes not been able to elicit voluntary compliance.[12]

Citizens comply with authority when compliance is more attractive than exercising outside options. If their outside options are extremely unattractive, this may be a low standard to meet. Thomas Hobbes famously argued that the alternative to obeying the Leviathan was a "war of all against all," a state of nature in which life was "nasty, brutish and short." Under those circumstances, the standard for legitimate government could not be set very high. Social contract theorists such as Locke and Rousseau argued that the citizen's outside options were considerably better, so they could expect more of the sovereign. Acemoglu and Robinson offer a formal model that neatly captures this debate. They model revolution as an outside option, and the public policies and constitutional constraints that emerge in equilibrium reflect the attractiveness of launching a revolution.[13] On one hand, the citizens' collective action problems strengthen the rulers' bargaining position, but on the other, inequality makes revolution attractive because of the possibility of redistribution. Democratic transitions occur – the elites give up formal power – because this is the only way elites can credibly commit to redistributing income.

In international relations, the weaker states' participation constraints may not be binding if the participation of major powers generates substantial externalities. For example, the WTO/GATT international trade regime diverts trade away from non-members, creating negative externalities that provide strong incentives to join the institution.[14] As the membership of these organizations has gradually grown, non-members have found it increasingly costly to remain excluded. This has driven down the participation constraint, so institutional insiders have been able to secure trade concessions from new entrants to the WTO that were much greater than they themselves had made in order to join. On the other hand, when the membership accumulates its own resources and becomes less dependent upon the leading power, exit options become more credible. Some of the larger developing countries enjoyed much greater bargaining leverage by 2000 than they had at the beginning of the 1990s, and were better able to resist the agenda proposed by the United States and the EU during the Doha Round of trade talks than they had been during the previous Uruguay Round.

[12] Stone 1996.
[13] Acemoglu and Robinson 2005.
[14] Oye 1992.

A participation constraint is a minimalist notion of legitimacy, which leaves out much of what we traditionally mean by the term. Legitimacy defined as voluntary participation does not necessarily imply fair procedures, fair substantive outcomes, transparency, or popular consent.[15] Legitimacy will be improved to the extent that organizations have these attributes, and their absence is a source of dissension; none of these is a prerequisite for order within a society of states, however.[16] What is necessary for an international organization to have this kind of minimalist legitimacy is that the leaders of states believe that voluntary participation in the organization and compliance with its norms and procedures will help them to achieve their objectives on average. This kind of legitimacy depends as much on the self-interested calculations of dictators as on the consent of democratic publics.

The United Nations Security Council (UNSC, or the Security Council) is a useful case in point. The Security Council is generally understood to have a legitimate right to approve the international use of force. National leaders act as if its sanction is important: François Mitterand insisted that France could not support the first Gulf War in 1991 without UNSC approval, and Tony Blair insisted on an effort to obtain UNSC approval for the second in 2003. Public opinion surveys taken around the world are more supportive of proposed uses of force that obtain UNSC sanction. However, the UNSC does not enjoy legitimacy because its decisions follow legal precedent faithfully (they do not), or because it follows transparent and uncorrupt procedures (it does not). Its decisions are based on political expediency rather than legal norms, and vote buying is rampant.[17] Nor is the UNSC legitimate because of the representativeness of its membership, which is questionable, or the popular sovereignty of its members, some of which are undemocratic. The kind of legitimacy the UNSC achieves has more to do with voluntary participation – or at least acquiescence – than with participatory democracy.[18]

In order to secure their participation, weak states must be compensated in some way for the losses they incur when powerful states exert informal control. Because great powers cannot commit to refrain from exerting extraordinary influence when their core interests are engaged, they can only compensate weak states by giving them a greater share of decision-making power during ordinary times. Therefore, weak states must receive a share of formal power that is out of proportion to their resources. Multilateral decision-making procedures are

[15] Buchanan and Keohane 2004.
[16] Bull 1977.
[17] Kuziemko and Werker 2006.
[18] Voeten 2005.

a deliberate institutional design that allows powerful states to credibly transfer control over routine bargaining.[19]

The negotiation over vote shares in the IMF in 1944 is a case in point. The United States controlled the only convertible currency during the Second World War, it financed the allied war effort, and most of the future members of what became the IMF were denied a seat at the table at Bretton Woods because they were occupied powers or military opponents. The negotiations over institutional design were carried out between the United States and Great Britain at a point when Britain's dependence on the United States was maximized. It was clear that the United States would have to provide the bulk of the resources for any cooperative monetary arrangements after the war, and that the contributions of other countries, even Britain, would be only symbolic at the outset. Under these circumstances, the United States could have constructed a wide range of institutional forms. However, the chief US negotiator, Harry Dexter White, took the matter of the legitimacy of the institution very seriously. The US intention at the outset of the negotiations was to make vote shares and quotas in the new organization strictly proportional to financial contributions in hard currency, which would have given the United States approximately sixty percent of the votes. However, in order to secure wider participation in the arrangement, the United States negotiators agreed to limit their vote share to thirty percent. White explained his thinking as follows:

> To accord voting power strictly proportionate to the value of the subscription would give the one or two powers control over the Fund. To do that would destroy the truly international character of the Fund, and seriously jeopardize its success. Indeed it is very doubtful if many countries would be willing to participate in an international organization with wide powers if one or two countries were able to control its policies.[20]

From the beginning, the legitimacy of the IMF was conceived as a participation constraint.

US vote share in the IMF has gradually declined as the membership has expanded and the economic recovery after the war and subsequent development gave other countries substantial resources to contribute. The entrance of new members eroded US vote shares, and successive rounds of quota revisions shifted more of the voting weight to Europe and Japan. However, US voting power has never been as low relative to its share of net contributions as it was at the outset, when only the United States and Canada were in a position to play the role of net creditors.

[19] Ruggie 1993.
[20] Gold 1972, 19, cited in Woods 2006, 23.

Contingent delegation

The familiar realist argument about international institutions is that states do not delegate authority to international organizations because they fear that cooperation will allow their rivals to make disproportional gains in military power.[21] This logic applies only to intense, bipolar military rivalries, where the use of force is likely and there are no incentives to cooperate with some rivals in order to compete with others.[22] In relationships in which the use of force is very unattractive, and which are characterized by substantial externalities so that cooperation is valuable, states have proven themselves willing to delegate substantial authority to international institutions.[23] As a result, international relations have become highly legalized in recent decades, and the features of international organizations have become important elements in the diplomatic repertoire.

A more sophisticated power politics argument is that international organizations are simply tools in the arsenals of powerful states. In this view, the formal governance mechanisms of international institutions are components of a polite fiction that hides their true purposes. Stephen Krasner argued during the 1980s that the scope for multilateral cooperation was severely limited because of the sharp divergence between the interests of developed countries in open markets and the interests of developing countries in shielding themselves from market volatility. International institutions, he argued, simply represented the interests of the powerful states.[24] The dramatic expansion of multilateral institutions that followed surprised Krasner, as it surprised most astute observers; but a cynic could still argue that it reflected the expanded power and influence of the United States after the Cold War more than any new legitimacy of the institutions themselves. To the extent that international regimes, international law, or other institutional arrangements mattered at all, they were epiphenomenal, because they reflected the underlying distribution of power.[25]

A closely related argument is that powerful states are able to avoid the use of overt coercion, which is costly, by means of subtler strategies that structure the incentives that other states face. Susan Strange argued that the United States exerted a much greater degree of influence in the international system than was at first apparent because it was able to create incentives for other states to act in ways that advanced its interests on their own initiative.[26] The creation and

21 Waltz 1979; Mearsheimer 2001.
22 Powell 1991; Snidal 1991.
23 Keohane and Nye 1977.
24 Krasner 1985.
25 Krasner 1983, 1999.
26 Strange 1988.

design of international institutions was one important aspect of this strategy, so that the apparent consensus and cooperation that arose in multilateral settings was really a symptom of effectively exercised hegemony. Where liberal scholars have tended to see cooperation in the international system, realists have seen domination, albeit a domination that was cloaked in a prudent regard for the interests of subordinate states.[27]

These arguments share some features with the argument developed in this book, but I want to draw a clear distinction between the power-politics view of international institutions and the theory of informal governance. The argument made here is quite distinct. The claim is that modes of formal and informal governance are robust and exist side by side, rather than that informal governance eclipses formal governance or renders it insubstantial. Indeed, in the international system, formal and informal governance represent two sides of a social contract between strong and weak states, and the equilibrium outcome requires that both parties benefit enough from their interactions to make the contract profitable. If weaker states were not convinced that the privileges of the powerful would be invoked sparingly, the entire architecture of international cooperation would crumble; and the more frequently these privileges are invoked, the more formal influence the powerful must cede in order to secure the consent of the governed.

However, powerful states are powerful by virtue of the fact that they have attractive outside options. In the language of economics, the opportunity cost of participating in an international organization is high when it is possible to achieve one's objectives unilaterally. When actors have attractive outside options and their preferences are strong, they cannot commit themselves to abiding by rules. Therefore, the commitment of powerful states to international law is always provisional, and in this sense, the delegation of authority to international institutions is always contingent. When powerful states perceive their critical interests to be jeopardized, they refuse to be constrained. Consequently, international organizations have evolved emergency override procedures that allow the great powers to assume control when their interests are intense in order to maintain their commitment to the game.

In a similar way, rulers who hold attractive extra-legal options can extract deference from elected legislators in authoritarian states and transitional regimes, and military officers can influence the behavior of elected officials in states that are vulnerable to military coups. The German Reichstag deferred to the kaiser on foreign policy and defense issues, because the kaiser possessed the extra-legal option of dissolving the Reichstag if it challenged his prerogatives on

[27] Gilpin 1981.

critical issues.[28] To take a more recent example, the Erdogan government of Turkey elected in 2003 exercised restraint rather than impose its preferred set of Islamic religious reforms, which might provoke a coup by the secular officer corps of the Turkish army.[29] In this sense, the outside options controlled by the kaiser or Turkish military officers – even if they are never exercised – play an important role in defining the equilibrium behavior of political actors and determining the significance of legal institutions. The substantive significance of these informal understandings can shift abruptly, however, if the attractiveness of the outside option changes. The understandings that General Augusto Pinochet relied upon to protect him in retirement after the transition to democracy in Chile rapidly eroded once it became clear that the army would not intervene to protect him. Similarly, the practical significance of the formal institutional arrangements negotiated at the Polish Roundtable in 1989 shifted dramatically during the summer and fall as it became clearer that the Soviet Union would not support an effort to reestablish Communism in Poland by force.

Each of these examples illustrates the way in which outside options interact with formal administrative arrangements to determine the practical distribution of authority. In this sense, the realist distinction between anarchy and hierarchy[30] could not be further from the truth, because every hierarchy incorporates elements of anarchy. Equilibrium play of the game depends upon the attractiveness of outside options that are not exercised. International organization is possible because international law does not consist only of "brittle stalks," which powerful states have to shatter in order to achieve their objectives.[31] Instead, it consists of flexible, evolving mechanisms that accommodate great-power interests when they flare acutely and temper them when they subside.

Delegation and institutional design

If international governance is to be provided over a particular issue area, an institutional design must be chosen. Should the rules of the regime be informal or legalized? Should commitments undertaken be permanent, or limited in duration? Should decision-making procedures be participatory or centralized? The

28 I am grateful to Ronald Rogowski for suggesting this example.

29 A Turkish student told me that she voted for Erdogan's party, in spite of his views about Islamic law, because she was convinced that the army would never allow him to legislate them. She worried that his secular opponents would not be similarly deterred from pursuing populist economic policies.

30 Waltz 1979.

31 Krasner 1999.

prevailing approach to studying institutional design has followed the logic of transaction-cost economics. According to this view, institutions exist to reduce transaction costs, and the variety of institutional designs reflects the variety of political market failures that they are intended to address.[32] Thus, for example, Barbara Koremenos argues that states choose to make agreements of limited duration when they anticipate that circumstances may change, making long-term agreements untenable.[33] Peter Rosendorff and Helen Milner explain escape clauses, which allow states to temporarily set aside their legal responsibilities, in much the same way: they represent an efficient response to uncertainty about the short-term domestic political costs of compliance.[34] Duncan Snidal and co-authors advance a wide range of hypotheses linking transaction costs to decisions to centralize or decentralize decision making, expand or contract membership and the substantive scope of agreements, and legalize commitments or leave them informal.[35]

The extension of the transaction-cost approach to the politics of delegation assumes that decisions to delegate authority balance the costs of agency against the costs of centralization. Principals make trade-offs between the costs of delegating decision-making authority to agents who may not share their preferences, on one hand, and the costs of making uninformed decisions, on the other. When agents must perform complex tasks and effective decision making depends heavily upon expertise, it is optimal for principals to cede substantial authority to their agents. When, on the other hand, agents perform repetitive or simple tasks and they enjoy no substantial information advantage over their principals, it is optimal for principals to closely control and monitor their behavior. This approach has been used to explain delegation of regulatory functions to bureaucratic agencies and the "industrial organization" of the United States Congress, and it has been extended to the study of international organizations.[36]

According to this approach, and to the transaction-cost approach generally, institutions are efficient by assumption, or if second-best, provide the best feasible set of incentives. For example, vertical integration of firms is an efficient response to commitment problems created by asset-specific investments,[37] and executive compensation packages are designed to efficiently align executives' incentives to take risks with those of investors.[38] There are powerful insights

32 Keohane 1984; Williamson 1985; Miller 1992.
33 Koremenos 2006.
34 Rosendorff and Milner 2001.
35 Abbott and Snidal 2000; Koremenos *et al.* 2001.
36 Hawkins *et al.* 2006.
37 Williamson 1985.
38 Milgrom and Roberts 1992.

here, and these claims may be correct in many cases; certainly impartial institutional designers should pay attention to incentives. Institutional designers are rarely impartial, however, and it may also be the case that vertical integration is a way to increase market power and that executive compensation reflects collusion between executives and board members. There is, furthermore, some danger of circularity in a functionalist approach that explains causes in terms of effects (e.g. explaining institutional features in terms of reductions in transaction costs), because some incentive problem can almost always be found to rationalize the existing state of affairs.

The functionalist transaction-cost approach is not very helpful for explaining institutional failures, because it only explains efficient adaptations to incentive problems.[39] It cannot shed light on the reasons why institutions might be designed inefficiently, or might deliberately be designed to fail. Historical accounts, on the other hand, tend to present the origins of international institutions as rather haphazard, marked by conflicts of interest, and shaped by the distribution of power that prevailed at the time.[40] To take a prominent example, the degree of legalization of the international trade regime has provoked sharp conflicts of interest since the dawn of the post-war era. A template for legalized cooperation in the proposed International Trade Organization was prevented from coming into force by opposition in the United States Senate, which blocked ratification of the treaty. Forty years later, developing countries objected to US- and EU-led plans to recast the informal trade regime of the GATT under the legalized aegis of the WTO, and acquiesced only after the United States and the EU threatened to revoke the trade privileges they enjoyed under the GATT unless they complied.[41] This episode sharply underlined the importance of power in determining institutional design.

Furthermore, there are difficulties with some of the assumptions necessary to make transaction costs drive the politics of delegation. It is conventionally argued that international institutions have an information or expertise advantage over their member governments, because their function is to provide information that facilitates cooperation.[42] However, the most convincing empirical stories about how institutions reduce transaction costs suggest that they do so by making authoritative determinations about what counts as defection from an agreement.[43] That is, institutions help to facilitate correlated strategies by resolving uncertainty about the definition of the rules. There are not many

39 Stone 2009b.
40 Keohane 1984; Helleiner 1994; Milner 1997; Moravcsik 1998.
41 Barton *et al*. 2006.
42 Keohane 1984; Hawkins *et al*. 2006.
43 Reinhardt 2001.

examples where institutions really have superior information. Most intergovernmental organizations, as for example the WTO, rely upon member states to put violations of rules on the agenda: they rely on "fire alarms" rather than "police patrols."[44] Even the EU, the most impressive international institution in terms of its bureaucratic capacity, cannot rival the analytic and data collection capacities of its member states. The IMF does not have a data-collection advantage over its members, which filter and often falsify the data that they feed to it, and arguably has no advantage over international financial markets, where major investors have the resources and incentives to procure information. The IMF management has an information advantage over its Executive Board,[45] but the degree of advantage varies significantly across countries. The Fund has developed procedures that allow it to withhold confidential information from the Executive Board, including internal memos. However, informal consultations allow the United States Treasury much more extensive access to information, and in important cases such as Mexico, Indonesia, Korea, Russia and Argentina, Treasury officials were directly involved in the negotiations.[46] Confidentiality in the IMF has more to do with centralizing control than with delegating.

Even when institutions have an informational edge over states, an agency problem arises only if the agents' types are unknown or the costs of shirking are substantial. If shirking is not very costly (i.e., discretion is important, but effort is not), the principal can achieve the desired policy by appointing an agent who is known to share the principal's preferences.[47] The problem of shirking is not very costly in international organizations relative to the value of the policy areas that they oversee.[48] With a staff of 2,700 at its peak – now about 2,400 – there is a limit to the amount of resources the IMF could consume through bureaucratic inefficiency. The EU is capable of spending more than any other international institution, and the issue of mismanagement of EU funds is significant enough to motivate conservative candidates in EU parliamentary elections, but it is not important enough to excite voters very much. All of this suggests that extracting effort from international bureaucrats is not a very important issue. On the other hand, a great deal is known about agents' types, to conclude from the recent public discussions over selection of EU commissioners, ECB presidents, IMF managing directors, and WTO directors. The IMF, for example, is a technocratic agency with staff selection procedures

[44] McCubbins and Schwarz 1984.
[45] Martin 2006.
[46] IEO 2003, 2004.
[47] Moe 1990.
[48] For a contrary view, see Vaubel 1986.

that lead it to pursue predictable objectives, so there is no need to closely monitor its daily activities.[49] Sharing a consensus around market-oriented reforms, the Fund's principals can safely delegate substantial operational autonomy and substantive authority. In ordinary times, the United States and the other shareholders have no compelling interest in intervening in the details of conditionality, and the Fund creates policies autonomously. Delegation is not costly for the principals because the agent's type is known.

On the other hand, the existence of multiple principals with divergent preferences is sufficient to create agent discretion, even in the absence of asymmetric information.[50] Discretion, in this formal sense, means that the agent is able to choose among a range of policies to implement. In the case of the EU, the Commission appears to exercise a substantial degree of agenda control when the status quo lies outside the voting core of the states represented in the Council, because it can make proposals within a wide range that will be approved by a qualified majority.[51] Nielsen and Tierney explain variations in World Bank implementation of environmental mandates in terms of variation in the consistency of the interests of the major players on the Executive Board.[52] Along similar lines, Martin argues that multiple principals account for the substantial degree of autonomy that the IMF staff enjoys in crafting the conditionality attached to its loans.[53] Each of these arguments relies on several assumptions that the informal governance model relaxes.

First, existing models of delegation assume that the formal rules represent the form of the game that is actually played. In contrast, informal governance assumes that the formal voting rules are in force only when the extraordinary procedures are not invoked. It remains possible for powerful states to limit their losses by circumventing the formal voting process: they exert informal influence when their interests are strongly affected, and in extreme cases they buy votes or threaten to exercise outside options.[54] Second, theories of delegation generally employ a static definition of the principals' interests: each principal wants to maximize profit, or minimize cost, or achieve an outcome as close as possible to a fixed ideal point.[55] In contrast, variation over time in the interests of powerful countries plays a key role in the theory of informal governance. It is this variation that creates the powerful countries' commitment problems, but

49 Barnett and Finnemore 2004; Chwieroth 2009.
50 Banks and Weingast 1992; Calvert *et al.* 1989.
51 Tsebelis 1994; Tsebelis and Garrett 2001.
52 Nielson and Tierney 2003.
53 Martin 2006.
54 Fang 2005; Voeten 2001; Achen 2006.
55 It would be equivalent to assume that shocks to principals' interests vary over time, but these shocks are realized only after the agent's decision is made.

also makes possible an inter-temporal exchange of influence over issues that vary in importance to different agents.

Finally, the formal models of delegation on which this literature is based presuppose a particular sequence of events, or extensive form of the game, in which a decision is made to delegate authority to an international agent, the agent subsequently makes a policy decision, and only then is the principal's uncertainty resolved. Under these assumptions, principals that delegate authority have made at least a temporary commitment not to interfere in the agent's decision, which is final – in fact, this is what is conventionally meant by delegation, as opposed to central control. In contrast, the theory of informal governance assumes that there are some principals, and always at least one, that are able to preempt the agent's decision even after delegation has occurred. Consequently, a collective decision to delegate authority to an international agent actually delegates some authority to the agent and some authority to the country or countries that are able to employ informal influence to override the agent's decisions. When the leading state's interests are intense, the leading state will exercise the delegated authority, and when those interests are not intense, the agent will exercise discretion.

Informal governance presents dilemmas for designers of international institutions. It is possible to delegate significant powers to international institutions, but they cannot really be made autonomous *vis-à-vis* great power intervention, and the more powers are delegated, the more attractive this intervention becomes. The danger embodied in delegation is not that the agency will run out of control, but that it will be captured by the most powerful state in the system.[56] In contrast to functionalist theories of delegation, which emphasize variations in transaction costs, and treat institutional design as a balancing act between the costs imposed by agency and centralization, the model of informal governance suggests that delegation depends on variations in the intensity of long-term conflicts of interest. States will only agree to delegate extensive powers to international organizations when they expect to share broadly similar objectives.

All international organizations involve some delegation of powers, but the array of power and interests circumscribes the form of delegation. International organizations can be delegated executive, legislative and judicial functions, and these differ substantially in the degree to which they are subject to informal manipulation. Executive authority is most immediately subject to informal influence, because the power to dispose of resources and implement policies inherently involves a range of legitimate discretion and subjective judgment.

56 For a contrasting view, see Vaubel 1986; Dreher and Vaubel 2004.

Furthermore, efforts to influence executive decision making are not necessarily improper and are not stigmatized as illegal. Judicial authority is least subject to manipulation – although the independence of international judiciaries is no more certain than that of domestic ones[57] – because legalization narrows the scope of the agent's discretion and efforts to influence judges are recognized as improper. Arbitration functions as an institutionalized means of resolving conflict only if it is believed to be tolerably fair. Legalization, therefore, shifts policy making from the arena of informal influence into the sphere of formal rules. Legislative functions are rarely delegated, and international organizations that have these functions generally leave legislation to the contracting parties, or states.

Where conflict of interest is perceived as systematic and lasting, weaker states will be reluctant to delegate much discretionary authority to agencies that subsequently might be captured by their stronger rivals. This accounts for the weak secretariat of the WTO, which presides over a bargaining milieu in which the parties expect to have many conflicting interests.[58] The WTO has much more limited autonomy than the IMF, for example, which has been delegated extensive executive authority. In addition, legalization has constrained the exercise of power in the trade regime. The IMF is a very non-legalized organization – the only legally binding and enforceable commitment countries make to the IMF is to repay the money they borrow – and in contrast the WTO is a legal forum. The most important function delegated to the WTO as an organization is dispute settlement, which is valuable to the membership because it legalizes and adjudicates trade rules. In doing so, dispute settlement makes the application of rules predictable and less subject to manipulation.[59] Legalization helps to defuse conflict, because it is easier for governments to comply with a legal judgment than to capitulate to a political demand from a foreign state. For example, Japan found it possible to comply with demands to liberalize agriculture imports when its policies were ruled GATT-illegal that would have been politically impossible to accept as demands issued by the United States in bilateral negotiations.[60] This function works because dispute settlement panels are believed to be technocratic and relatively free of improper informal influence.

In this view, the relative autonomy of international financial institutions is

[57] See Carrubba 2005, but also the contrasting view of Voeten 2008.

[58] Barton *et al.* 2006. Economic arguments for the optimality of unilateral free trade notwithstanding (e.g. Krugman 1997), trade politics is conflictual. The reasons have to do with a combination of political economy incentives for protectionism and terms-of-trade effects (Bagwell and Staiger 2002).

[59] Barton *et al.* 2006; Davis 2010.

[60] Davis 2003.

not a result of disagreement among the major shareholders, but of the fundamental agreement of the shareholders on the general principles of financial stabilization, market openness, and liberal economic reform. This makes it possible for the members to delegate substantial executive authority. Because this authority is discretionary, it creates opportunities for powerful states to exert informal influence; but in practice the wide range of common interests limits the costs of such intervention.

The EU is a quite different case. European states have delegated substantial authority to the EU in areas where they have broadly congruent interests, including even legislative powers, but have allowed it only a limited role in setting foreign policy, where national differences are deeper and more lasting. In foreign policy, decision making remains intergovernmental and informal. The EU has gone further than any other international organization in legalized delegation. Rulings of the European Court of Justice have supremacy over national law and courts and have direct effect on European citizens, and they have expanded into ever-widening circles of policy areas. Legalization of cooperation was necessary, because the relatively flat distribution of power in Europe empowers several countries to exert informal influence, which would have made the costs of informal governance prohibitive. Legalization has served to defuse controversies, and has prevented the most powerful states in the EU from exercising undue informal influence in areas in which conflicts of interest were endemic. Informal influence continues to play a key role in the EU legislative process, however, as well as in negotiations over new phases of integration.

Delegation is often seen as a response to commitment problems. Temptations to defect are predictable in many areas of international cooperation, where commitment is optimal *ex ante* and reneging is optimal *ex post*. This situation, known in economics as a time-consistency problem, arises whenever current policies affect the pay-off to decisions made in the past.[61] The best solution to time-consistency problems is a commitment device. Facing such dilemmas, farsighted national leaders may attempt to tie their hands – or those of their successors – by delegating authority to an international organization. The best empirical example is the delegation of monetary policy to the independent European Central Bank. The existence of time-consistency problems is a key functionalist explanation for international organization, and in this case it was the weakness of monetary reputations in many of the EU member countries that provided the impetus for delegation. However, it is a feature of the anarchical international environment that such commitment devices are generally unavailable when they are most needed, and when available, are

[61] Kydland and Prescott 1977.

always imperfect. Even when they attempt to delegate important functions to international institutions, states always retain the capacity to renege, and the most independent international institutions remain vulnerable to the efforts of member states to influence their policies.

In practice, delegating executive functions to international institutions creates more commitment problems than it resolves, because the principals are rarely committed to institutional independence. In the case of crisis lending, for example, conflict among the major players has less to do with the content of the rules than with when to make exceptions to them. In general, central bankers oppose bail-outs of financial institutions because they create moral hazard, but in particular cases they support them because the costs of large bank failures are politically unacceptable and may be systemically threatening. In the same way, IMF Executive Directors prefer in general to safeguard the integrity of the institution, but in particular cases, shareholders find it convenient to use IMF programs as an inexpensive form of foreign aid.[62] In an emergency, the IMF can mobilize more resources and act more expeditiously than the US Agency for International Development (USAID), and it can lend without the approval of the United States Congress, so it is an invaluable instrument of foreign policy influence for the United States president. The United States has drawn upon its influence at the Fund to attempt to induce recipient governments to support its foreign policy objectives, and at times it has pressured the Fund to be lenient because it has been reluctant to risk destabilizing friendly regimes. Although the United States shares an interest in stabilizing the global economy with the other G-7 countries, it disagrees with them about how important other interests are – such as strategic objectives in the Middle East – that are extraneous to the concerns of international finance but temporarily come into conflict with the long-term objectives of the IMF. Common long-term interests in promoting economic development and open markets suffer when the Fund's priorities are subordinated to other objectives, because this undermines the credibility of the Fund's loans-for-reforms contract. In numerous cases of IMF lending to Russia, Egypt, Turkey and Pakistan, the United States traded its leverage over the IMF for concessions on other issues that seemed more pressing at the time than economic reform. In others, such as Argentina in 2001, US policymakers urged the IMF to waive conditionality in order to try to stave off a default that could rock the international financial system, only to deepen the crisis when it arrived. The most influential post-Communist countries – those that received the most economic aid from the United States – were subject to the least rigorous enforcement and violated their conditions most often, and consequently

[62] Marc Leland, Assistant Treasury Secretary in the Reagan administration, referred to the IMF as "a convenient conduit for US influence" (Cohen 1986, 229).

suffered from higher inflation and more devaluation.[63] Efforts to consolidate democracy in Russia and Ukraine suffered because of the resulting instability. Similarly, African countries that had ties to the United States, Britain or France were subject to less rigorous enforcement of IMF conditionality.[64] The evidence suggests that the IMF fails to enforce its conditions because its principals revoke its authority when enforcing conditionality becomes inconvenient.

The IMF has a commitment problem because it was optimal for its most powerful principals to design an institution that they could control. This is not a problem that is limited to the IMF; to varying degrees and in a variety of forms, it emerges in all international organizations. The IMF is a special case, but it is a useful case to illustrate the problems of international organization generally. The IMF has a high degree of autonomy and delegated authority, which is possible because of the broad international consensus about its fundamental purposes. Because so much authority is delegated, it has developed robust forms of informal governance that run parallel to its formal governance procedures. This makes it useful for illustrative purposes. On the other hand, it represents an example of the limits of delegation under the most fortuitous circumstances, and an example of what off-the-equilibrium-path play might look like in thinner organizations, if as much authority were delegated to them as to the IMF. US control of the IMF represents a cautionary tale for reformers who might seek to strengthen the regulatory powers of the WTO.

Conclusions

The discussion so far leads to four main conclusions; formalizing the argument in the next chapter will generate additional testable hypotheses. First, international organizations operate according to two parallel sets of rules. Formal rules represent the broad interests of the membership, and reflect the preferences of weak states out of proportion to their resources; informal rules provide exceptional access to decision making for powerful states when their core interests are affected. Second, effective institutions depend on voluntary participation, so they must be at least minimally legitimate. While powerful states can exert informal influence, it would be a mistake to conclude that institutions simply reflect the interests of the powerful. The allocation of voting rights has to balance the fact that powerful states have attractive outside options, while

63 Stone 2002.

64 Stone 2004. In each of these studies, the rigor of enforcement is measured in terms of the length of program suspensions when programs go "off track." Chapter 9 revisits these claims using better data and a tighter test of the hypotheses generated by the model of informal governance.

even weak states must be offered enough to prefer participation to exit. Formal rules and standard procedures determine the status quo that prevails when the leading state chooses not to intervene, and it cannot intervene too often without undermining the value of the organization. Third, important features of institutional design depend on the distribution of power and interests in the issues at stake. Because any powers delegated to an international organization can be usurped by powerful states, extensive delegation of executive authority will only occur when the interests of the key actors are closely aligned. When interests are more conflictual, delegation takes legalized forms that are more difficult to manipulate. Finally, international organizations are subject to time-consistency problems. This follows from the previous three propositions. If powerful states are unable to commit to rules when their interests are intense and weaker states defer to them, international organizations will inherit their principals' commitment problems.

The opportunistic manipulation of international organizations is a problem that is deeply rooted in the structure of the international system. As long as the distribution of power is highly unequal, some states will enjoy much more attractive outside options than others, so they will be unable to commit to abiding by formal rules when their interests are strong. Weaker powers tolerate the development of informal governance mechanisms that allow powerful countries to impose their preferences because the participation of the most important states increases the value of international cooperation. Consequently, time-consistency problems are not simply an unfortunate defect of institutional design, which can be corrected by better social engineering. Time consistency is a fundamental problem of world order, which is built into the informal governance of international organizations. Informal governance is a component of the best response strategies that support international organization as a solution to collective action problems. As this chapter has argued, and the next chapter will demonstrate formally, informal governance is in equilibrium.

The expected frequency of the leading state's intervention determines the amount of delegation that is possible in international organizations, so delegation is limited in issue areas such as trade, where the protagonists expect to face frequent and sharp conflicts of interest. However, delegation makes informal influence less costly to exercise. Consequently, informal governance procedures are most prominent in organizations that enjoy the most delegated authority, in spite of the fact that they preside over issues where long-term interests are well aligned. Ironically, the leading state's commitment problems have the most scope to affect international cooperation in the issue areas where the international community has the greatest common interests.

3

A model of informal governance

The argument is that international organizations are best understood as equilibrium outcomes that balance the power and interests of the leading state and the member countries. Institutional design is endogenous to this interaction, and includes membership, formal voting rights and informal governance procedures. The model that follows gives specific content to this claim by specifying how three particular forms of power interact. *Structural power* represents the outside options of the leading state and the externalities that its participation generates for other members.[1] *Formal voting rights* set the policy of the organization and create the parameters within which informal influence is exercised. *Informal influence* consists of participation in decision making and special access to information, and it allows the leading state to override the common policy when its vital interests are affected.

Hybrid institutional forms involving both formal and informal governance mechanisms are the norm because they make it possible to accommodate the interests of both strong and weak powers. Informal governance can be legitimate because the degree of conflict of interest between the leading state and the membership varies within the range of issues or cases that fall under an organization's competence, so the member countries tolerate a degree of informal influence in cases of special concern to the leading power in return for a larger share of decision-making authority in ordinary times. This tacit contract depends upon the restraint of the leading state, however, and the legitimacy and credibility of the organization can be eroded if informal influence is used too frequently.

The argument is laid out in the form of a formal model. Formalization makes it possible to define our terms precisely. Concepts such as power and legitimacy have diverse meanings, and defining them in mathematical terms makes

[1] Strange 1988.

it possible to indicate precisely what they signify in a particular argument. Furthermore, formalization makes it possible to detect logical errors that might be obscured in a prose argument – it imposes "accounting standards" for arguments,[2] assuring that conclusions really follow from assumptions. Beyond assuring clarity and logical consistency, however, a formal model is a uniquely powerful tool for discovering unexpected implications of arguments. Game theory is not useful for some purposes, such as explaining the origins of preferences or worldviews, but it is an ideal tool for exploring the effects of complex strategic interactions.

The model presented here is designed to be as simple as possible in game theoretic terms, involving no incomplete information and no dynamically evolving state variables, but it has a lot of moving parts. Precisely how the elements of institutional design influence one another would not be obvious without a formal analysis. For example, if US structural power increases, what is the effect on the distribution of formal voting rights? It turns out that this leads to a decrease rather than an increase in US formal control rights, because the United States comes to depend more heavily on informal influence. States with substantial structural power have greater informal influence, and they compensate for this by giving up formal voting rights in order to induce participation by a wider range of states. On the other hand, when the leading state's temptations to exercise informal influence grow, this leads to a decline in informal governance and a redistribution of control rights in favor of weaker powers, but also to a decline in the organization's legitimacy and significance. The precise meaning of these claims will be made clear below.

The key features of the model are as follows: (1) An international organization imposes a policy that is determined by weighted voting, but the United States has the ability to override the policy in a particular case, at some cost. The temptation to override the common policy is a random variable, so in a particular case it may or may not be attractive for the United States to do so. Voting represents formal control and the US override represents informal influence. (2) The member countries vote to determine the cost that the United States pays when it overrides their policy, so informal influence depends on the consent of the membership. (3) The United States can exercise an outside option that does not depend on multilateral cooperation, and chooses a level of investment in the organization, which provides positive externalities to the other members. This ability to impose costs on the membership by partially exiting the organization represents US structural power, and deters the membership from setting the cost of informal influence at a prohibitive level.

[2] Powell 1999.

(4) The United States proposes the distribution of vote shares in the international organization, and the members decide whether to participate under those terms. Assigning this bargaining advantage to the United States represents the unique role that the leading state plays in designing any organization in which it participates, in addition to the advantages due to the distribution of institutional memberships and vote shares inherited from the Cold War. This simplification of the bargaining protocol is not necessary in order to derive the main results, however. The key feature of the model is that institutional design is endogenous.

The model

The model is an extensive-form game of full and perfect information, with players the United States and n other countries. The sequence of play is as follows: The United States offers a vector of vote shares in an international organization to a subset $K \subseteq N$, and the members of K choose whether to participate. Subsequently, the members vote to set a cost, c, that will be imposed upon the United States if it chooses to override the organization's policy in a particular case. The United States then chooses its level of participation in the organization. Nature subsequently initiates a crisis, which is of variable importance to the United States, and the United States decides whether to preempt the expected policy in this case. Finally, if the United States has not exercised an override, the members vote to set the institution's policy. This sequence is illustrated in Figure 3.1. Countries i have ideal points a_i on the interval $(0, 1)$, and members of the organization receive utility:

$$u_j = \gamma \sum_i z_i - (1 - \lambda) z_j - |x - a_j|,$$

where z are the contributions made by each country i, λ is a political rent derived from voting power in the organization, γ is the degree of US participation in the organization, and x is the policy that is implemented. Non-members receive zero.

US utility differs from that of other countries in two respects. First, the United States is able to partially exit the organization, reducing its contribution and the weight it puts on the organization's policy to a proportion represented by $\gamma \in (0, 1)$. In addition, the United States receives a benefit, $b \sim U(0, \bar{b})$, if it overrides the standard policy and imposes $x = 0$. When it overrides the policy, the US incurs a cost, c, which is chosen by the membership. The US

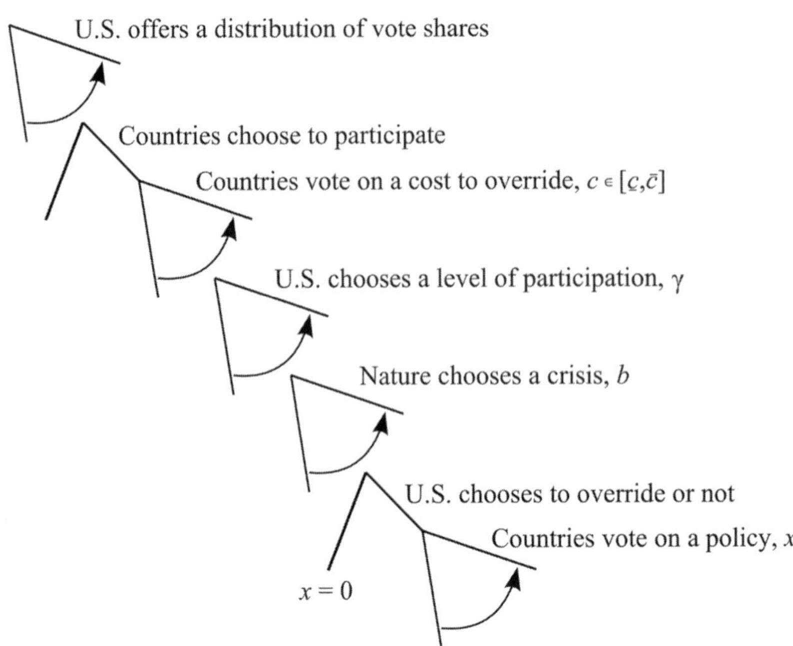

Figure 3.1 The sequence of play.

indirect utility function is as follows:

$$u_{US} = \gamma\Big(\sum_i z_i - (1-\lambda)\gamma z_{US} - |x - a_{US}| + I(b-c)\Big) + (1-\gamma)(R),$$

where R is a reservation utility available by exercising an outside option and I is an indicator variable, taking the value 1 if the United States decides to override the organization's policy and 0 if it does not.

Equilibrium analysis

The equilibrium concept is subgame perfection (SPE), and the best responses are found by backward induction. At the final node, if it is reached because the United States has not chosen to preempt, the countries vote on a policy, and the pivotal voter chooses the policy that corresponds to its ideal point, $x = a_p$.

At the previous node, the United States chooses to preempt the expected policy if the utility of overriding and setting a policy of zero exceeds the utility of not overriding:

$$-|0 - a_{US}| + (b - c) > -|x - a_{US}|.$$

There are two possible cases, depending on whether the pivotal voter prefers a policy lower than the US ideal point ($a_{US} > x$), or a policy greater than the US ideal point ($a_{US} < x$).[3] The threshold value of b that invokes the US override is:

$$b^* \equiv \begin{cases} c + x & \text{if} \quad a_{US} > x, \\ c - x + 2a_{US} & \text{if} \quad a_{US} < x. \end{cases}$$

It will be useful to note that the *ex ante* probability of overriding, p, is:

$$p = \begin{cases} 1 - (c + x)/\bar{b} & \text{if} \quad a_{US} > x, \\ 1 - (c - x + 2a_{US})/\bar{b} & \text{if} \quad a_{US} < x. \end{cases}$$

At the previous decision node, the United States chooses a level of participation, γ, to maximize the expected value of:

$$\gamma\Bigg(\sum_i z_i - (1 - \lambda)\gamma z_{US} - |x - a_{US}| + I(b - c)\Bigg) + (1 - \gamma)(R).$$

This yields the equilibrium level of US participation:

$$\gamma = \begin{cases} \frac{\sum z_i + 1/\bar{b} - R - a_{US} - c + (c+x)^2/\bar{b}}{2(1-\lambda)z_{US}} & \text{if} \quad a_{US} > x, \\ \frac{\sum z_i + 1/\bar{b} - R - a_{US} - c + (c-x+2a_{US})^2/\bar{b}}{2(1-\lambda)z_{US}} & \text{if} \quad a_{US} < x. \end{cases}$$

At the previous decision node, the countries choose the cost, c, which the United States incurs when it chooses to override the organization's chosen policy, taking into account the effect of this choice on the US decision to override and on the level of US investment in the organization. The pivotal voter maximizes:

$$\gamma \sum_i z_i - (1 - \lambda)z_j - |x - a_j|,$$

which yields the expectation,

$$\gamma \sum_i z_i - (1 - \lambda)z_j - (1 - p)|x - a_j| - pa_j.$$

[3] The two cases are equivalent when $a_{US} = x$.

Maximizing with respect to c yields the optimal cost. Again, there are two cases:

$$c = \begin{cases} \frac{\bar{b}}{2} - x - \frac{a_p(1-\lambda)z_{US}}{\sum z_i} & \text{if} \quad a_{US} > x, \\ \frac{\bar{b}}{2} + x - 2a_{US} - \frac{a_p(1-\lambda)z_{US}}{\sum z_i} & \text{if} \quad a_{US} < x. \end{cases}$$

At the prior node, countries choose to participate if the utility of participating is greater than zero:

$$u_j = \gamma \sum_i z_i - (1-\lambda)z_j - E(|x - a_j|) \geq 0.$$

Because γ and c are continuous functions of x, this can be rewritten as a pair of conditions on x:

$$\underline{x}_j \leq x \leq \bar{x}_j.$$

Each country i chooses to participate as long as the pivotal voter is not too far from its ideal point, where "too far" depends upon the size of a country's contribution and the other parameters of the model. This interval is the country-specific participation constraint.

At the first decision node, the United States offers a distribution of vote shares to a set of contributing countries. In equilibrium, votes are offered only to countries that will agree to participate, and the distribution of votes determines the pivotal voter such that the relevant participation constraint is satisfied for all participants. For any distribution of country ideal points and contribution sizes there exists one or more feasible coalitions, where a feasible coalition is defined as a set of countries including the United States whose participation constraints have a non-empty intersection that includes the ideal point of at least one of the members of the set (the set that includes only the United States is always a feasible coalition). The United States offers a vector of vote shares that assigns the coalition member with the ideal point in the intersection of the feasible set that is closest to its own as the pivotal voter. From the US perspective, the utility-relevant characteristics of a coalition are its size and the ideal point of its pivotal voter, from which it is possible to calculate the endogenous variables of the model. Therefore, the United States is able to calculate the utility received from each feasible coalition, and chooses the coalition and pivotal voter that offers the highest utility.

There is no general solution for the distribution of votes because the countries can have arbitrary ideal points and contribution sizes, but it is possible to use the first-order conditions to characterize the trade-off that defines the US equilibrium strategy. US utility increases with the size of the coalition, which determines the benefits of collective action, and US utility decreases as the pivotal voter moves further from the US ideal point.

There are two cases. If $a_{US} > x$ in equilibrium, expanding the coalition would require the United States to shift vote share to countries that prefer still lower levels of policy, x. Expanding the coalition increases US utility, and making policy concessions (weakening the policy) decreases US utility, so the optimal size of the coalition is determined by this trade-off. If $a_{US} < x$ in equilibrium, expanding the coalition would require the United States to shift voting power to countries that prefer levels of the policy that are higher than the United States prefers. Expanding the coalition continues to be beneficial, but now increasing the stringency of the policy reduces US utility. Again, there is a trade-off between the size of the coalition and control over its policy, and it is optimal for the United States to balance the costs and benefits of expanding the coalition. To close the model, I assume that if the United States is indifferent between two possible coalitions, it chooses the one with the pivotal voter whose ideal point is closest to its own.

Discussion

The key insight of the model is to capture how structural power, formal control and informal influence interact. Informal influence is ubiquitous in international organizations, but this does not mean that formal control rights are unimportant; rather, formal rights of control determine the parameters within which powerful countries are allowed to exercise informal influence. In the model, although the leading state retains the option of overriding consensual procedures, the member countries choose the cost that the leading state pays when it chooses to exercise that option. In this sense, informal governance is subject to the consent of the membership. How formal voting rights are used, however, plays out in the shadow of structural power. Countries have structural power if they enjoy attractive outside options to multilateral cooperation and their participation in joint endeavors provides positive externalities to other participants. In the model, this is represented by the leading state's outside option, R, and its ability to influence the pay-off to multilateral cooperation by choosing the degree of its participation, γ. Countries with substantial structural power must be appeased, and in the model this deters the member countries from making the cost of overriding the institutional policy prohibitive.

The leading state has substantial influence over the design of institutions, and for the sake of simplicity the model assumes that the United States has proposal power and therefore holds all of the bargaining power. Nevertheless, the United States is willing to cede substantial formal control to member countries in order to secure their participation in the institution. It does so in spite of the fact that the member countries have different policy preferences and that they prefer to constrain the US ability to exercise informal influence. The United States is able to make these concessions because it anticipates that the members will be deterred from exploiting their formal control rights to prevent informal influence from being exerted when the US interest in doing so is very strong.

This confidence, in turn, rests on US structural power. The comparative statics of the model trace out the effects of shifting structural power.[4] Thus, for example, as the attractiveness of the US outside option increases, the United States shifts away from participation in the organization ($d\gamma/dR < 0$), which imposes costs on the rest of the membership. In response, the member countries reduce the cost that they impose when the United States chooses to override their policies in order to restore the incentives for the United States to invest in the institution ($dc/dR < 0$). The frequency with which the United States overrides the common policy increases ($dp/dR > 0$), and the balance shifts from formal to informal governance. The joint effects of reduced US participation and increased use of the US override undermine the value of the organization for the rest of the membership, making other countries less willing to participate ($du_i/dR < 0$). Thus, increased unilateralism and the shift towards informal governance undermine the legitimacy of the international organization.

In order to compensate for the decreased value of the organization to its members, the United States becomes willing to cede them a greater share of voting rights to shore up declining legitimacy. Whether it will in fact cede voting rights depends upon the distribution of ideal points of potential members, but the US best response shifts because countries become less willing to participate and because the increase in US structural power relaxes the trade-off between expanding the coalition and accepting greater constraints on US informal influence. Thus, surprisingly, increasing US structural power causes the United States to be more willing to give up formal vote share, shifting the pivotal voter further from its ideal point in order to expand the coalition of members. Conversely, as US structural power declines, the United States becomes less inclined to exercise its exit options, and the membership constrains the exercise of its informal influence as well. As US structural power

[4] Comparative statics are the effects of an exogenous variable on an endogenous variable, defined as the total derivative dy/dx, at the point of equilibrium. To convey the intuition behind the results I discuss them as if the best responses occurred sequentially, but in fact these relationships hold simultaneously in equilibrium.

declines, formal governance becomes more important relative to informal governance, the legitimacy of the institution improves among the membership, and the United States retains more formal control.

Another comparative statics exercise allows us to explore the implications of misbehavior by the leading state in the system. Informal governance rests on an implicit contract: the leading state will participate if it is allowed to exert informal influence, and the member countries consent to grant informal influence if it is not abused. If the leading state exercises its power to override the institutional policy too frequently, it undermines the value of the institution for the other participants. The implications follow from the comparative statics on the US temptation parameter, $\bar{b}$. If there is an exogenous increase in the expected benefit of overriding, this increases the probability that the United States decides to override ($dp/d\bar{b} > 0$), which leads the member countries to increase the cost that the United States pays when it does so ($dc/d\bar{b} > 0$). The member countries will not increase the cost sufficiently to fully offset the increased temptation, however, because increasing the cost leads the United States to exercise its outside options and reduce its level of investment in the organization ($\partial\gamma/\partial c < 0$). The combination of a higher probability that the common policy will be overridden and lower US participation lowers the value of participating in the organization for the other members ($du_i/d\bar{b} < 0$). In order to induce them to continue participating in the organization, the United States may (again, depending upon the distribution of country sizes and their ideal points) be compelled to offer to redistribute vote shares in the organization, shifting the pivotal voter further from its own ideal point. This appears to be exactly what happened in the IMF in 2008, where voting rights were redistributed in order to compensate for a perceived drop in the legitimacy of the organization that was linked to US micromanagement of the Asian crisis of the late 1990s and a series of crises in Russia, Argentina, Brazil and Turkey.[5]

Extensions

Formal modeling is an exercise in making choices. The objective is to incorporate the features that appear to be substantively most important to the subject at hand while retaining as much generality and tractability as possible. Occam's razor applies: simplicity is a virtue, and the simplest game that captures the key intuition of an argument is generally preferable to a model that incorporates unnecessary features. However, we can often learn important things by

[5] Further discussion of this is deferred to Chapter 10.

extending a basic model in various directions. The model presented here is the simplest game that captures the key insights of informal governance, and a number of extensions are possible.

Multiple leading states

There are m leading states, j. One of the leading states makes a proposed distribution of vote shares that all other members must accept or decline. Each leading state has the option of partially exiting the organization by choosing γ_j, enjoys the ability to override the organization's policy, and has a utility function with the same form as that of the United States in the model above, with the temptations of the leading states to override distributed independently. The leading states decide simultaneously whether to override the common policy, and state j receives the benefit and pays the cost of overriding only if it decides to override. If any leading state exercises an override, $x = 0$. In the utility function of all non-leading member states, the term γ is replaced by $\sum \frac{\gamma_j}{m}$. This model allows us to consider cases such as the WTO, which has two leading powers, and European institutions, which have had three or more at various points in time.

The formal derivation of the parallel results is omitted, but follows the same procedure as above. There are two important findings. First, introducing additional leading states leads to an increase in the equilibrium level of c. This can be interpreted as a shift in the organization's governance that deemphasizes informal governance and emphasizes formalized decision making. This follows from two considerations: (1) the frequency of overriding for any cost threshold increases as the number of leading states with independently distributed temptations to override increases, and (2) an override by any particular leading state creates a negative externality for all of the others, so increasing costs leads to a smaller reduction in participation by the leading states ($\partial\gamma/\partial c$ is reduced). In equilibrium, everyone prefers to make informal influence harder to exercise in order to restrain everyone else. Second, introducing additional leading states reduces the level of investment in the organization by each of the leading states. This can be interpreted as unwillingness to delegate extensive powers to an organization. This follows from the fact that an increased number of leading states override the common policy more frequently at any given level of c, making the organization less valuable, and that the equilibrium value of c is higher, making overriding less attractive. Outside options become more attractive because other states exercise informal influence and because it becomes more costly to do so oneself.

The substantive significance of these findings is to relate the number of leading states (or quasi-state groupings such as the EU) within an issue area to the design of international organizations and delegation of powers to them. The EU is an example of an organization with a relatively large number of leading states, which facilitates common investment in some issue areas by legalizing cooperation and making informal influence difficult to exercise. Where informal governance is the norm, common policies are very weak, as in foreign and defense policy. The WTO is an example of an organization with two leading powers, the United States and the EU, which retain informal influence but refuse to invest the organization with substantial executive or legislative powers. When important functions are delegated to the WTO, this is done through legalized adjudication procedures that minimize the possibility of exercising informal influence. These implications will be discussed further in later chapters.

Repetition

The game is infinitely repeated with common discount factor δ. Let $s = \{$vote shares, participation, c, γ, b^*, x, reversion$\}$ be a strategy profile for this game, where *reversion* specifies how the strategy next period depends upon the outcome this period, and let s^* be the profile that forms a Nash equilibrium in the stage game. Let s^{**} be a strategy profile of the repeated game that will be called a *cooperative equilibrium*, such that $b^*(s^{**}) \geq b^*(s^*), c(s^{**}) < c(s^*)$, and all players revert to s^* for the rest of the game if any player deviates from s^{**}. The strategy profile s^{**} forms a subgame perfect equilibrium of the repeated game for δ sufficiently high.

Proof Define continuation values as follows: V_L^N is the continuation value of a leading state for playing the Nash strategies of the stage game every period, and V_F^N is the corresponding continuation value for a follower state. V_L^* and V_F^* are the continuation values if all leading and following states play according to s^{**}. For δ sufficiently high, the profile s^{**} forms an SPE if $V_L^* > V_L^N$ and $V_F^* > V_F^N$ and the reversion strategies form an SPE.

Suppose that $b^*(s^{**}) = b^*(s^*)$ and $c(s^{**}) < c(s^*)$. In that case, $V_L^* > V_L^N$, because the leading state pays a lower cost in every period in which it chooses to override the common policy. Because the continuation value is higher in the cooperative equilibrium, however, for high enough discount factors the leading state would be willing to exercise restraint to maintain cooperation, so there exist $b^*(s^{**}) \geq b^*(s^*)$. Because the expected utility in every period is higher under the cooperative equilibrium, $\gamma(s^{**}) > \gamma(s^*)$. These results imply that $V_F^* > V_F^N$, because overriding occurs less frequently in the cooperative equilibrium and the leading states' participation is greater. The reversion strategies that support this equilibrium themselves form an SPE because they form the unique Nash equilibrium of the stage game.

The extension of the model to a repeated game captures the notion that the optimal functioning of institutions depends upon a social compact between powerful and weak states that is based upon an enlightened view of their respective interests. In a single-shot game, each state chooses strategies that maximize its short-run interests. In the context of repeated interactions, however, powerful states are willing to exercise restraint in order to sustain the benefits of cooperation in the future. Weaker states nurture this restraint by reducing the costs that they impose upon the powerful when they override common policies, so long as powerful states only do so when the temptation exceeds a particular threshold. There is an accepted range of legitimate deviations from formal rules, and an outer range of illegitimate deviations, and the difference turns on the circumstances of domestic politics or international strategic concerns that create the temptations.

Other possible extensions

A more complex extension would be to a dynamic game with a persistent state variable. For example, it would be possible to repeat the game but make institutions sticky, so that vote shares, the cost of overriding the common policy, or both are difficult to change. This extension would generate interesting insights about the development of institutions over time, and would allow us to make stronger claims about how the development of institutions depends upon countries' strategies. The current model can explore the effect of changing US preferences on institutions through comparative statics: if the expected benefit from manipulating the institution rises, countries respond by increasing the cost of overriding, and the United States responds by reducing its investment in the institution. This allows us to point to a key danger to international organizations, which is that the temptations of the leading power can lead to their gradual marginalization. A dynamic model would take the analysis a step further by exploring how the states of the world – participation, cost, etc. – can evolve over time in response to countries' actions. For example, we could learn whether changes are persistent or ephemeral, and whether some states are absorbing. Most of the specific properties of the dynamics, however – as opposed to the fact that the equilibrium is dynamic and its character shifts in response to country actions – would be highly dependent upon specific modeling assumptions, and would not therefore produce very general conclusions.

In addition, a number of extensions are possible involving imperfect monitoring of outcomes, incomplete information and signaling. Imperfect monitoring is a relatively trivial extension of the single-shot model: if the US decision to override is imperfectly observed (for example, the fact that an override has been exercised is observed with probability q), countries simply choose a cost level sufficient to induce the same equilibrium strategies as in the model analyzed above. However, in a repeated version of the model, where retrospective punishment strategies can achieve higher levels of restraint by the United States, imperfect monitoring will reduce the degree to which reputational equilibria impose restraint. For any discount factor, the possibility that overriding will not be detected lowers the threshold temptation necessary to provoke the United States to override the common policy, bringing the equilibrium strategies closer to those of the single-shot model. However, adding imperfect monitoring does not seem to enrich the substantive conclusions that we can draw from the model.

A variety of models involving incomplete information and signaling are possible. Extending the single-shot model to include incomplete information about the US temptation parameter is not particularly useful, because no informative signaling equilibria are possible. In a repeated setting, however, such an extension would again make it possible for the United States to build a reputation for restraint. This would also allow the model to generate insights about dynamics: US decisions to override the institutional policy would erode the cooperativeness of institutions, gradually leading to institutional procedures that restricted informal manipulation, which in turn would induce low levels of US investment. The particulars of the dynamics, however, would be dependent upon arbitrary modeling choices such as the number of repetitions and the nature of the uncertainty about US preferences.

In summary, the most substantively important extension of the model is to include multiple leading states. The main insight to be gained through repetition is the potential to generate restraint on the part of the leading states. The optimal functioning of international institutions depends upon mutual restraint: powerful states refrain from exercising informal influence outside of a recognized zone of legitimate deviations from the formal rules, and in turn weak states refrain from imposing formal rules that would curtail their privileges. This restraint does not qualitatively change the actors' behavior, however; it simply shifts the threshold for the temptation necessary to induce the leading state to intervene and the level of cost imposed when it does so. Indeed, the cost imposed when the leading state overrides the common policy in the static game can be interpreted as a reduced form parameter representing reputational costs in repeated interactions.

Other extensions of the model would generate substantively similar insights at the cost of introducing considerable additional complexity. Dynamic games (repeated games with state variables that evolve over time) and signaling models make it possible to explore dynamics and characterize equilibria in which future expectations and behavior depend upon current actions. A key insight of these extensions is that the quality of international institutions can evolve over time in response to choices that countries make, and in particular, that institutions can deteriorate if the United States overuses its prerogatives to exercise informal influence. The static game generates a similar insight, however. Varying the temptation parameter – the range of possible benefits from intervention – induces the member countries to be more cautious and set higher obstacles to informal influence, which in turn undermines the incentives for the United States to participate substantially in the organization. This is simply a comparative statics exercise, and says nothing about the dynamics of institutional evolution; but sharp conclusions about dynamics would in any case be dependent upon arbitrary modeling choices. The simpler model captures the essence of the matter.

Conclusions

International organizations have become increasingly important actors in international politics. Some critics have emphasized their autonomy,[6] while others regard international organizations as instruments in the hands of powerful states.[7] The approach presented here is decidedly state-centered. This is not to deny that the details of international governance owe a great deal to the strategies and beliefs of international agents.[8] However, the broad policies and many of the important details are worked out through formal and informal governance procedures that are established by states and in which states are the important actors. There are no international rogue agencies, because states remain the fundamental actors in international relations. The most powerful states retain the ability to control informally even formally autonomous institutions, and lack the ability to irrevocably delegate authority. The autonomous agencies are problematic not because they follow their own agendas, but because they can be captured by powerful states.

The puzzle for a state-centered theory of international organization is to explain why weaker states participate in international organizations, if their

[6] Vaubel 1986; Barnett and Finnemore 2004.
[7] Krasner 1985; Strange 1988.
[8] Abdelal 2007; Chwieroth 2009.

policies simply reflect the preferences of the powerful. The solution is informal governance. Informal governance facilitates an inter-temporal exchange between weak and powerful states. Weak states receive sufficient input into the formal governance structure to form a stake in it and to assure that they will benefit from the policies of international organizations on average, if not in every instance. Powerful states are willing to share power, because institutions are only useful to powerful states to the extent that they elicit voluntary participation. However, the most powerful states participate only when they are assured that they can assume control, albeit at some cost, when they deem that their core interests are affected.

Informal governance is in continuous tension, because the manipulation that makes power sharing tolerable for the leading state undermines the legitimacy and credibility of international organizations. However, legitimacy is essential whether international organizations are to serve their core purposes or be useful as instruments of power, and delegation is possible only to the extent that the participants expect that manipulation will be relatively infrequent. There must be sufficient agreement about common purposes that weaker states can expect to benefit from cooperation. International organizations are legitimate because, in equilibrium, the leading state chooses not to manipulate them under ordinary circumstances.

Ultimately, the terms of informal governance are themselves subject to negotiation and revision. If the United States exploits its ability to manipulate an international organization too flagrantly, other countries may use their formal voting rights to revise the organization's procedures and make this more costly. However, they are deterred from making informal influence too difficult to exert, because this would erode the usefulness of the organization for the United States, and ultimately lead it to be marginalized. The member countries implicitly consent to manipulation by the leading state or states, because they make this the price of their participation.

There are, therefore, three distinct forms of power in play in international organizations: structural power, formal control, and informal influence. Structural power represents the outside options a country enjoys and the externalities its participation in an institution creates for others. Powerful countries have attractive alternatives to multilateral cooperation and their participation in common endeavors magnifies the benefits of cooperation for all, so their interests must be accommodated. Formal control rights are embedded in the legal rules of international organizations, and may or may not correspond to variations in structural power. Countries that are strong in terms of structural power may nevertheless choose to disperse formal control widely in order to create legitimacy. Informal influence arises through participation in the decision-making process, informal consultation with the agents who are delegated authority to make decisions, and privileged access to information. Informal influence is invariably unequal, and cannot be wholly prevented by any constitutional scheme, but it can be reduced by promoting transparency and making decisions by majority voting. Most international organizations are not designed to be transparent or majoritarian, however. Countries with substantial structural power are accorded opportunities for informal influence in order to make participation attractive to them, which makes it possible for them to give up formal control of the organization without jeopardizing their core interests.

PART TWO

CASES

4

Informal governance in the IMF

The degree of the IMF's autonomy is controversial. The IMF was not designed to be the independent world central bank that Keynes envisaged; from the beginning, its members, most notably the United States, expressed a preference for a member-controlled organization rather than a supranational one.[1] However, the Fund's management and staff have gradually gained autonomy from the shareholder countries represented on the Executive Board, and critics of the IMF fear that this autonomy goes too far.[2] An alternative critique assumes that international organizations simply reflect the interests of a few powerful states, or of one. An impressive amount of evidence indicates that major shareholders are able to skew the distribution of IMF loans and to subsequently undermine the enforcement of conditionality.[3] Similarly, countries that enjoy special relationships with major IMF shareholders may be able to avoid extensive conditionality when they borrow from the Fund.[4] In almost all cases, the evidence indicates that the powerful shareholder that exercises influence over the IMF is the United States.[5]

How does a country that holds only seventeen percent of the voting power in an organization exercise a controlling interest in its activities? The argument made here is that the aspects of the IMF's formal design that make it appear to be so autonomous, and that allow it to exercise considerable

1 Pauly 1997.
2 Martin 2006.
3 Thacker 1999; Barro and Lee 2005; Dreher and Jensen 2007; Eichengreen *et al.* 2006; Stone 2002, 2004. For a review of the recent quantitative literature on IMF lending, see Steinwand and Stone 2008.
4 Polak 1991; Gould 2003, 2006; Copelovitch 2004; Dreher and Jensen 2007.
5 My work on Africa found that France and Britain intervened on behalf of some of their former colonies with which they maintained close political ties (Stone 2004). Subsequent interviews at the Fund have confirmed this pattern but underscored that it is limited to Africa. In other regions, the United States firmly repulsed other G-7 countries that sought to interfere, as Japan discovered in Indonesia and Korea.

discretion in ordinary times, also make it extremely vulnerable to capture by a determined state that enjoys an organizational advantage. IMF standard operating procedures delegate substantial authority to management, weaken the Executive Board to the point that it is unable to exert effective oversight, and create substantial informational asymmetries among the shareholders and between the shareholders and management. Delegation, weak oversight and lack of transparency lower the costs when the United States assumes operational control, because its influence is difficult to observe.

In large part, the exercise of informal influence in special cases is made possible because of the broad consensus among the major shareholders about the IMF's objectives, which reduces the incentives for the medium-size players to monitor US activities. The United States exerts control of the IMF through informal participation, in a way that is similar to the way minority shareholders can effectively control publicly held corporations if they are willing to exert sufficient effort. The smaller shareholders are content to free-ride, because they know that their interests are unlikely to come into conflict with those of the United States in most cases. When these interests do come into conflict, the United States has an overwhelming advantage over other states in its capacity to participate informally in IMF decision making, and the informal practices of the Fund amplify that advantage.

IMF governance for general policies diverges from the pattern for lending decisions. General policies, institutional reforms and constitutional changes are analogous to legislative processes. The process of making these decisions involves minimal information asymmetries, little delegation to IMF staff, and direct involvement by the member countries; most importantly, the outcome of these decisions is of immediate interest to all members. Consequently, informal influence is minimized, and voting rules significantly influence the outcomes. On the other hand, lending decisions are of primary importance to the borrower, involve substantial information asymmetries among the other members, and involve broad delegation to IMF management and staff. Under these circumstances, informal power becomes effective when it is exercised. This provides the basis for an inter-temporal exchange: the United States retains the ability to decisively influence lending decisions, at the cost of giving up substantial control over formal decision making.

Formal rules and informal procedures

The IMF follows a complex set of formal procedures that are centered on the Executive Board, which are designed to provide legitimacy and democratic accountability to its decisions. IMF governance functions in practice according to these formal procedures during decisions about general policies, institutional reforms and constitutional changes. Voting rules play a key role in the IMF's formal procedures, and although formal votes are rarely taken, the decisions made by consensus reflect the distribution of votes and the majority requirements that apply to particular kinds of decisions.

Voting in the IMF is based on the same quota system that determines member countries' financial contributions and credit access limits. The quotas of new members are determined by formulas based on national product, trade volumes, openness, and financial reserves, which are intended to reflect both the members' capacity to contribute and likely need to draw on Fund resources. The formulas are essentially arbitrary, however, have been adjusted over the years, and are periodically subject to renegotiation, which underscores their political origin. The original quota formulas arose from an American effort at Bretton Woods to cloak in technocratic calculations its political judgments about what share of control it was necessary to cede to each of the major powers in order to secure their participation. The author of the original formula, Raymond Mikesell, recalls that Harry Dexter White charged him with devising a formula that would yield a quota of approximately 3 billion dollars for the United States, provide half that amount for Great Britain, and grant third and fourth place to the Soviet Union and China, respectively – parameters that had been set by the president and the secretary of state.[6] No guidance was provided on what data should be used for the formula; Mikesell found that the formula had to weight national output significantly to achieve the desired results, but he introduced trade openness to get closer. The proposed quotas were adjusted in a number of cases through bilateral bargaining, and several were adjusted subsequently during the Bretton Woods negotiations, so that the actual quotas deviated substantially from those produced by the formula. Mikesell was initially instructed to keep the formula confidential when he presented the proposed quotas at the Bretton Woods conference. Describing his presentation to the Bretton Woods delegates, Mikesell recalls:

> I…gave a rambling twenty minute seminar on the factors taken into account in calculating the quotas, but I did not reveal the formula. I tried to make the process appear as scientific as possible, but the delegates were intelligent enough to realize that the process was more political than scientific.[7]

Many of the delegates were not satisfied with their proposed quotas and

[6] Mikesell 1994, 22.
[7] Mikesell 1994, 35–6.

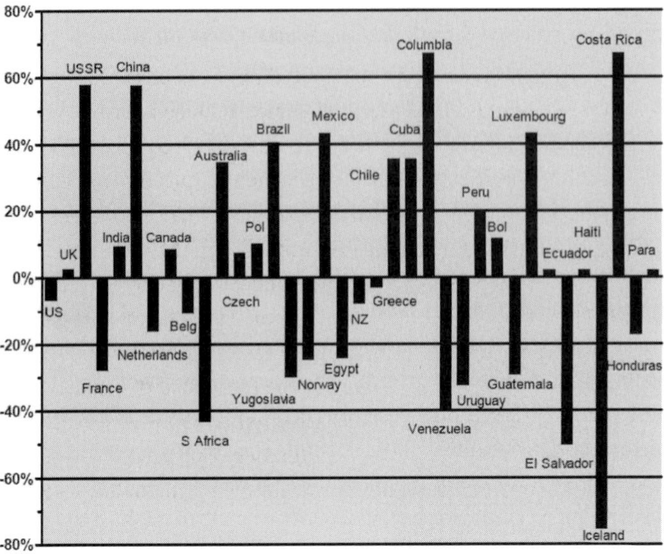

Figure 4.1 Deviations of Bretton Woods quotas from the formula.

Source: Report to the IMF Executive Board of the Quota Formula Review Group. April 28, 2000: 17 (www.imf.org); author's calculations.

demanded revisions, some of which were granted in bilateral negotiations. The French delegate, Pierre Mendes-France, objected strongly that the French quota had been set at a lower level than China's, but he failed to achieve a revision.[8] Figure 4.1 illustrates the wide range of variation of actual quotas determined at Bretton Woods around the quotas predicted by the formula. While there remained a strong correlation between actual quotas and quotas predicted by the formula, the wide range of variation reflects the fact that bargaining dominated the process.

In the years since the Bretton Woods conference, the US share of quotas has steadily declined as new members joined the IMF and faster growth in other countries changed the proportions of world trade and output. In addition, the quota formula has been revised several times. When necessary, however, the veto threshold has been adjusted downwards to assure that the United States retained effective veto power. It has played a significant role in formal policy making that the United States has always controlled a minority of shares, so it

[8] Mikesell 1994, 37.

could not directly control policies, but has controlled a share that was substantial enough to block adoption of new policies.

In contrast to general policy decisions, lending decisions are not made strictly according to formal rules. Instead, the balance between formal and informal governance varies significantly. In routine cases, the Executive Board delegates substantial authority to IMF management, which in turn delegates detailed decision making to staff. In cases that are important to major shareholders, on the other hand, the informal mechanisms for influencing IMF policy become decisive. The formal rules are further eclipsed when lending occurs in the midst of a crisis, and informal governance reaches its apex when the crisis occurs in a systemically important country. The more high-level attention a program attracts among the leading shareholders, the more the substance of decision making is shaped outside the formal process. The informal mode of governance diverges sharply from the formal one, and the differences are substantively important in terms of the distribution of authority within the organization and among the member states.

The formal rules are based upon universal participation and representation of the membership, democratic decision-making procedures for policy formulation and oversight and a voting mechanism weighted according to contributions to the Fund's capital. In contrast, the informal governance practices of the IMF centralize decision-making authority, limit effective participation and restrict the flow of information. The locus of effective decision making moves outside of the Executive Board to forums that better reflect the international distribution of resources, and management's formal proposal power is exercised informally by individual shareholders, which shape proposals before management brings them to the board. Shareholder countries' influence over decision making is not directly proportional to the distribution of vote shares and is not simply a function of the formal voting rules. Instead, participation in decision making varies depending upon the institutional capacity of the shareholding state and access to information. The Fund's informal norms strengthen the appointed management of the Fund *vis-à-vis* the bulk of the membership, but assure in practice that the G-7 countries acting in concert, and often the United States acting on its own, are able to exercise effective control over the Fund when they regard this as necessary.

In particular, three institutional features that might appear to strengthen the Fund's autonomy – avoidance of voting, a strong chair, and the centralization of information – in reality serve as backdoors that allow the United States to exert a controlling influence over lending decisions.

Voting is generally avoided on the Executive Board. Instead, the managing director, acting as chair, ascertains the "sense of the meeting."[9] Votes were called periodically in the early years of the Fund's existence, but this subsequently became very rare; for example, only five votes were taken between 1954 and 1972.[10] In principle, any Executive Director (ED) may call for a formal vote at any time, but a strong norm has arisen, which all of the EDs support, which discourages exercising that right. When voting occurs, the Executive Board minutes reflect the concern that this not become common practice:

> When votes have been requested since 1953, there have been expressions of regret, even by the executive director calling for the vote, at the departure from the "normal traditions" of the Executive Directors, and expressions of hope that it would be possible to continue to resolve issues "by the usual process of discussion."[11]

The practical implications of this practice vary across types of decisions. In discussions of general policies, this has usually meant that the weighted distribution of formal voting power was diluted, because the large shareholders made an effort to build oversized coalitions, and preferably to reach decisions unanimously, rather than impose their will by taking close votes. As an early IMF study concluded, "decision by 'the sense of the meeting' moderates the effect of weighted voting power."[12] During lending decisions, on the other hand, the norm of avoiding voting means in practice that almost all proposals pass unanimously. In effect, the Executive Board ratifies whatever the IMF management proposes.

According to the IMF's formal procedures, the managing director exercises a remarkable degree of gate-keeping power and proposal power as chairman of the Executive Board. No lending item can come before the board without the managing director's approval. In addition, amendments to country lending items are not allowed because they have been negotiated with country authorities before they are brought to the board for ratification. When the managing director is able to choose his proposal autonomously, such procedures assure that he can control the agenda and choose his most preferred policy from the feasible set. However, informal participation allows influential shareholders to control the substance of the management proposal, assuming the formal proposal-setting prerogatives of the chair for themselves. This allows the United States

9 Rule C-10 of the Rules and Regulations, adopted in 1946, provides that "The Chairman will ordinarily ascertain the sense of the meeting in lieu of a formal vote. Any Executive Director may require a formal vote to be taken with votes cast as prescribed in Article XII, Section 3(i)." Quoted in Gold 1972, 197.

10 Gold 1972, 196.

11 Gold 1972, 198.

12 Gold 1972, 198.

to exert effective control by participating much more actively than the other shareholders. The United States has a tremendous organizational advantage over other countries because it has a more extensive diplomatic corps, particularly important private financial institutions, numerous advantages in gathering information, and all of the advantages of having the IMF located in the United States capital, in addition to issuing the international reserve currency and commanding the resources of a superpower. Perhaps more important than these organizational resources is the informal deference that the other directors and the IMF staff accord to the United States. With the exception of France and the United Kingdom, which exercise substantial influence in their respective spheres in Africa, the United States is usually the only active participant.

The privileged position of the United States is strengthened by rules that centralize information. There are extensive formal rules that insulate negotiations about IMF programs from participation by shareholders through their EDs. Except for the borrower's representative, EDs do not participate in missions to countries or the negotiation of programs. In addition, they are not privy to the confidential documents that are key to the negotiations, the mission briefs that determine the parameters of the negotiator's discretion and the back-to-office reports about the progress of negotiations.[13] This centralization of information generally prevents EDs from influencing conditionality, but it does not prevent the United States from being fully informed. For example, the United States ED routinely interviews chiefs of mission before and after missions to Latin American countries, and in extraordinary cases such as Mexico, Russia, Indonesia and Korea, senior US Treasury officials were intimately involved in the details of the negotiations.[14] Confidentiality provides the IMF management with an information advantage over the Executive Board and a measure of autonomy,[15] but simultaneously allows the United States to centralize control.

[13] This may seem surprising; after all, the principal should want full access to information in order to monitor the agent effectively. When interviewed, however, IMF officials unanimously agreed that these documents were never provided to EDs. EDs reported that they never asked to see them, and they would not expect staff to comply if they did. There was broad agreement that these rules were necessary to safeguard the integrity of the bargaining process, because the directors could not commit not to reveal the staff's bottom line to the borrowing country if they knew what it was.

[14] IEO 2003. Although in principle any ED can request special briefings with staff, in practice only the US and French EDs regularly do so, and the French ED interviews staff only about missions to francophone Africa. An ED from a small European country explained that if he made such a request, it would be granted politely, but privileged information would not be forthcoming. If he persisted in asking for special briefings, he would expect to see a memo circulated requesting that EDs forebear from overburdening staff. In other words, his understanding was that the EDs were formally equal, but some were more equal than others.

[15] Martin 2006.

The Executive Board

According to the IMF's Articles of Agreement, the highest constitutional authority of the organization is the Board of Governors, but this body has delegated most of its authority between annual meetings to the Executive Board. The Executive Board exercises most of the functions of a board of trustees, and its decisions form the case law of the IMF and interpret precedents. The Executive Board consists of resident EDs (originally twelve, and currently twenty-four), of whom five are appointed by the largest shareholders, namely the United States, Japan, Germany, Britain and France, and 19 are elected by the rest of the membership for two-year terms.

The G-7 deputies, the deputy ministers of finance responsible for international affairs, have become the effective locus of decision making in cases of crisis lending.[16] The rank and expertise of EDs varies substantially, but most of the EDs from the leading shareholding countries are civil servants, and financial decisions in major crises are made at the political level. The deputies comprise the level where technical expertise meets political responsibility, and when decisions are too hot to make on their own responsibility, the deputies have the access within their governments to reach a decision within twenty-four hours. The G-7 deputies have formal meetings six times per year and know each other well, so they are able to conduct important business by conference call. The G-7 countries seek to avoid open disagreements in order to avoid sending destabilizing signals to markets, and having reached a common position, the G-7 countries almost always vote as a bloc on the rare occasions when votes are recorded. Except for rare cases, this takes most of the drama out of Executive Board meetings. The role of the G-7 has shifted somewhat in recent years, as the EDs from the EU have intensified their consultations and coordinated their positions, and as the G-20 has assumed new prominence in the wake of the global financial crisis of 2008. The G-7 deputies continue to be a critical locus of IMF governance, however.

By the 1990s, there were three distinct groups of EDs on the Executive Board, and they behaved quite differently. The G-7 EDs almost always supported the proposal made by management, because their positions had been incorporated into the proposal before a formal board meeting took place. If the positions of the G-7 countries clashed, this almost never took place on the board.[17] There is variation in the roles of EDs within the G-7; for example, the

16 This is often the case when prominent institutional reforms are considered, as well as in crisis lending. For example, the Heavily Indebted Poor Countries (HIPC) initiative, which offered substantial debt relief, was developed by the G-7. Interview with IMF senior staff.

17 The exception is the case of Mexico in 1995, which is discussed in Chapter 7, and is well documented in Copelovitch 2010. The dispute only came into the open because the United

Canadian ED tends to be more senior than his G-7 colleagues. The ED from the United Kingdom represents the Chancellor of the Exchequer and the alternate represents the Bank of England, so they sometimes take different positions. The Canadian and Italian ED are elected by multi-country constituencies, and the other G-7 EDs are appointed by their home countries. Representing multiple countries gives an ED a greater range of independence.[18]

The EDs from developing countries have a distinct role because they represent borrowers rather than net creditors to the Fund. Consequently, their main function is to represent their constituents to the board as borrowers. Because they represent multiple countries and their constituents participate actively in Fund programs, a significant portion of the workload handled by their offices involves accompanying IMF missions to the countries they represent. The developing country EDs follow a strong norm of solidarity, which makes them reliable supporters of management proposals to make Fund resources available to members. Developing country EDs generally do not have time to inform themselves on country matters beyond reading the staff report unless the matter involves one of their own constituents, and they do not receive the institutional back-up from their capitals that G-7 EDs enjoy. Although larger numbers of constituent countries come with larger staffs, the developing country EDs are the most thinly stretched because they have so many missions to which to send representatives. In effect, the only EDs who are likely to express opposition to proposals to use Fund resources at the board are those from small developed countries who represent multiple constituencies. These are the EDs who have been most active in probing the assumptions of Fund programs, and they are the ones who are most likely to abstain when a program is controversial. They are the most independent from their home capitals, because they represent constituencies of several countries, and they are not dependent on the goodwill of management or of the developing country EDs because they do not anticipate borrowing from the Fund. They are required to represent the interests of their constituents, however, which sometimes requires them to swallow their policy preferences. For example, the Dutch ED was critical of the program for Russia in July 1998, but did not participate in the discussion because his constituent, Ukraine, was up for discussion at the same time. The small European countries enliven the discussion and raise the level of debate, but they do not represent a real constraint on the management's ability to promote its agenda. Abstentions

States pushed a last-minute increase in the size of the loan to Mexico onto the agenda without allowing time for discussion by the G-7 deputies. Even in that case, one has to read between the lines of the Executive Board minutes to perceive the degree of disagreement among the directors.

[18] Interviews with former and present EDs; interviews conducted for IEO 2003.

do not block adoption of a decision, but they are rare nevertheless, and voting against a management proposal is almost unheard of.

Management

In IMF parlance, "management" refers to the managing director and the deputy managing directors – everyone else in the organization aside from the Executive Board members and their offices is "staff." The IMF management exercises a remarkable degree of formal proposal power, particularly in decisions that affect particular member countries. In most voting systems, a wide range of outcomes is possible given a distribution of voting power and preferences, and therefore whoever controls the power to make proposals is able to control the outcome.[19] The Executive Board is chaired by the managing director or by one of his deputies, and as chairman of the board, the managing director conducts the business of the board and generally has the last word. The management proposes all action items, and lending decisions are made on the basis of an up-or-down decision that does not allow amendments to be made at the board, because letters of intent have been negotiated and signed by the country authorities before the board meeting. In principle, the board could reject a proposal and send it back for renegotiation, although this might be disastrous in a crisis case; but even in ordinary lending, this has not occurred in recent memory.[20] Decisions of the board are written beforehand by staff in the form of the chairman's summing up, which is not circulated before the meeting but instead is read to the board at the conclusion of the meeting, sometimes with amendments that express issues raised during the meeting.[21]

This formal arrangement suggests a very independent institution with a powerful executive. However, informal consultations allow the leading shareholders to shape the agenda and craft proposals before they come to the board. Influence in this informal process is not circumscribed by the formal power inherent in vote shares and the formal voting rules. If only the formal rules were operative, the management would still seek to craft its proposals to guarantee a majority, and potential veto players – particularly the United States, as the

[19] McKelvey 1976, 1979. Kalandrakis (2006) demonstrates that in a general bargaining model with sequential voting, there exist proposal rules that generate every possible distribution of the surplus, given any distribution of vote shares and discount rates.

[20] Interview with IMF staff.

[21] This is an interesting difference between the Fund and the World Bank, which otherwise has the same basic governance structure and the same distribution of vote shares. In the World Bank, the equivalent document is reviewed and sometimes revised by a subcommittee of the EDs before it goes to the board.

largest shareholder – would exercise disproportionate influence. An important implication of the formal voting rule, however, is that this influence would only operate in a negative sense: veto players could influence proposals that they could credibly threaten to otherwise oppose. There is some evidence, which is discussed in the concluding section of this chapter, that US influence over general Fund policies is dependent upon the ability to exercise veto threats in precisely this way. However, in decisions affecting individual countries, this is not the case. In country matters, the United States has an impressive degree of positive power. For example, it is able to promote lending even when the other leading shareholders are skeptical, and it can heavily influence the content of programs even when it has a strong interest in seeing them move forward.

The consequence of this system is that influence in the IMF over decisions that affect particular countries corresponds more closely to informal participation than to formal voting power. An example of asymmetric participation emerged in interviews with staff who indicated that the US ED always requested a special briefing before a country item regarding a Latin American country came to the board. In addition, in important cases, including Argentina, Brazil and Mexico, the US ED requested meetings to debrief the chief of mission before and after each trip abroad.[22] The US ED does not have any more access to confidential documents than the other EDs, but with these extensive briefings she was able to effectively monitor the progress of negotiations. The United States has a huge advantage over its peers in influence over the IMF because the Fund is located in the heart of the federal government, so contacts are almost costless. As a result, the briefings that the ED convened generally involved representatives of Treasury and several other US government departments, so the US government was engaged on many levels. Other EDs also have access to staff when they choose to exercise it, but the behavioral pattern is that they do so much more rarely. The degree of direct involvement of their capitals is generally much lower as well because of distance and time zones. A prominent exception, however, is that the French ED becomes deeply engaged in items involving francophone African countries, and missions to Africa often stop in Paris in order to brief the French Treasury.[23] During crises, the G-7 EDs are routinely briefed before the other countries, because it is understood that the key unofficial forum for making decisions about international finance is the G-7 deputies. This norm of prior consultation was only violated once in

[22] Interviews with IMF staff.

[23] Similarly, British EDs intervene on behalf of Commonwealth countries in Africa. For example, the British ED played a key role in restarting IMF lending to Kenya in the 1990s. Interviews and informal discussions with staff.

recent memory, in the case of Mexico in 1995, and the result was stormy.[24] In some cases management held briefings for the G-10 EDs rather than just the G-7 in order to address objections by the smaller European countries that they were being left out of the loop, and in the cases of Mexico, Indonesia, Korea and Argentina the board held additional, informal meetings in order to strike a balance between sharing information with the entire board and maintaining confidentiality.[25] However, these broader consultations supplemented rather than replaced the private consultations between major shareholders and management, and the most important contacts took place at a higher level than the EDs. The US Assistant or Deputy Treasury Secretary has frequent contact with the IMF managing director and his first deputy, and when the leadership of Treasury is effective, as it was during the Clinton administration, the line between the US government and IMF management becomes blurred.

Information asymmetry

Informal governance in the IMF relies on the high degree of secrecy that is reinforced by discipline within the IMF staff. The original rationale for secrecy was that under the Bretton Woods system of pegged exchange rates the Fund handled confidential information about future exchange rate adjustments that had significant market value. Long after the demise of this system, the Fund still occasionally handles very valuable information, but the market value of Fund documents has significantly eroded, and its shelf life is very short. Nevertheless, the IMF maintains an elaborate classification system for secret documents, and breach of confidentiality is regarded as a very serious offense within the organization.[26] The staff has a free-wheeling internal discussion of

[24] Interviews with IMF staff.

[25] Informal board meetings are called to share information and allow discussion when a formal board decision is not needed. They are closed, so the audience is restricted, and very limited minutes are kept. The fact that the meetings took place is recorded in the Executive Board minutes. Interpretation is from interviews with IMF staff.

[26] IMF documents are classified as public; for official use only (for example, staff reports circulated to the Executive Board); confidential (for example, Executive Board minutes and letters of intent, mission briefs, back-to-office reports, and much interdepartmental correspondence); strictly confidential (for example, the Whittome Report cited below and minutes of restricted board meetings); and secret (for example, correspondence with authorities, and mission briefs and back-to-office reports prepared during the Asian crisis). Each category of documents has an associated handling procedure, and the higher levels involve numbered copies and locked cabinets; only the lower levels are held in the archives. Documents regarded as internal – all documents circulated within individual departments and most of the interdepartmental memos generated during program development – are not registered on the Cyberdocs internal database of IMF documents, so the only record of their existence is in the department that holds them. During the Mission to Indonesia in 1997,

policy options, but it presents a monolithic view to the Executive Board, and the same is true at various levels within the organization. Subordinate staff members do not dispute the position taken by the chief of mission or the front office of a department when addressing management,[27] and staff closes ranks around management when it interacts with EDs. Staff members acknowledge that they would not express an opinion on or off the record to an ED that differed from management's official position. EDs, for their part, recognize that they cannot elicit unofficial opinions from staff, and rarely try.[28] They acquiesce in a system in which they are denied access to most categories of internal Fund documents, such as mission briefs, back-to-office reports and interdepartmental correspondence. This arrangement is intended to protect the integrity of the staff's technical judgments and to avoid undermining the Fund's position as trusted confidante *vis-à-vis* member countries. The effect, however, is that management is able to control the access of EDs to staff opinions and analyses.[29]

Informal governance predominates over formal governance throughout the project cycle in systemic crises. The roles played by the Executive Board, individual EDs, and the governments of major shareholders differ during pre-crisis surveillance, decisions about the use of Fund resources, the design of conditionality, and the enforcement of conditionality, but the problems involved in surveillance provide a stark illustration of the weakness of the Executive Board.

Surveillance

The IMF devotes considerable resources to bilateral surveillance of the policies of its members. Every member country is visited according to a regular schedule by an IMF mission, which prepares a staff report and reports to the

World Bank officials reacted with incomprehension when told by their IMF colleagues that they could not have access to documents that they themselves had written because they were now classified as confidential (Blustein 2001). This clash of organizational cultures is telling.

27 An exception within staff is the special role of the Strategy, Policy and Review Department, formerly Policy Development and Review (PDR) Department, which has the role of reviewing draft mission briefs and approving programs proposed by the area departments. A representative of this department accompanies every mission, and writes a report that provides management with an independent channel of information.

28 Interviews with former EDs and IMF staff.

29 In recent years the Fund has taken a number of important steps to increase transparency, including publishing letters of intent associated with IMF lending programs and providing public access to the Monitoring of Agreements (MONA) database on the internet. Although these steps have increased the external transparency of the institution, they have not changed the information asymmetries within the Executive Board, because all of this information was already available to ED.

Executive Board. The Executive Board devotes an average of 23 percent of its meetings and 22 percent of its time to Article IV surveillance that does not involve any use of Fund resources.[30] This surveillance has a variety of purposes, but a major focus in emerging markets is to detect early warning signs of developing crises and recommend corrective action before a crisis becomes full blown and requires drastic policy corrections. Assessments conducted after crises, however, invariably point to important failures to detect the warning signs. There is some selection bias here; when surveillance is more effective, crises may be avoided, so focusing on crises exaggerates the rate of surveillance failure. Nevertheless, a growing number of important cases have been documented in which surveillance has failed, and it is important to ask whether something about the IMF's governance hampers the surveillance effort. In addition, recent quantitative studies have found that IMF forecasting is systematically biased.[31]

The first evaluation of crisis management conducted by the Fund, the Whittome Report, found a disturbing pattern of surveillance failures in Mexico that led up to the 1994–95 crisis. Sir Alan Whittome, a retired Fund insider, concluded that "the culture, procedures, and incentives that have grown up in the Fund were inimical to an early recognition of the dangers facing Mexico."[32] Carefully reviewing the data available to the staff and when it became available, Whittome concluded that giving Mexico the benefit of the doubt was reasonable until the fall of 1994, when data that had been available to the Mexican government at the beginning of the summer were finally reported to the IMF, showing that reserves had declined and monetary policy had deteriorated. By the end of September the Fund staff had clear evidence that Mexico's macroeconomic policies were inconsistent with sustaining its exchange rate target, and that either an exchange rate realignment or a currency crisis had become inevitable. In spite of the data, however, the information that the staff provided in its report for the upcoming Article IV review failed to signal that anything had changed.

Whittome diagnosed the problem with surveillance in terms of three sets of issues. First, there was concern that anything presented in writing to the board has a large audience, because Executive Board documents are widely circulated in member countries and often find their way into the hands of the press. In the context of a potential crisis that could be triggered by the leakage

[30] IMF Secretary's Department. *Selected Workload Indicators of the Executive Board, Number and Hours of Board Meetings, 1997–2007*. Table 1.

[31] Dreher *et al.* 2008; Fratzscher and Reynaud 2007.

[32] Whittome, L. Alan. *Report on Fund Surveillance of Mexico, 1993–94* (Whittome Report). EBS/95/48. March 23, 1995: 35.

of sensitive information, therefore, anything critical of a member country that was sent to the Board had to be written in such dense code that it was difficult to separate the signal from the noise.

Second, EDs frequently act as protectors of member countries, and take issue with Staff reports that are perceived as critical. Staff is naturally risk averse about confronting member countries with critical analysis, especially when the country is in a vulnerable position that would make it react strongly. Earlier in 1994 EDs had criticized staff of the Western Hemisphere Department for "badgering" Argentina about its current account deficit (an issue that reemerged with a vengeance in 2001), and this had a chilling effect on the staff monitoring Mexico. In addition, during the Article IV consultations with Mexico in 1993, the ED representing Mexico had asked that language referring to the deterioration in the quality of data available from Mexico be removed from the staff report. Since no one objected and the report was edited to create a more favorable impression, the staff was justified in inferring that there was no interest on the board in receiving negative assessments of Mexico's policies.[33]

Finally, the staff's extraordinary discipline, which allows it to keep valuable information confidential and to present a unified view to the outside world, has the disadvantage that debate is shut off when management takes a position. As a result, the information that the Executive Board receives is systematically biased in favor of the management proposal. The management had frequently praised Mexico as an example of successful economic reform, and Mexico had made a great deal of progress. In 1994, furthermore, the managing director wrote letters placing his seal of approval on Mexican requests for financing from the United States and Canada. "It would not then be surprising," Whittome concludes, "if the staff found it awkward to raise doubts about the direction in which the economy was headed."[34]

The discrepancy between the reports sent to the Executive Board and the operational data on which they were based was sufficiently stark that it has led some observers to conclude that IMF staff must have suffered from "groupthink."[35] The IMF's policy advice to Mexico, Ngaire Woods argues, "had solidified into one optimistic scenario, which was adopted as an article of faith." She goes on to argue that Fund staff showed a systematic failure to recognize warning signs – a "faith-based blindness or seeming groupthink" – that reflected a dogmatic devotion to a narrow set of economic theories.[36] Reading IMF staff reports to the Executive Board could indeed convey this impression,

[33] Whittome Report, 30–1.
[34] Whittome Report, 25.
[35] Woods 2006, 60.
[36] Woods 2006, 63.

if they are taken to represent the staff's true views. Within the staff, however, there was wide appreciation of the dangers of Mexico's economic mismanagement, and the warning signs were not missed; they were simply downplayed in official reports. Reports to the Executive Board are not used as an opportunity to ring alarm bells.

A serious effort was undertaken to improve surveillance after the appearance of the Whittome Report. The Fund modernized its access to financial data and made a substantial effort to improve data reporting standards in member countries by establishing the Special Data Dissemination Standard (SDDS) in 1996. After the Asian crisis, the Fund went further by beginning to publish letters of intent, the documents that codify IMF conditional lending programs, on the internet. However, the staff continued to filter the information it passed on to the board. In each of the crises covered in this book, staff concealed from the board the problems it faced in obtaining access to confidential data, censored the data that it provided to the board because of concerns that the data would leak, and downplayed the severity of exchange rate risks in its reports to the board.

The most sensitive data concern central bank reserves. The Fund pressures countries to disclose this information, but countries facing impending crises often distort their central bank balance sheets to hide their vulnerabilities from the market, and are unwilling to disclose accurate data to the Fund. As noted above, this was a key problem in Mexico in 1994. Similarly, the Fund was unable to gain access to critical information about the balance of usable reserves in Russia (1996–98), Thailand (1997) and Korea (1997). A Fund surveillance team failed to recognize the risks that the Asian crisis would spread to Korea as late as October 1997, because the Koreans created a rosy impression of their finances, which only gradually crumbled as more information came to light. During the routine Article IV consultations in mid-October, before Korea asked for emergency assistance, it reported official reserves to the Fund of approximately $30 billion, or two months of imports.[37] It was not until late November that the mission was informed that a substantial portion of the Bank of Korea's gross foreign reserves was not usable for foreign exchange operations because they had been deposited in off-shore subsidiaries of commercial banks to allow them to service their short-term debt.[38] The staff report, which was dated December 3, dramatically revised the estimate of available reserves.

37 IMF – Korea. *Briefing Paper for Negotiation of a Stand-By Arrangement*. Prepared by the Asia and Pacific Department (in consultation with other departments). Approved by Wanda Tseng and Joaquin Ferran. November 21, 1997: 5.

38 The estimate used in Fund documents at the time was 25%. Blustein cites a figure of 40% (2001, 130, 140).

Taking the encumbrance of those reserves into account, the staff report concluded that usable reserves had fallen to a critically low level of $7 billion.[39] Because it had failed to detect how vulnerable Korea was, the Fund was forced to scramble to assemble political support for a rescue package that had to be much larger than it had expected.

The staff report, however, skated lightly over the fact that the Koreans had hidden the true dimensions of their problem from the Fund mission just a few weeks before. The report identified the "opacity of Korea's financial data" as a key structural problem, but this is a common observation in these reports, and did not signal the degree of frustration staff felt with the Koreans over this episode.[40] Certainly, some EDs were aware that the Koreans had been hiding their vulnerability from the Fund, but they did not learn about it from the staff report.

The fragility of Korean finances in December 1997 intensified concerns about secrecy and limited the information that staff reported to the board, as usable reserves fell to $3.9 billion on December 18 before recovering to $8 billion. The staff report for the December 3 program, cited above, was leaked to the Korean press, and the Korean government decided to publish it in response in order to control the damage, a decision that provoked a heated debate on the Executive Board.[41] In the run-up to the expanded program announced on December 27, therefore, management instructed staff to remove data on the daily level of Korean reserves from the staff report, citing concerns that the information could be leaked to the press.[42]

Beginning several years before the 1998 crisis, the Central Bank of Russia (CBR) engaged in an elaborate set of financial transactions designed to hide from the IMF and the market the fact that it was using substantial amounts of its reserves to buy state bonds, or GKOs.[43] When the deception came to light, the head of the CBR and his deputies insisted that IMF staff had to have been

[39] *Korea: Request for Stand-By Arrangement*. Prepared by the Asia and Pacific Department (in consultation with other departments). Approved by Hubert Neiss and Joaquin Ferran. December 3, 1997: 11.

[40] *Korea: Request for Stand-By Arrangement*. Prepared by the Asia and Pacific Department (in consultation with other departments). Approved by Hubert Neiss and Joaquin Ferran. December 3, 1997: 12.

[41] *Republic of Korea – Request for Publication* EBM/97/118-1 – Final. December 9, 1997.

[42] Fischer, Stanley. *Korea – Draft Staff Report*. Office Memorandum to Mr. Boorman and Mr. Aghevli. December 27, 1997: 1.

[43] Price Waterhouse Coopers 1999, cited in Stone 2002, 143. The CBR held some of its reserves in numbered off-shore accounts in foreign banks that were wholly-owned subsidiaries, and sold $1.2 billion of Russian state debt to them, which allowed it to meet IMF targets for central bank net domestic assets and net international reserves. The IMF was informed of the transaction, but not informed that the foreign banks involved were owned by the CBR. The IMF hired the consulting firm to investigate after the new Russian government revealed the deception in 1998, and briefly posted the report on its website.

aware that these transactions were illegitimate, but had chosen not to pursue the matter.[44] The Russian officials claimed that IMF staff had colluded in their efforts to misrepresent their holdings of reserves, so that they would appear to have met the conditions for disbursing loan installments during the critical Russian presidential election of 1996. According to Sergei Aleksashenko, first deputy chairman of the CBR at the time, "Approving the tranche in 1996 was a political question for the Fund and for the Central Bank. No one was interested in knowing the details about the operations."[45] IMF officials rejected this interpretation.

Staff failed to give the Executive Board clear early warning signals about exchange rate risks in each of the crises discussed in this book. When it had the data and recognized the problem, the Fund staff wrote reports to the Executive Board that couched the warnings in cautious language about risks that was not readily distinguishable from the language used when there was no substantial evidence of danger. In the cases of Brazil and Argentina the evidence gradually mounted that the countries were engaging in fiscal policies that were inconsistent with their respective announced exchange rate regimes, a crawling peg in Brazil and a currency board arrangement in Argentina. However, even when the crises began to loom on the horizon, the staff never stated that the exchange rate was misaligned or warned that a significant policy change was necessary in order to avoid a dramatic correction. In Brazil, staff reports pointed to a loss of competitiveness, which could be a sign of an overvalued exchange rate, and reports touched on issues of debt sustainability, but there was never a "bottom-line judgment" about the risks of a crisis.[46] Staff members involved in those assessments emphasized that there was a strong presumption against challenging the authorities' opinion about their exchange rate, and that it would be unwise for staff to claim that the exchange rate was overvalued without compelling evidence that a crisis was imminent.[47] In Argentina, the Fund's advice consistently focused on labor market rigidities, rather than emphasizing the fundamental issue that the exchange rate peg was unsustainable in the presence of substantial fiscal deficits and a volume of public debt that could not be serviced without continued capital inflows.[48] The Treasurer's

44 The CBR officials argued that it was apparent that there were no foreign banks interested in buying large quantities of Russian bonds in 1996, so Fund staff had to know that the transaction with its subsidiary, FIMACO, was illegitimate, and they did not ask for clarification. Interviews with Sergei Dubinin, November 17, 1999; with Sergei Aleksashenko, November 16, 1999; and with Aleksandr Potemkin, November 14, 1999, cited in Stone 2002.

45 Interview with Sergei Aleksashenko, November 16, 1999, cited in Stone 2002, 144.

46 Transcript of interview conducted for IEO 2003, 2.

47 Interviews with IMF staff.

48 Interviews with IMF staff involved with Argentina. One respondent disagreed with the interpretation that the staff had concealed information from the board, but agreed that staff had

Department and Research each expressed objections to the 1998 program during the internal review, but their concerns were not reflected in the staff report.[49] In all cases the fear of leaks from the board played a significant role in degrading the clarity of the messages that the board received, particularly in writing, which is the main form in which the board receives information from the staff. Staff in the Western Hemisphere Department accurately understood what was happening in Brazil and Argentina, correctly analyzed the danger of continuing with their current strategy, and were well aware of the risks. However, a warning about the exchange rate could not be put into a staff report, because it would find its way into the press.

In some cases, the perceived need to avoid offending country authorities or the need to close ranks behind management prevented the staff from sending danger signals that would have helped inform the board about the risks involved in a program. Regardless of the signal they received, staff pooled on a strategy of sending an ambiguous signal to the board. In several cases, the effect was that the IMF embarked on risky programs and the staff and management did not inform the board how risky they believed them to be. It is unlikely that the IMF would have made very different decisions had staff reporting been more forthright. The key informal decision makers in these cases had access to more candid assessments, both from their own sources and directly from management. The fact that the Executive Board received filtered analysis, however, undermined the quality of its work and made it less relevant to decision making in crises than it otherwise would have been.

The limits of board access to critical information and how they evolve over time are illustrated by the use of side letters. Side letters are private written agreements between management and country authorities that supplement formal conditionality, but are considered too sensitive for a variety of reasons to include in letters of intent. Side letters were originally devised as a way of preventing such information from leaking when it was presented to the board, and often not only the content, but even the existence of side agreements was not communicated to the board. Between 1997 and 1999 there were 28 side letters, usually covering exchange rates, interest rates, intervention in the financial system, expenditures, or enterprise restructuring. One side letter covered capital controls, three covered trade policy, and three covered price increases. There was intense pressure to reform this practice after the Asian crisis, and in 1999 the board passed a new set of guidelines for side letters that called for reducing their use and limiting it to issues that were market-sensitive. In addition,

to be very careful how concerns are conveyed to the board, and that the main signal sent about the exchange rate regime was that it required more labor market flexibility.

49 IEO 2004, 37 (web version).

it prescribed that the existence of side letters or oral agreements must be communicated to the board, and EDs must be permitted to read the side letters in a restricted session and return the copies to management. However, management is permitted to remove information from the copy circulated to the board if "disclosure would: (a) seriously hamper the authorities' capacity to conduct economic policy; or (b) confer an unfair market advantage upon persons not authorized to have knowledge of the information."[50] A Policy Development and Review Department (PDR) report on the use of side letters prepared in 2002 indicated that the new policy had been followed, and that the use of side letters had declined from 18 percent of countries using Fund resources to 7 percent. In at least two cases side letters were not used – oral agreements were used instead – because country authorities "were reluctant to use side letters because of the wider distribution under the revised procedures and doubted that the existence of the letter would remain undisclosed."[51] One case in which the board was not informed of the existence of an oral agreement was the augmentation of the program for Argentina in September 2001, in which Argentina committed to discussing a new policy framework – i.e., reevaluating its fixed exchange rate – with the IMF if its reserves fell below a threshold, which was set just above the level of outstanding Fund credit. Although the board was not informed, the G-7 deputies were, and some EDs knew about the agreement because their governments informed them.[52]

Policy issues

In contrast to the previous discussion of country items, the decision-making procedure for general policy issues conforms closely to the IMF's formal governance model. Although the norm of consensus decision making remains strong and management tries to avoid contentious votes on the Executive Board, dissenting votes are more common, and decisions correspond more closely to the vote shares of the members and the formal voting rules. In particular, the United States frequently does not prevail when it champions policy changes, although it can use its position as a veto player to prevent changes that it opposes or to bargain for policy changes when its approval is needed in order

50 "Use of Fund Resources – Side Letters." Executive Board Minutes. EBM/99/108. September 23, 1999: 62.

51 "Review of Side Letters and the Use of Fund Resources." Prepared by the Policy Development and Review Department in consultation with the Secretary's Department and Legal Department. EBS/02/89. May 28, 2002: 2–3, 6.

52 IEO 2004, 53, 56. There remains some dispute about whether a side letter or an oral agreement was used in this case. An ED who was informed about the agreement at the time insisted that it was an oral agreement.

to expand IMF quotas. Deference to management is much weaker on general policy issues than on lending, and the board takes a more active role in formulating policy.

To take a trivial example, there has been a long-term disagreement on the board about the compensation and size of Fund staff. The United States has consistently taken the position that costs should be contained by maintaining a lean staff, and that Fund staff were excessively compensated. Staff compensation does not have direct budgetary consequences for the shareholders, because the IMF's operations are financed by the interest it charges on its loans. However, as the provider of the largest share of the Fund's capital, US officials have traditionally felt that they contributed the largest share of the costs. In addition, US officials have taken a jaundiced view because Fund compensation exceeds the compensation of US government officials with similar levels of seniority and is tax free. EDs from developing countries, on the other hand, have preferred high levels of compensation for Fund staff. EDs and their staff are compensated according to Fund salary schedules, and they sometimes migrate from the Executive Board to staff positions. Developing-country views on this issue have generally prevailed when compensation changes have not required supermajority votes, reflecting the preferences of the majority of the board members. During 2007 and early 2008 the Fund was hit by a budget crisis, however, because demand for its loans had hit a record low, and the interest from the remaining loans was not sufficient to finance Fund expenses. In the corridors of the IMF, a frequently heard quip was that the Fund needed to "find another Turkey" – because Turkey had been a frequent user of Fund resources and its outstanding loans were about to be repaid. In order to balance the budget, the Fund sought Executive Board permission to convert some of its gold reserves into an investment account to generate income, but this required a supermajority vote. As a result, the United States was able to insist upon budget austerity, which led to a 10 percent cut in staff levels.

A more consequential example was the evolution of the Fund's policy regarding capital controls. The Fund's Articles of Agreement grant each member country the right to impose capital controls at its own sole discretion, in contrast to current account controls, which they are encouraged to phase out. In fact, the consensus view at Bretton Woods was that capital controls were a desirable instrument for managing the volatility of international capital flows, and the agreement foresaw the possibility of cooperative use of capital controls to prevent currency crises.[53] It was well understood at the time that commitment to fixed exchange rates and full employment was inconsistent with free

[53] Helleiner 1994; Chwieroth 2009.

capital mobility, although these relationships were formalized later.[54] It was not until the 1960s that the economics profession began to seriously question the wisdom of using capital controls, and the consensus that they were harmful did not emerge until the 1970s. The United States became an early advocate of abolishing capital controls during the Nixon administration after closing the gold window in 1971 and floating the dollar in 1973. European countries and Japan relied upon capital controls to manage the turbulence of the 1970s, however, and a clear majority on the Executive Board favored their continuation. Current account imbalances swelled after the abolition of the Bretton Woods system of fixed exchange rates, and differential responses to the oil shocks of the 1970s strained European efforts to stabilize their exchange rates. Meanwhile, American efforts to talk down the value of the dollar led to capital outflows that complicated the German Bundesbank's efforts to contain inflation. As a result, European countries, with strong support from Japan, sought a new IMF policy designed to implement cooperative capital controls in the spirit of the original Bretton Woods agreement. Any progress was blocked, however, by the stolid opposition of the United States.[55] While the United States was unable to achieve any movement in IMF policy in its own desired direction because it was isolated on the issue of capital controls, it was able to rely on its formal voting power to veto any policy shift in the opposite direction.

Recent research makes a convincing case that staff developed its own views, which coincided with those of the majority in the 1970s, because the views of the economics profession penetrated the organization with a lag as new staff members were recruited from among the graduates of top economics departments. Staff began encouraging developing countries to dismantle their capital controls in the 1980s, largely because the prevalent view in economics that capital controls were harmful to development had finally percolated through the Fund.[56] During this decade, however, important shifts in the positions of the G-7 countries permitted the staff to develop a new line. The shift to the right in French economic policy under Mitterand – the famous "U-turn," in which France opted for economic liberalism combined with European integration when the market proved in 1983 that Keynesianism in one country would not work – played a key role in shaping the new consensus.[57] France had been the last major hold-out against liberalization within the European Community, and had blocked the Anglo–German–Dutch proposal to liberalize capital flows in the early 1980s. With this policy shift, the way was open for agreement on

[54] Mundell 1960.
[55] Helleiner 1994, Chapter 6.
[56] Chwieroth 2009.
[57] Abdelal 2007.

the Single European Act of 1986 and the 1988 directive to abolish capital controls in Europe by 1992.[58] Meanwhile, Japan dismantled many of its capital controls under US pressure, and the Organization for Economic Cooperation and Development (OECD) adopted a strict set of requirements that members abolish capital controls. Michel Camdessus came to the Fund as managing director determined to liberalize capital flows.[59] The Clinton administration intensified the longstanding US preference for abolishing capital controls under Treasury Secretaries Robert Rubin and Lawrence Summers, but it was the fact that this view had become consensual that now made it possible to make progress on this agenda. By the 1990s, even many developing countries had dismantled their capital controls and adopted liberal economic policies.

The fate of two recent initiatives with regard to capital controls illustrates the ways in which policy issues differ from the treatment of country items in IMF governance. The first was the development of the proposal to transfer jurisdiction over capital controls to the Fund in 1997. The authorship of this proposal is controversial – Abdelal ascribes it to Camdessus, Chwieroth attributes it to the IMF staff, and journalistic accounts credit US pressure – but it is clear that it enjoyed the support of the IMF and at least the tacit support of the Clinton administration, although administration officials subsequently claimed that they had been skeptical. It moved through the various stages of IMF governance, from the Executive Board to the Interim Committee (the predecessor of the IMFC) relatively smoothly. The new policy guidelines were set to be finalized in spring 1998, but the eruption of the Asian crisis intervened and shook the consensus on the board. Nevertheless, sufficient momentum had been achieved that the proposal seemed likely to pass, and Camdessus continued to support it staunchly. By this point, even if it was not the original author of the proposal, the Clinton administration was strongly committed to it and pushed it forward. However, in the spring of 1998 a group of Congressmen led by Richard Gephardt threatened to withhold support for legislation to support an increase in IMF quotas, which requires House approval, if the new proposal for capital controls went forward. The United States withdrew its support, and the proposal promptly died.[60]

Over the next few years, abolishing capital controls became less popular in the economics profession, which began to emphasize the benefits of sequencing economic reforms and improving financial market institutions before

58 Moravcsik 1998, 262–63, 269–73, 333–47.

59 Abdelal 2007.

60 Gephardt was Democratic House minority leader at the time, so his support was essential to a Democratic administration seeking a quota increase. He was a leader of the protectionist wing of the Democratic Party and took a skeptical approach to the international financial institutions.

liberalizing capital flows. Nevertheless, IMF staff remained firmly committed to the virtues of liberalization. When the Executive Board called on the Fund to develop Medium Term Strategy (MTS), therefore, one of the few substantive changes to IMF strategy that the staff proposed was to renew the proposal to grant the IMF jurisdiction over member country capital controls. The MTS went through an extensive interdepartmental review process and was proposed to the Executive Board by management, which had an incentive to anticipate objections. Nevertheless, the proposal was rejected at the Executive Board, and management was directed to redraft the MTS. In the end, the extensive staff work and the product of the interagency review was rejected wholesale, and management commissioned a narrow team of drafters to draw up a revised document that was much less substantive.[61]

These examples illustrate the view, which is widespread within the Fund, that the formal decision-making procedures are decisive during decisions about general policies. In the case of capital control policy, the US role seems to have been exactly what we would expect from its role in the formal decision-making structure. As the leading shareholder, it is able to block initiatives that it opposes, as it did to proposals to strengthen capital controls in the 1970s, and as it finally did to the proposal to give the Fund authority over capital controls in 1998. However, while US support is necessary for positive initiatives, it is not sufficient; policy changes only when a majority supports it. The United States was unable to shift IMF policy on capital controls to keep up with changes in its own views in the 1970s, and by the time US preferences for liberalization began to be implemented in the 1980s, reducing capital controls was no longer a strong US policy priority.[62] The emergence of a broad consensus among the countries represented on the Executive Board by the 1990s provided the space for the IMF management to promote liberalization under Michel Camdessus, and was more important than the Clinton administration's zeal for liberalization.

The development of the IMF practice of conditional lending provides an illustration of the interaction between formal and informal decision rules, because it involved both decisions about general policies, in which voting rules were decisive, and the gradual development of precedents related to individual countries, where informal influence was much more pervasive. The treaty establishing the IMF adopted at Bretton Woods in 1944 did not provide for conditional lending, although some of its language implied that access to Fund resources need not be automatic. For the first few years of its existence the IMF lent its resources without applying any formal conditions aside from seeking

61 IEO 2009.
62 Chwieroth 2009.

the approval of its Executive Board, and conditional lending was not established until 1952. The United States, which at this time was the primary net creditor to the IMF and held 30 percent of IMF quotas, insisted that loans should be accompanied with binding conditions, arguing that this was necessary in order to safeguard Fund resources. The United States was not initially able to prevail over the determined opposition of the other members, however, which expected to be net borrowers and therefore to be subject to the conditions.

Frank Southard, the US ED, announced the first steps towards conditionality as US policy in May 1948, in the form of guidelines for eligibility to draw on Fund resources, and almost immediately began applying these principles in individual country cases.[63] The other countries refused to adopt conditionality as a formal Fund policy, however, and the United States did not have the votes to establish the policy unilaterally. On the other hand, the United States was able to effectively use its 30 percent vote share to block action, and it brought Fund lending to a halt in 1950. In a form of partial exit, the United States used unilateral lending under the European Recovery Program as an alternative to IMF lending, and attached substantial conditionality to its support. The staff and management were alarmed that the impasse would render the IMF a dead letter, and advanced several compromise solutions that were rejected in 1949 and 1950. Finally, after substantial debate and several drafts, the Executive Board adopted the policy establishing the Stand-By Arrangement (SBA) as a conditional lending facility in 1952.[64]

Conditionality policy developed gradually during the 1950s. Phasing IMF programs, or disbursing loans in tranches, was first introduced in 1956, and the current practice of making disbursements conditional on meeting formal performance criteria was introduced in 1957. The application of phasing and conditions was uneven, however, and was most widely used in western hemisphere SBAs. The success of these programs was generally dependent upon substantial amounts of supplementary financing by the United States, and the United States was therefore strongly interested in program design and in a strong position to influence it. The US ED, William Dale, argued in 1966, "By establishing performance criteria related to public finance, credit policy, and the balance of payments, stand-by arrangements have in many cases provided an essential part of the basis on which sizable amounts of US assistance have been committed."[65]

Meanwhile, European countries' preferences about the design of condition-

[63] Gould 2006, 45.
[64] Gould 2006, 45–7.
[65] EBM/66/13. February 23, 1966: 5. IMF archives, quoted in Gould 2006, 78.

ality shifted as their roles shifted from net borrower to net creditor. Most west European countries had convertible currencies and current accounts by the end of the 1950s, and were much less dependent upon US financing than they had been early in the decade. As a result, policy on conditionality was much more consensual by the time of the first review of IMF conditionality in 1968 than it had been in the early 1950s. In fact, the EDs representing Germany and Canada appeared to be somewhat more enthusiastic about conditionality than the US ED, who suggested that conditionality might have gone too far and been too intrusive.[66] Germany had current account surpluses by the 1960s, and its main macroeconomic concern was preventing the resulting capital inflows from creating inflation. The guidelines adopted represented a compromise, instructing staff to limit binding conditions to the "minimum necessary," abolishing conditionality for low levels of access to IMF resources, and calling for greater uniformity in the application of conditionality.[67] Uniformity, in particular, is a concern of developing country EDs. However, the guidelines also represented an acknowledgment by the membership of the legitimacy of conditionality, and established the principle that all upper-tranche programs should have binding conditions.

Subsequent reviews of conditionality in 1979 and 2002 similarly called for reductions in the number of conditions and more uniformity of treatment, but also codified new practices that had arisen in the interim, such as medium-term lending in 1979 and financial sector conditionality in 2002. Meanwhile, applying the principles adopted in 1979 under rapidly changing conditions led to a dramatic expansion of conditionality in the 1980s and 1990s. The size of financial imbalances rose much more rapidly than IMF quotas, and long-term users of IMF resources accrued substantial debts, so that the majority of borrowers entered the upper credit tranches that called for substantial conditionality. The Reagan administration exploited the opportunity that this afforded to expand conditionality and give it a distinctive supply-side emphasis.[68] The nominal expansion of IMF quotas in 1983 was limited to 22 percent, so that inflation drove borrowers into higher credit tranches, and during the expansion the United States exercised unusually strong formal control over IMF policies because its vote share is sufficient to block quota expansions. Discussions within the Executive Board in July and August 1983 were initially deadlocked, as the United States resisted calls from developing countries to expand quotas and raise access limits in the wake of the Latin American debt crisis. France and Britain crafted a compromise within the G-7 under which access limits

66 Gould 2006, 78.
67 Gould 2006, 79.
68 Kahler 1990.

were raised, but countries that exceeded the old limits would be subject to more stringent conditionality.[69] Two-thirds of IMF loan disbursements involved substantial conditionality by the end of the 1980s, compared to only one-quarter in the 1970s.[70] Based on archival research, Erica Gould estimates that the average number of performance criteria in an IMF program jumped from 7.1 during the period from 1974 to 1982 to 12.1 between 1983 and 1990.[71] Throughout the development of conditionality, it appears that the policy has only imperfectly represented US preferences, but has gradually come closer as the majority of the Executive Board became creditors and their preferences shifted to more closely resemble those of US representatives.[72]

The Executive Board plays a much more active role in debating and amending changes in general policies than it does in approving programs for individual countries. Whereas country lending items generally pass the board with minimal discussion, management proposals on policy issues are subject to intense scrutiny because they directly engage the interests of the whole membership. Executive Board policy decisions do not have the force of law, but they are more analogous to legislative than to executive decisions because they apply to wide ranges of cases, and they are watched carefully because they set general precedents. The aspects of executive delegation that facilitate informal participation – confidentiality, urgency and tight agenda control – are missing in general policy discussions. This different treatment of policy issues, which are subject to formal voting and open discussion, and country-specific executive decisions, which are subject to informal governance, has important implications for the distribution of influence within the organization. US influence over general policies reflects the US' status as the largest shareholder, but is restricted to a degree that is commensurate with its vote share. In contrast, US influence is much more decisive over country matters that directly concern only one or a few members.

69 Boughton 2001, 881–82.
70 Boughton 2001, 561.
71 Gould 2006, 60.
72 Gould (2006) interprets this history differently, but her data and historical evidence are consistent with the argument made here. She argues that the United States had a preference for weaker conditionality because the United States intervened to weaken conditionality in numerous cases, and countries that received substantial amounts of US foreign aid were subject to less conditionality. The argument here is that this is evidence of informal influence that leads to exceptions for favored states (see Chapter 8), but that the United States had a general preference for more stringent conditionality. The ability to make exceptions is only valuable if the general rule is onerous.

Conclusions

A critical argument of this book is that institutions are endogenous. Informal governance practices arise and persist because the states that participate in international organizations make trade-offs between the costs of ceding control to powerful actors and the costs of inducing those actors to withdraw from multilateral cooperation. The IMF Executive Board has the formal power to change these practices, and it engages in periodic self-assessments and makes reforms to its procedures, as it did when it began publishing letters of intent and discussing side letters. However, there are good reasons for the Executive Board to avoid disturbing the status quo.

First, the status quo works pretty well for the significant shareholders most of the time. They have a consensus view, with some allowance for differences of emphasis, about what sorts of economic reforms developing countries should be encouraged to adopt, and management shares this consensus, so there is no compelling incentive to monitor closely. Management's preferences are known, and shirking is not a relevant concern, so there is no significant principal–agent problem that would deter delegation. In the average country most of the time, furthermore, the United States does not exert special influence because it has no compelling incentive to do so and because manipulation of the process involves some costs. Thus, the costs of informal governance are usually modest for most of the shareholders. Furthermore, the mid-sized shareholders have a weight in discussions about general policies that is much greater than their weight in the international economy, so the costs of informality are outweighed by the benefits of enjoying a disproportional share of decision-making power in an international forum in which the United States is heavily invested.

Second, although individual EDs might prefer to increase the competency of the Executive Board, they do not have the authority within their own governments to initiate substantial reforms. Within the G-7, decision making on important issues occurs at the level of the G-7 deputies, who substantially outrank their respective EDs. This suits the United States because it finds it easier to achieve consensus within the G-7 than in a wider and more public forum, and it suits the other G-7 countries because membership in the G-7 gives them privileged access to information and a place at the table when the important issues are discussed. Developed countries outside the G-7 find the arrangement less satisfactory and are more likely to raise reform proposals, but also have less influence and less ability to introduce changes. Developing countries, until recently, have complied with these arrangements because they were net borrowers rather than net creditors, so they were willing to participate in spite of their relative underrepresentation. This has been shifting as countries such as China, India and Brazil have become increasingly important players in the world economy, and the shift of the locus of governance from the G-7 to the G-20 promises to increase their role in the future. However, when countries have shifted from net borrower to net creditor status in the past, their interests have generally aligned more closely with those of the United States, ensuring that it was relatively easy to maintain a consensus among the states that were powerful enough to change the rules.

Ultimately, institutional design depends upon the distribution of power and interests. Informal governance persists because it is useful for the United States to be able to manipulate IMF policies under special circumstances, and other countries acquiesce in institutional arrangements – a strong management, a weak Executive Board, and substantial secrecy – that make the costs of manipulating the organization low enough to be tolerable for the leading power.

5

The World Trade Organization

Comparative cases provide useful counterpoints to the IMF, illustrating the broad sweep of the theory of informal governance, and also demonstrating that the theory can help to explain the substantial differences across international institutions for diverse issue areas. The cases chosen are the World Trade Organization and the European Union (EU). Important aspects of informal governance emerge in each of these organizations. Indeed, in each case, the informal practices play an essential role in institutional design, and ignoring them would lead to fundamental misunderstanding of how each institution functions. However, informal governance plays very different roles in each case, and I argue that the model presented in Chapter 3 sheds light on the variety of international organizations.

The comparative statics of the model make strong predictions about institutional design. The expectation of long-term conflict of interest and the dispersion of structural power impose limits on the willingness of states to invest in jointly controlled institutions and lead to more formalization. However, we do not necessarily expect weak institutions to be associated with formalization because of the intervening effects of the returns to cooperation. When the returns to cooperation are high, states become willing to invest substantial powers in institutions even when the existence of multiple leading powers increases the costs of delegation. However, in order to minimize these costs, they choose formalized institutions that make delegating extensive powers more acceptable. Consequently, whenever extensive delegation arises under circumstances of multiple leading powers with substantially conflicting interests, it should take legalized forms.

These expectations are consistent with the existing practices in the World Trade Organization (WTO), which came into force in 1995, and the General Agreement on Tariffs and Trade (GATT), which was inaugurated in 1947 and continues under the WTO. Both trade regimes have had a weak central secretariat with few delegated powers, because the major players anticipate that an institution with substantial powers would be subject to capture, and they anticipate frequent conflict of interest over trade policy. Executive powers are weak. Similarly, the process of GATT/WTO rule-making is not highly formalized. Rules are made by the conference of the parties through a process of informal bargaining conducted by state representatives. There is no legislative delegation. Delegation is limited to the quasi-judicial interpretation of rules. On the other hand, the delegation of authority to the WTO's dispute settlement procedure is far reaching, and the trade regime has become more formalized as the scope of this delegation has increased. The number of GATT disputes subject to the procedure has increased dramatically since the creation of the WTO, and GATT trade law has grown rapidly to cover an ever-expanding policy area. At the same time, the commitments adopted by new members of the WTO have become much more extensive than they were under the GATT, and some of these commitments have been the subject of subsequent disputes. The contracting parties have been careful to limit their delegation of authority to legal and quasi-judicial forms that are relatively difficult to influence informally, but within this sphere they have allowed extensive delegation.

This chapter discusses three aspects of GATT/WTO policy-making: dispute adjudication, trade rounds and accession. Dispute adjudication is the most formalized and involves the greatest degree of delegation. Trade rounds, the GATT legislative process, are informal and are negotiated by the parties on their own behalf. The accession process for new members, on the other hand, is both formalized and controlled directly by states. Informal influence plays an important role in each of the three dimensions of policy-making, but it is most limited in the highly legalized process of dispute adjudication.

GATT/WTO dispute adjudication

Outside of the EU, GATT trade law is the most rapidly expanding area in international law, and the area of international law with the greatest substantive effects. The Uruguay Round culminated in eighteen major agreements and numerous protocols, which totaled over 26,000 pages of text. The establishment of the WTO in 1995 formalized the GATT Dispute Settlement Understanding and has led to a dramatic increase in the substantive scope of trade law, the complexity of the law, and the activity of the WTO Dispute Settlement Body.[1] The decisions rendered have become much more detailed and complex, typically running to hundreds of pages in length, compared to GATT decisions

[1] Davis 2010.

that were typically a dozen pages long. The rapidly expanding case law now reaches well over 30,000 pages.[2] This is among the most striking instances of a trend towards the legalization of international politics, in which states have chosen to formalize their commitments to each other and delegate the resolution of particular conflicts to international jurists.[3] By the middle of 2009, 395 cases had been brought before the Dispute Resolution Body under the WTO rules. The majority of these cases have been resolved informally, after briefs were filed and formal arguments were heard, but before the panel ruling was issued. The rulings in cases that have run their course, however, have consistently favored trade opening, and have established a growing basis of international precedent that expands the reach of GATT law. Of the 142 cases that have been ruled on by panels, 125 rulings, or 88 percent, have found at least one violation of GATT rules.[4] Rulings by the Appellate Body have further expanded the sphere of judicial delegation, in some cases well beyond what the parties originally intended.[5]

US plans for the post-war era included a formalized International Trade Organization (ITO) with comprehensive rules covering trade and investment and the power to adjudicate disputes, which was prevented from coming into force by the refusal of the US Senate to ratify the treaty.[6] This episode illustrates some of the dilemmas associated with extraordinary power. The British and American negotiators agreed on the principle of formal dispute resolution, although the British insisted on an option to reintroduce quotas for balance of payments reasons, and US negotiators demanded safeguards.[7] However, the balance of payments surplus that gave the United States such extraordinary structural power in the aftermath of World War Two made the British and other trade partners reluctant to embrace multilateral liberalization, so that the best deal the Americans were able to negotiate was a messy compromise that US export-oriented business regarded as worse than the status quo. In particular, the British refused to compromise on the discriminatory system of Imperial Preferences, and US negotiators conceded that the ITO would operate under

[2] Shaffer 2009, 168–9.

[3] Abbott and Snidal 2000; Keohane *et al.* 2000.

[4] World Trade Law database, www.worldtradelaw.net/violationcount.asp, accessed July 22, 2009. The source lists complaints, rather than reports, because in a few cases multiple reports were issued because there were multiple complainants.

[5] Steinberg 2004.

[6] William Diebold wrote in 1952, "The core of the postwar trade policy of the United States was the ITO..." (1952, 36). The United States proposed the initial draft at the time of the British Loan of 1945 and organized multilateral negotiations involving fifty countries that eventually led to the signing of the Havana Charter in 1948. The treaty was never reported out of committee in the Senate, however, and in 1950 the Truman administration quietly acknowledged that it would not reintroduce it for ratification.

[7] Milner 1997, 143–8.

a one-country–one-vote system, which was far from representing the bargaining leverage the United States exercised outside the forum. In order to achieve wide adherence to the Havana Charter, furthermore, US negotiators made concessions on a number of issues that preserved protectionist policies. US international business closed ranks in opposition to the treaty, convinced that the United States could negotiate more market opening on a bilateral basis by using its market power.[8] The US Council of the International Chamber of Commerce singled out discriminatory trade practices that would be preserved under the ITO and argued that the ITO Charter "places the United States in a permanent minority position owing to its one country-one vote procedure." It went on to argue that "membership in the ITO based on this Charter would make it impossible for the United States to engage in an independent course of policy in favor of multilateral trade."[9] The ITO appeared less attractive than the US outside option. This outside option included continuing to use an alternative multilateral regime, the provisional GATT, which had been designed to be a component of the ITO but had come into use before the ITO was put up for ratification. The first GATT round in 1947 led to average tariff reductions of approximately one-third.[10] Even if the GATT unraveled after non-ratification of the ITO, however, US export-led businesses and foreign investors calculated that their interests would be protected better under bilateralism than under a flawed multilateral regime.

The fall-back position, the GATT trade regime created in 1947, was very informal. The GATT 1947 had no formal enforcement powers, its provisions were not enforceable in domestic courts, and it was never submitted to the US Senate for ratification. Initially, it had no formal dispute resolution procedure and relied on informal consultations, but within a few years it developed the practice of appointing expert panels to make rulings on legal complaints by the members. This grew into an elaborate dispute resolution procedure under which members could submit disputes to panels of trade lawyers for arbitration, but the defendant had to voluntarily participate in the process for it to go forward, and the panel ruling was not binding because either side could unilaterally reject it. Nevertheless, members turned to the dispute resolution process hundreds of times under the GATT regime, and compliance with panel rulings was very high. Violations were generally resolved by mutual agreement.[11] The compliance rate no doubt reflected the strong selection effects imposed by the

[8] Gardner 1980, 375–6; Diebold 1952, 20.

[9] Executive Committee of the United States Council of the International Chamber of Commerce. *Statement of Position on the Havana Charter for an International Trade Organization*. May 9, 1950: 2–3. Cited in Gardner 1980, 377.

[10] Odell 2000, 168.

[11] Hudec 1993; Reinhardt 2001.

procedure, since a country could block the formation of a panel or veto the panel decision rather than allow the procedure to run its course and then refuse to comply, but the participants apparently valued the ability of the procedure to resolve disputes more than the stakes in a particular dispute often enough to make an informal regime effective. The creation of the WTO in 1995 formalized the dispute resolution procedure, putting an end to the defendant's right to block adoption of a panel ruling and establishing a standing Appellate Body to review appeals. These changes invigorated the dispute procedure and increased the frequency of filings: 395 cases have been filed in the fourteen years since the WTO was created in 1995 (28.2 per year), compared to 535 complaints during the entire forty-six year history of the GATT until that point (11.6 per year).

By the time of the Uruguay Round (1986–94), the balance of power and interests had shifted, and neither the United States nor the European Community regarded the informal regime as adequate. The complexity of the international trade regime had increased enormously and the emphasis in the negotiations had shifted from bound tariff rates (which by now were quite low outside of agriculture) to non-tariff barriers to trade, so that violations of the regime became less transparent, and the importance of dispute resolution was magnified. After losing a series of high-profile GATT disputes in the early 1980s, the United States had come to rely increasingly on the threat of imposing unilateral trade sanctions, an outside option that was inconsistent with the norms of GATT.[12] Section 301 of the Trade Act of 1974 required the US Trade Representative to draw up an annual list of countries that were applying unfair trade practices, and to impose automatic trade sanctions if they failed to adjust them. This strategy had some success in securing market access, but antagonized US trade partners.[13] The European Community and Japan regarded reining in US unilateralism as one of their top priorities for the Uruguay Round.[14] Meanwhile, since the European Community had emerged as a counterweight to the trading leverage of the United States, US officials had come to recognize the advantages of a legalized regime that would bring about mutual restraint. In terms of the model of informal governance, both the benefits of cooperation and the dispersion of structural power had shifted in ways that favored delegation to a formalized institution.

The US Trade Representative made specific proposals to strengthen the

[12] In "United States – Sections 301–310 of the Trade Act of 1974," WTO DS152, the panel ruled in 2000 that the Trade Act was not in violation of GATT rules, but retaliation under it would be a violation if not authorized by a WTO panel ruling (Davis, forthcoming, 42).

[13] Bayard and Elliott 1994.

[14] Barton *et al.* 2006, 69–71.

GATT dispute resolution procedure at the beginning of the Uruguay Round, and in 1990 it was the United States that proposed the package of reforms that was ultimately embodied in the WTO, including automatic adoption of panel reports and the creation of the Appellate Body. The US position on legalization was ambiguous, however. On one hand, US decision makers believed that other countries were more likely to violate GATT provisions, so strengthened procedures would benefit US interests. On the other hand, however, US negotiators insisted on the legality of the Super 301 procedure, which was very popular in Congress.[15] When it proposed legalization, the United States linked these reforms to adoption of sweeping changes to the substantive rules of the trade regime that reflected US interests – the introduction of GATT rules on trade in services, intellectual property rights and treatment of foreign investment – so this was an offer to exchange substantive reforms for procedural constraints. Leading developing countries objected to the substantive rules (GATS, TRIPS and TRIMS), and attempted to block the progress of the trade round on those grounds, but did not object to legalization.[16]

There is a vigorous debate about the fairness of the dispute resolution procedure. Some of the same organizational advantages that allow the United States to exert informal influence in the IMF operate here as well. Proxies for organizational capacity strongly predict the initiation of GATT disputes.[17] In addition, developing countries are less likely to achieve early settlements – a negotiated settlement before the formal panel ruling – which is when the settlements that are most favorable for the complainant typically occur.[18] The costs of pursuing disputes are not trivial for developing countries. In Brazil's case contesting US subsidies for cotton, the legal fees amounted to $2 million. In the dispute between the United States and the EU over illegal subsidies to Boeing and Airbus, fees paid to private law firms reached $1 million per month.[19]

The appeals process may provide additional opportunities for powerful countries to influence the outcome. Although the process of forming dispute panels is transparent and difficult to influence, panel rulings can be appealed to the standing Appellate Body, and this body frequently modifies the original ruling. Steinberg argues that the leading trading powers influence the Appellate Body by selecting its members.[20] In addition, the Appellate Body has incentives to accommodate the interests of powerful countries to prevent its rulings

[15] Hudec 1993, 194.
[16] Hudec 1993.
[17] Some studies use the size of country delegations to the WTO in Geneva, while Busch *et al.* (2010) use a capacity index based on survey data.
[18] Busch and Reinhardt 2000, 2003.
[19] Shaffer 2009.
[20] Steinberg 2004, 249.

from being openly defied, so it modifies panel decisions in ways that are expected to minimize the possibility of such conflict.[21] Garrett and Smith argue that the Appellate Body has been particularly active in modifying rulings that went against the United States or the EU, and the legal reasoning behind a ruling is often changed to avoid offending powerful players even if the ruling itself stands, which can have an impact on the development of case law and precedent for the future.[22] There is no strong body of quantitative evidence that indicates a pervasive pattern of biased rulings, however, and it appears that the legalized setting of dispute settlement limits the degree of informal influence.

Having initiated a dispute, successfully prosecuted the case, and finally prevailed, the complainant now faces the task of compelling compliance. The WTO has no direct enforcement mechanism; it simply authorizes an appropriate sanction to be applied by the complainant. The ability to compel therefore depends upon the complainant's market power. How much the respondent complies by liberalizing its trade policies depends on the ability of the complainant to retaliate, which is a function of its imports from the complainant.[23] These difficulties are foreseeable, and structural power apparently affects decisions to initiate disputes. Substantial imports from a trade partner are associated with increased incidence of disputes; joint membership in a regional trade agreement and dependence on aid from the target country are associated with fewer disputes.[24]

The most important participants in the dispute settlement procedure, both under the GATT and under the WTO, have been the United States and the EU. The United States initiated 26.4% of disputes under GATT and 22.5% of those under the WTO, and the European Community/EU initiated 18.5% under GATT and 20.0% under the WTO. The median member initiated one GATT dispute and no WTO disputes.[25] Much of this variation, however, could be accounted for by the size and diversity of US and EU exports, which provide more numerous opportunities for trade conflicts.[26] Consistent with this interpretation, the United States has been targeted as a respondent in WTO disputes more frequently than it has initiated them (26.8% of cases), and the EU was also a frequent target (16.2% of cases). Guzman and Simmons argue that

[21] Steinberg 2004.
[22] Garrett and Smith 2002.
[23] Bown 2004.
[24] Bown 2005.
[25] The data cover 1975–2009, and are from Busch and Reinhardt (2003) for the GATT period and from the World Trade Law database of WTO trade disputes, available at www.worldtradelaw.net. There have been 395 disputes launched as of July 21, 2009.
[26] Horn *et al.* 1999.

Table 5.1 *Initiators of WTO disputes, 1995–2009.*

	Disputes	Share	Cumulative
United States	89	23%	23%
European Communities	79	20%	43%
Canada	30	8%	50%
Brazil	23	6%	56%
India	16	4%	60%
Mexico	16	4%	64%
Argentina	14	4%	68%
Japan	12	3%	71%
Korea	12	3%	74%
Thailand	10	3%	76%

Source: World Trade Law database of WTO trade disputes, available at www.worldtradelaw.net.

because developing countries are constrained in their legal capacity, they must be selective about the disputes they initiate, so they are more likely to select high-income countries as respondents.[27] They find that concern about retaliation does not seem to deter countries from initiating disputes, although Busch and Reinhardt find evidence that such retaliation apparently occurs.[28] Although the top ten disputants initiate three-quarters of all disputes, the range of countries that were significant participants in GATT disputes has significantly widened under the WTO. This trend has continued over time, and developing countries have launched the majority of disputes in the last few years.

However, there are important lacunae in the areas covered by the formalized dispute resolution procedure, which have allowed the major trading states to safeguard their domestic interests. First, there are areas of trade in which the rules are not enforced by tacit mutual consent. When devising the WTO's adjudication procedures and rules covering export subsidies, for example, the United States and the EU could not be certain whether they would ultimately be directed against Boeing or Airbus. Because both sides preferred not to roll the dice, there was a longstanding informal ceasefire over enforcement of WTO rules against either aircraft producer until the issue became caught up in the 2004 US presidential campaign.

In addition, compliance with dispute resolution has been rendered less costly by the slowness of the dispute procedure. As a case in point, the Boeing–Airbus litigation, which has been the most costly in WTO history, has lasted long enough to shield the parties from any costly adjustments. A panel report was

27 Guzman and Simmons 2005.
28 Busch and Reinhardt 2002.

issued in September 2009 that supported US allegations filed in 2004 that the EU and its members had spent billions of euros in illegal "launch aid," or low-interest loans provided to support the development of new airplane models. European governments had invested approximately $13 billion to develop the Airbus A380 model, for example, and France, Germany and Britain have since committed to investing 2.9 billion euros to support development of the new A350. However, an EU countersuit alleges that Boeing has been provided with over $24 billion in subsidies through military and space agency contracts and Washington State tax breaks. Even after five years of litigation, the WTO ruling does not finish the process of resolving the conflicting claims, and meanwhile the economics of the airplane industry has shifted dramatically, leading both suppliers to outsource much of their manufacturing to countries in Asia.[29]

In many cases, the slowness of the process makes it possible for countries to temporarily deviate from their obligations when domestic pressures are intense, but avoid sanctions by complying with a ruling that only arrives after political circumstances have changed. During the 2004 presidential election, for example, the Bush administration imposed levies on imports of steel products in order to garner votes in the swing-vote states of Ohio, West Virginia and Pennsylvania. The EU challenged the measure in the WTO and ultimately won, and drew up plans to impose retaliatory sanctions targeted at US congressional districts with insecure Republican incumbents. The free-trading Bush administration had no desire to extend long-term protection to the steel industry, however, and complied with the WTO ruling after the election was over. Similarly, China recently announced that it would comply with a WTO ruling overturning its protectionist levies on imported automobile parts, but the delay caused by the adjudication process apparently allowed China to achieve most of its objectives. The United States initiated the dispute procedure in March 2006, and a dispute resolution panel was established in October, which waited until July 2008 to rule. China appealed the ruling, and lost the appeal in December, but was given until September 1, 2009 to comply. While the three-year dispute process dragged on, the prohibitive tariffs on imports of auto parts had convinced major automobile makers to build new plants in China and transfer technology, which had been the objective of the tariffs. Corporate spokesmen in the automotive industry indicated that the Chinese decision to comply with the WTO ruling was not expected to have any effect on their operations.[30]

Anti-dumping rules provide the most attractive safety valve for countries

[29] "Five-Year Dispute on Aircraft Claims Loses Its Urgency." *New York Times*. September 4, 2009: B5.

[30] "After Carmakers Adapt, China Trade Dispute Ends." *New York Times*. August 31, 2009: B3. China lowered its tariffs for imported cars when it joined the WTO in 2001, but retained applied rates of 25% for imported cars and 10% for imported parts. In 2005 China imposed

that face sharp domestic opposition to liberalization. The anti-dumping provisions of the GATT are intended to prevent predatory pricing practices, the practice of selling goods abroad at depressed prices in order to drive competitors out of business. These provisions allow importing countries to impose countervailing tariffs if three conditions are met: (1) the export price is lower than the home price for the same product, (2) the importing country is able to demonstrate material injury to its import-competing industry, and (3) a causal link is established between the first two conditions. The standard of evidence to establish these claims is low, however, and the underlying data are sufficiently malleable that in practice anti-dumping actions have come to be a respectable way for WTO members to apply short-term trade protection.[31] The evidence that predatory pricing is in fact occurring in the majority of anti-dumping cases is very weak, and the incidence of anti-dumping actions is not well explained by the price data that are supposed to justify them. In the ten years following the establishment of the WTO there were 2,840 anti-dumping investigations reported to the WTO, most of which resulted in the imposition of anti-dumping duties or price undertakings.

The anti-dumping regime may be functional for GATT as a whole because it provides an escape clause that allows countries to avoid paying high political costs to comply with the regime. Indeed, there is evidence that anti-dumping provisions increase liberalization.[32] When domestic circumstances change in ways that make trade agreements unenforceable, it is better to have a mechanism that allows countries to deviate from their commitments legally than to insist upon rigid application of the rules. The existence of such forms of insurance against high political costs may make the contracting parties willing to accept deeper cuts in their tariff levels than would otherwise be the case. This is consistent with a broader functionalist interpretation of escape clauses,[33] and addresses an incentive problem – uncertainty about domestic costs – that might otherwise significantly reduce the breadth of cooperation.[34]

The international debate about anti-dumping actions, however, has been cast as a conflict between developed countries, which use these measures when it is politically expedient, and developing countries, which suffer the costs and are unable to effectively respond. A coalition of countries that are targeted by anti-dumping measures much more frequently than they use them – for the most part, developing countries and countries that are highly dependent on exports

the higher rate on car parts intended for assembly in China, and the WTO ruling found that this violated its treaty commitments.

31 Silberston 2003.

32 Kucik and Reinhardt 2008.

33 Rosendorff and Milner 2001.

34 Downs *et al.* 1996.

– has advanced the issue of reining in anti-dumping actions as a key element of the Doha trade round agenda.[35] Opposition to this agenda has been led principally by the traditional users of anti-dumping measures, including the United States, which initiates 12.2% of all anti-dumping cases, Australia (5.7%) and Canada (4.2%).[36] The EU and the United States were the most frequent users of anti-dumping during the WTO's first decade, but in recent years developing countries have initiated the majority of cases, and the majority of those have been targeted at other developing countries. Anti-dumping measures are an escape clause that is uniquely valuable to powerful trading states, because it is the only way under GATT law to impose penalties on only a single trading partner. Powerful countries find them more useful instruments than weak countries, because powerful countries are less subject to retaliation. About one-half of anti-dumping investigations are initiated against trading partners that had previously launched an anti-dumping investigation against the initiator.[37] Anti-dumping measures represent a form of override of the ordinary trade-policy process that can be used by powerful states when interests are intense, and in that sense serve an analogous function to informal participation in the IMF.

The WTO dispute resolution procedure, like any legal system, provides the best protection for those who are in the best position to participate. Legal capacity and informal influence tilt the playing field, and the game is played out in the shadow of very unequal capacity to retaliate. Nevertheless, the legalized procedure appears to safeguard the interests of weak countries to a much greater degree than they could achieve through bilateral bargaining. One measure of the fairness of the procedure is that the complainant almost always prevails regardless of the identity of the complainant and the respondent, which indicates a low incidence of frivolous complaints and a high degree of legalization of the dispute process. Another is that, despite the fact that countries have unequal retaliatory capacity, rulings receive a very high degree of compliance, even from powerful states. A third is that developing countries have initiated an increasing number of disputes, which suggests that they find this an effective means of defending their interests. The leading powers in the trade regime

[35] The so-called FAN group, or Friends of Anti-dumping Negotiations, consists of Brazil, Chile, Colombia, Costa Rica, Hong Kong, Israel, Japan, South Korea, Mexico, Norway, Singapore, Switzerland, Taiwan, Thailand and Turkey. This is a group of intensive initiators of WTO disputes, which accounts for 26.6% of all disputes, and includes all of the most active initiators of WTO disputes that are not among the top ten users of anti-dumping measures. There have been a total of 3,427 investigations during the 1995–2008 period. The top ten users of anti-dumping have been India (564), US (418), EU (391), Argentina (241), South Africa (206), Australia (197), Brazil (170), China (151), Canada (145) and Turkey (137).

[36] Moore 2002, 2005.

[37] Prusa and Skeath 2002.

have elected to be bound by law in the application of their treaty obligations in order to constrain each other and in order to increase the legitimacy of a regime that they find valuable.

GATT rule making

In contrast to the substantial delegation of authority to quasi-judicial bodies in dispute resolution, there is no substantial delegation of legislative authority under the GATT/WTO regime. Bargaining between states determines the rules, and bargaining remains a substantial obstacle to international cooperation. Every GATT round has faced delays and teetered on the edge of collapse before it was finally successfully concluded. Some meetings ended in dramatic failure, as in Cancun, where the parties staked out irreconcilable positions. An important question is how, and to what degree, this bargaining is effectively constrained by the formal rules of the GATT regime. The GATT articles, subsequently codified in the treaty that launched the WTO, impose constraints on the use of bargaining power which are designed to promote trade liberalization and simultaneously reassure weaker countries that they will not be subjected to extortion by states with substantial market power. Weak states might otherwise fear to join the multilateral regime, since liberalizing their trade policies makes them more vulnerable to efforts by powerful states to shift the terms of trade. Liberalizing might, for example, lead private actors to make asset-specific investments that increase sensitivity to world prices.[38]

Economists Kyle Bagwell and Robert Staiger have set forth a compelling argument in a series of articles and a book that the rules of the multilateral trading system substantially constrain the use of market power by states and facilitate Pareto-efficient outcomes.[39] Their argument starts with the original, but by now familiar, demonstration that the conflict of interest over trade policies that can be resolved through cooperation concerns terms-of-trade externalities. That is, conflict arises because import restrictions shift the relative prices of imported and exported goods so that the importer gains more of the surplus from trade. If countries preferred to set particular domestic prices but were unconcerned about their terms of trade, they could achieve those prices through an appropriate mix of taxes and subsidies that did not impose any externalities on their trade partners. Conflict arises – along with the potential for cooperation – only because national governments are not indifferent to their terms of

[38] Maggi 1999.
[39] Bagwell and Staiger 2002.

trade. For example, governments have budget constraints that make them prefer tariffs to subsidies, and using tariffs shifts the costs of supporting domestic producers onto a trade partner. The terms of trade externality can be measured in terms of access to export markets, which has effects on profits and employment in the export sector, and market access is the currency of international trade negotiations.

Bagwell and Staiger use their terms-of-trade theory to argue that two key provisions of the GATT regime, reciprocity and Most Favored Nation (MFN) treatment, substantially neutralize the advantages of market power in trade negotiations. Reciprocity requires that policy adjustments maintain a bilateral balance of market access. For example, concessions made in bargaining should lead to equal levels of expected exports; if one country withdraws a trade concession, the other is justified in withdrawing a concession worth an equivalent amount of exports; and if one country violates its commitments, the authorized retaliation should affect an equivalent volume of exports. This has the effect of minimizing externalities that travel through world prices, because reciprocity rebalances the terms of trade between trade partners. MFN treatment requires that any concession made to one GATT member must be extended to all others. This has the effect of preventing third parties from being harmed by concessions that other GATT members make to each other.

Starting from a non-cooperative Nash equilibrium in which two countries unilaterally impose tariffs that are best responses to each other, a variety of agreements can be reached along a contract curve that makes both parties better off, but only one of these is efficient in the sense that it guarantees the maximum amount of trade consistent with giving both governments their preferred local price. Bargaining power could shift the agreement along the contract curve away from that efficient point, giving superior terms of trade to the more powerful state. However, Bagwell and Staiger argue, Article XXVIII of the GATT provides for rules for renegotiation that effectively neutralize the advantages of such an agreement for the stronger side. Under Article XXVIII, the weaker partner could unilaterally withdraw concessions until it reached its desired local price. Its trade partner would be authorized to retaliate, but the retaliation would be limited by reciprocity, maintaining constant terms of trade, so the weaker country would be better off at this new point than at the previous agreement. The resulting trade policies would be off of the contract curve, so they would be subject to renegotiation. The only point that is renegotiation-proof, according to this argument, is the efficient point on the contract curve, which does not reflect bargaining power.

This is an ingenious argument, and it captures an important insight about GATT rules: the expectation of reciprocity generally acts to reduce the significance of market power in bargaining. However, it is a mistake to confuse the formal rules of the institution with its behavioral regularities. Reciprocity allows for multiple interpretations, so the principle is not guaranteed to balance the terms of trade. In addition, the composition of concessions withdrawn can be chosen strategically to impose high political costs, as the EU's plan to target swing districts in its steel dispute with the United States illustrates. Furthermore, the stronger partner can withdraw additional concessions of its own if it chooses to do so, and its superior market power may deter deviations from the original bargain. Market power remains relevant, and the system remains one of power-based bargaining, although the exercise of power is tempered by norms and rules.

Bagwell and Staiger advance a similar argument for the efficiency-enhancing properties of MFN treatment. MFN is often argued to generate free-rider problems, since trading partners that do not participate in bilateral bargaining nevertheless reap the benefits of any concessions that are made. Bagwell and Staiger argue, however, that MFN treatment eliminates hold-up problems that would otherwise prevent liberalization in a multilateral setting.[40] Suppose the United States and Brazil negotiate a trade agreement. If the United States subsequently negotiates an agreement with Argentina, competition with Argentine exports may reduce Brazil's exports to the US market. Anticipating this problem, Brazil expects any concessions it receives from the United States to depreciate in the future, which makes it more reluctant to make concessions of its own. MFN treatment ameliorates these problems, because any concessions made to either country are enjoyed by both.

There is another important insight here: the principle of MFN reduces the opportunities for countries to shift costs to each other. This offers important protection to weak countries, because they face more severe hold-up problems. The effects of trade agreements with large countries have disproportionate effects on small economies, causing substantial shifts in economic activity and investment. Consequently, liberalizing trade under bilateralism shifts substantial bargaining leverage to countries with large economies, and MFN treatment tends to reduce these power advantages. Again, however, it would be a mistake to take the principle of MFN at face value. Tariff schedules are sufficiently complex that trade partners can design agreements narrowly enough to exclude their competitors. The concessions that Japan and Europe made to the United

[40] Bagwell and Staiger (2002, 83) argue that when both MFN and reciprocity rules are respected, there is a single world price due to MFN and this price is fixed due to reciprocity, so liberalizing agreements create no externalities. As a result, they cannot impose terms-of-trade externalities on third parties, whether beneficial or harmful. The argument is based on a three-country, two-good model of trade, however, and it is not clear that it would generalize to a more realistic setting.

States in the agriculture negotiations in the Tokyo Round, discussed below, were a case in point. Deviations from strict nondiscrimination allow powerful countries to continue to shift costs to non-participants, and this is used to create bargaining leverage.

In sum, the rules of the multilateral trade system moderate the use of market power, but power-based bargaining continues to dominate in GATT rounds, allowing the large economies to control the agenda and to achieve their objectives by partially exiting the regime or threatening to do so. The formal agenda for GATT rounds is determined by a consensual process in which all members submit requests for market opening, but the operational agenda is set by the leading trading states. The United States lost its hegemony in trade by the late 1960s, and subsequent negotiating rounds involved meetings with small numbers of important trading states. Europe has acted as an increasingly unitary actor, and by the time of the Tokyo Round that was launched in 1977, the European Community had emerged as a rough equal to the United States. Most of the proposals that shape the trade agenda are first developed by the US Trade Representative or the European Commission, and progress in negotiations is made by first reaching agreements between those two key actors, and subsequently widening the sphere of agreement to bring in more parties: the Quad countries (including Canada and Japan), the G-7 and the Organization for Economic Cooperation and Development. The final package has historically been hammered out in the "Green Room," a caucus including 20 to 35 of the most important trading countries, and the exclusion of most developing countries from the key caucuses has allowed the developed countries to set the agenda and control the outcome.[41] In contrast to the formal agenda-setting process, the informal process is based on trading power – the ability to consume – and the ability of particular countries to participate depends on the extent to which their consent is necessary to make the trade regime function effectively.[42]

The gradual shift in trade power and the increasing number of members have led to continuous adjustments of this informal process, requiring wider consultations. As a result, the time required to reach agreement in trade rounds has steadily increased: two years for the Dillon Round (1960–1), four for the Kennedy Round (1964–7), seven for the Tokyo Round (1973–9) and nine for the Uruguay Round (1986–94). The Doha Round, launched in 2001, continues with no end in sight. China, Brazil and India have emerged as important players in the Doha process and have blocked efforts by the United States and Europe to move forward without a comprehensive agreement on agriculture.

The use of exit options plays a key role in this process. The leading powers

41 Steinberg 2002, 355.
42 Steinberg 2002.

can achieve their objectives either multilaterally or through a series of bilateral agreements, so they generally attempt to divide the opposition to their proposals by engaging in simultaneous bilateral or regional negotiations. Although such discriminatory deals run counter to the fundamental norm of the GATT, which was non-discrimination embodied in universal MFN treatment of all members, bilateral and regional preferential trade agreements (PTAs) have enjoyed legal standing under GATT rules from the beginning. The threat of exclusion from PTAs gives smaller or poorer countries incentives to compete with each other to reach agreement with the major powers. The tactic of reaching bilateral agreements to lay the groundwork for a multilateral agreement explains the eventual acquiescence of developing countries to the Trade Related Intellectual Property Rights Agreement (TRIPS), the provision that extended trade law into the area of property rights, although most developing countries saw this as disadvantageous.[43] Similarly, as the Doha Trade Round has run into obstacles, the United States and the EU have launched intensified efforts to negotiate bilateral investment treaties (BITs), and the United States has launched efforts to expand the North American Free Trade Area (NAFTA) and to negotiate a Central American Free Trade Agreement (CAFTA) and a Free Trade Area of the Americas. The negotiation of preferential trade agreements has been shown to increase during the active phases of GATT rounds, which suggests that they are seen as a strategy to increase multilateral leverage.[44]

The negotiations over agriculture in the Uruguay Round serve as an illustration of the central role of the United States and the EU. Launched at the initiative of the United States in 1986, the Uruguay Round quickly stalled over European resistance to US demands for liberalization in agriculture. The US position received a boost when fourteen agricultural exporting nations – the Cairns Group – refused to complete a package deal without substantial progress in agriculture.[45] However, it was the willingness of the United States to walk away from the negotiations in 1990, which had already reached important agreements on issues such as TRIPS and trade in services, that forced the EU to reevaluate its stolid defense of its Common Agricultural Policy (CAP). Germany finally abandoned its support for the French position of opposing any reform, and over French objections the EU Council of Ministers approved a text proposed by the GATT General Secretary, Arthur Dunkel, as the basis

43 Shaffer 2005.

44 Mansfield and Reinhardt 2003.

45 The group was formed in August 1986 and included Argentina, Australia, Brazil, Canada, Chile, Colombia, Fiji, Hungary, Indonesia, Malaysia, New Zealand, Philippines, Thailand and Uruguay.

for reopening negotiations. In November 1992 the United States threatened to impose unilateral trade sanctions on European agricultural products. Although the threat was not carried out, this led to a series of meetings between US and European trade officials that culminated in an agreement announced at Blair House on November 20 that broke the impasse and set the stage for a drastic restructuring of the CAP. As Christina Davis writes, "This negotiation represented bilateralism within the multilateral process."[46] Once the Americans and the Europeans had agreed to an acceptable formula, the rest of the membership followed suit.

In spite of the key roles played by the major powers, it is possible to argue that the formal agendas of GATT rounds are consequential. Davis argues that the formal features of bargaining rounds in the GATT vary in important ways that account for differences in the success of trade liberalization.[47] When the agenda for a GATT round embodies a credible commitment that all aspects of the round must be adopted as a single undertaking, this forms a credible linkage across issues that facilitates Pareto-improving international exchanges of concessions. This credible linkage activates latent lobbies within countries that are interested in expanding trade, which changes the balance of power between protectionist and export-oriented interest groups. In addition, the shift from narrow to broad trade agreements can lift jurisdiction from agencies that have been captured by narrow producer interests and transfer it to inter-agency committees that represent broader constituencies. As an example, she shows that the Tokyo Round had a very loose agenda that did not constrain the parties to resolve agricultural disputes in order to move forward on other issues, and it made little progress on dismantling Japanese quotas or scaling back subsidies under the European CAP. The agenda for the Uruguay Round was much more constraining, in contrast, and the result was substantial progress on previously intractable issues.

What seems to have varied most between Tokyo and Uruguay, however, was not the formal rules but the balance of informal bargaining power that determined whether linkages were credible. In both cases, the United States attempted to link concessions by Japan and Europe on agriculture to a package deal on industrial tariffs and other issues. In the Tokyo Round the linkage failed because Europe and Japan were unprepared to make the concessions US negotiators demanded in agriculture, and the United States backed down from its insistence on a package deal in a July 1977 meeting with EU trade representatives.[48] The result was that tariffs were reduced an average of only 7 percent on

[46] Davis 2003, 302.
[47] Davis 2003.
[48] Davis 2003, 72, 144, 257–64.

agricultural products in the Tokyo Round, compared to 39 percent reductions on tariffs for manufactured goods. As further evidence of bilateralism, the concessions that Japan and the European Communities made on agriculture were a response to bilateral US pressure, and in spite of the formal principle that MFN status extends concessions made by one country to all GATT members, some concessions were narrowly designed to cater to US exporters without allowing other countries to benefit.[49] In the Uruguay Round, in contrast, US negotiators refused to retreat from their demands in agriculture, and it was the European bargaining position that crumbled.

The most dramatic use of outside options in the trade regime was the action taken by the United States and the EU to close the Uruguay Trade Round. Developing countries resisted the sweeping package of reforms introduced along with the creation of the WTO, which included a General Agreement on Trade in Services (GATS), an accord on government procurement (GPA), Trade Related Investment Measures (TRIMS) and TRIPS. In previous GATT rounds developing countries had been able to largely resist wholesale reform of the trade regime, and had been able to free-ride to a certain degree on liberalization measures that were negotiated among the major players and subsequently extended to all of the membership through MFN treatment.[50] In the conclusion of the Uruguay Round, however, the United States and the EU jointly withdrew from the 1947 GATT regime, making continuation of the trade privileges of any GATT member *vis-à-vis* the United States and the EU contingent upon joining the WTO and acceding to all of the associated agreements concluded in the Uruguay Round.[51] This maneuver amounted to an end run around the formal consensus rule governing GATT trade rounds; as long as such a tactic is available, and the leading powers are in agreement, there is no further need to wait for consensus. The tactic succeeded because the United States and the EU possessed such an overwhelming share of world market power that none of the member countries could afford to be excluded, and the threat was credible because the global competition with the Soviet Union for the allegiance of developing countries had ended with the conclusion of the Cold War.

WTO accession

The most formalized part of the WTO/GATT rule-making procedure is its provision for adding new members, but this also incorporates important elements

49 Davis 2003, 152–3, 263.
50 Oye 1992.
51 Steinberg 2002; Barton *et al.* 2006.

of informal governance. The economic stakes involved in admitting new members can be very high, because each country admitted to a free trade area diverts trade from some of the existing members as well as creating trade. Even more important during the Cold War were the strategic implications of admitting non-aligned or Communist countries to one of the central international institutions. Consequently, the United States preferred an informal consensus rule, under which it could effectively veto the accession of any new member; and in practice, the United States served as the gate-keeper during the Cold War. There have been three waves of accessions since the GATT was launched with eighteen members in 1947. The first occurred in 1950, and led to the admission of four close US allies (West Germany, Italy, Greece and Turkey), three neutral European democracies (Sweden, Austria and Finland), and four Latin American countries close to the United States (Nicaragua, Haiti, the Dominican Republic and Peru). The second occurred in the 1960s as a result of decolonization, and 29 of the 39 countries admitted in the 1960s came through the accelerated Article 26 procedure for former colonies. Of the remainder, several were close US allies (Portugal, Spain, Iceland, Israel, South Korea). Two were Communist countries, but Yugoslavia (admitted in 1966) had broken relations with the Soviet Union, and Poland (admitted in 1967) was a calculated effort to drive a wedge in the Soviet bloc. The third wave of accessions followed the end of the Cold War, as 26 countries joined between 1992 and the establishment of the WTO in 1995, and 25 more joined subsequently under the WTO. Twenty-two of the former group consisted of former colonies that joined under Article 26, but most of the rest of these new members were directly or indirectly attributable to the end of the Cold War.[52]

The formal rules of GATT/WTO accession concentrate bargaining leverage in the hands of current members, but disperse it widely throughout the membership. The formal accession process begins when the applicant country submits a memorandum about its economy to the GATT/WTO secretariat. These memoranda became more extensive and covered broader areas of economic policies after the creation of the WTO in 1995. Any interested country may join the working party, which poses a series of questions to the applicant about its economic policies, which must be answered, and there can be as many question and answer rounds as necessary to satisfy all of the members of the working group. This process usually takes several months, but in the case of Russia

[52] Sixteen of the new members are former Communist countries. Four (Vietnam, Cambodia, Angola and Mozambique) are countries with whom the United States has normalized relations as a result of the end of the Cold War or the resolution of internal conflict related to the Cold War.

it dragged on for more than a year.[53] At the conclusion of the question and answer process, the applicant conducts bilateral negotiations with each member of the working party. Concurrently with these negotiations, the working party may have a series of meetings. In the majority of accession cases, working party meetings are unnecessary, and the average number of meetings is two, but in extreme cases this process can become extended: the China Working Party met 23 times, and the Ukraine Working Party met 17 times. The working party prepares a report that codifies all of the commitments that the applicant has made, as well as schedules specifying the applicant's bound tariff commitments for goods and services. These reports can be quite extensive – 219 pages in the case of Ukraine, and 178 in the case of China – but the median length is 39 pages, and some are very short. The Working Party Report for Ireland was one page in length. All of these commitments become integral parts of the applicant country's accession package, and therefore can be used as the basis for legal rulings in subsequent GATT disputes. The formal basis for admission to the WTO is a two-thirds vote of the membership, but in practice an application is never brought to a vote before the working party report is completed, which requires the consent of every member of the working party.

This informal norm has important substantive implications. International institutions generally evolve through a political process that privileges insiders, who are then able to impose many of their preferences on countries that join subsequently. In the case of trade agreements in particular, there is a persuasive argument that gradually expanding the membership helps to overcome free-rider problems by diverting trade away from non-members. Because the cost of exclusion rises as membership increases, the later members are willing to make greater and greater concessions in order to join.[54] Downs *et al.* have analyzed a similar situation in which voting takes place after successive rounds of expansion, and voting rules that privilege the status quo shift agenda power to earlier members of the organization.[55] The GATT/WTO membership procedure, however, is tilted more heavily against prospective members, because the informal decision-making procedure allows influential members to hold up any applicant and demand substantial concessions.[56]

The consensus rule has a lot of explanatory power. First, it shields early members from the need to make concessions to new entrants. Early members of the GATT were developed countries, which tended to share a preference for

53 Hoekman *et al.* 2002.
54 Oye 1992.
55 Downs *et al.* 1998.
56 The formal rule is that the members can admit a new member with a two-thirds majority vote, but the informal practice is that WTO decisions are made through consensus. Voting is only used when consensus decision-making fails, and voting has not been used yet in the WTO.

lower tariffs for industrial manufactured goods, which they exported, and for higher tariffs for textiles and agricultural goods, which were produced more cheaply abroad. Subsequent rounds of trade negotiations have expanded the range of goods and services covered by the regime, until the Uruguay Round extended it to cover services, foreign direct investment, and intellectual property rights. As new members have joined the regime in the 1990s, they have been required to accept the status quo and harmonize their trade policies with those of the WTO in return for equal treatment with existing members; the existing members have not been required to make corresponding concessions. As a result, the international trade regime remains asymmetric, tolerating high subsidies and barriers to trade in agricultural goods. Annual US cotton subsidies, for example, have exceeded total US foreign aid to sub-Saharan Africa for a number of years.

In addition, the consensus rule accounts for the slowness of the GATT/WTO accession process, which averages seven years. The membership tolerates a slow and cumbersome set of bilateral negotiations over issues that often concern only a handful of members rather than accelerate the process in order to reap the benefits of more rapid market liberalization. With the exception of the streamlined accessions of former colonies under Article 26, the accession negotiations have not been noticeably longer for the average country under the WTO than they were under the GATT, but they have been extended for some of the most important countries, including China (15 years) and Russia (14 years and counting as of this writing). Accession is noticeably slowed for countries that are important trading partners for numerous members and consequently have large working parties. Applicants that have large working parties also make many more commitments and much deeper cuts in their bound tariff rates than the average accession country. China, the extreme outlier, accepted 144 commitments as part of its accession package in addition to its bound tariff commitments, compared to a mean of 19, and granted initial negotiating rights on 5,113 HS-6 product subheadings (almost all of them), compared to a mean of 1,243.

It is inaccurate, however, to describe the WTO accession process as a unanimity rule. If the unanimity rule represented the actual game form, any member could demand concessions equal to the applicant's reservation value for joining the organization. Under such circumstances, it would be hard to explain why some countries choose not to be members of some working parties. In practice, a series of primary and secondary norms has arisen that regulates which countries block accession proceedings and for what reasons. One primary norm is that the leading exporter – the principal supplier – of each product leads the negotiations on that product, which is a rule that assures that the

United States and the EU are the main participants. Candidates concede initial negotiating rights on a wide range of products to particular member countries during the accession process, which means that they must negotiate with those members if they subsequently seek to change their bound tariff rates. Another primary norm is that the accession process is not invoked as a pretext for extracting concessions on non-germaine issues; otherwise, every member would have an incentive to raise spurious objections in an effort to extort monetary bribes or other side payments. This norm is subject to an important secondary norm, however, which is that the United States and the EU may violate it, but other members may not. China's accession was delayed for years because its human rights record made the US Congress reluctant to extend permanent MFN status. The United States publicly linked dropping objections to Russia's WTO membership to Russia's cooperation with US efforts to establish air bases in Uzbekistan to prosecute the 2001 war in Afghanistan, and again drew a linkage between Russia's candidacy and Russia's cooperation with the Iraq war in 2003. The EU used WTO membership as an overt bargaining counter with Russia as well, dropping its objections to Russia's subsidized domestic price for natural gas in return for Vladimir Putin's agreement to ratify the Kyoto Protocol on global climate change. More recently, Russia's candidacy was once more frozen in the wake of its military conflict with Georgia in 2008.

The case of China again illustrates the operation of the informal norms of the accession process, and the limits to how far they can be pushed by different members. The United States was capable of delaying China's accession to the WTO indefinitely, and for a time it appeared that it might do so over the issue of human rights. Once the United States and the other major participants announced that they had completed their negotiations with China, however, Mexico remained able to delay China's accession for more than a year. Mexico had a significant interest in keeping China outside the global trading regime because they competed with each other as sources of low-cost labor.[57] Mexico's membership in the NAFTA preferential trade arrangement and the US extension of permanent MFN status to China lowered the economic impact of China's accession, but China's membership in the WTO was still expected to undermine Mexico's exports to the United States much more than it would benefit Mexico in other ways. Mexico competed with China in assembly of electrical machinery (23% of Mexican exports), telecommunications equipment (10%) and computers (3%), and was rapidly losing market share.[58]

The presenting issue was that Mexico had initiated a large number of antidumping actions against China that were related to NAFTA and were widely

[57] "China Puts Mexican Trade in Line of Fire." *Financial Times*. January 10, 2001.
[58] Kraft 2007, 123.

believed to be illegal under GATT rules. Mexico demanded a fifteen-year transition period after China's entry into the WTO before it would be required to drop these actions. China balked at this demand, but a compromise allowed Mexico a six-year transition period before WTO anti-dumping rules would apply in 21 SITC 4-digit industries. These concessions did not really address the root issue that motivated Mexican opposition to China's WTO accession, however, because they addressed the concerns of import-competing industries rather than those of exporters to third markets, particularly to the United States. Even before the compromise had been reached, furthermore, Mexico announced publicly that it would not seek to block China's accession over the issue. While Mexico could delay, it could not credibly threaten to block China's entry, and even threatening to do so was judged unacceptably costly. By this point the rest of the membership had backed China's entry into the WTO, and Mexico acknowledged that it did not have sufficient weight in the world trading system to stand in the way indefinitely.

Conclusions

The WTO presides over one of the most conflictual issue areas in the international economy. Special interests can always be found that demand protection for their industries, and shifting macroeconomic trends and electoral calendars can make these demands salient in ways that are largely unpredictable and often non-transparent to outsiders. Long-term mutual interests can be achieved through cooperation, but the short-term incentives are always to defect. International trade was the issue area that inspired Robert Keohane's conceptualization of international politics as a repeated prisoner's dilemma.[59] Furthermore, the trade regime was an issue area in which power was dispersed, at least by the 1990s, roughly equally between the United States and the EU.

Under these circumstances, delegation of extensive rule-making authority or executive power to an international organization appeared to run excessive risks, but the costs of a thin, informal regime were reflected in extensive cheating and unilateralism. The compromise that seemed to best balance the risks was to reinvent the international trade regime in a legalized form, but to limit its authority to the adjudication of disputes. The result has been a decrease in unilateralism, a remarkable geographical expansion of the regime, and a deepening of the substantive scope of trade law. All of this was accomplished by the bold, coordinated exercise of market power by the United States and the EU,

[59] Keohane 1984.

backed by the tacit support of Canada, Japan and some other important trading states, which credibly threatened to exclude from the international trade regime any country that refused to adopt the new set of rules.

The formula works because the GATT/WTO dispute resolution procedure is moderately fair, moderately constraining, and moderately deferential. The procedure allows great powers to exercise some of their advantages, and the appeals procedure introduces strategic deference to their core interests. Bargaining between developed and developing countries continues to be asymmetric, even when it takes place in the shadow of law. However, the procedure is fair enough that the parties continue to use it, and developing countries have been increasing their participation and challenging the policies of the most powerful countries in the world. Because it is a legalized system, informal influence is constrained by legal norms and delegitimized, so rulings frequently go against powerful countries, and they usually comply with adverse rulings.

In contrast to adjudication, the legislative rule-making function of the WTO is informal and closely held by states. The process is marked by informal agenda power and the implicit, or sometimes explicit, threat of powerful states to exercise outside options. The origin of the WTO in the threat by the United States and the EU to exclude countries from the trade regime that refused to agree to its new rules underscored the fact that international organizations depend on the distribution of power.

The most formalized aspect of the WTO's legislative process is the accession of new members, but it is the informal norms that effectively allow powerful countries to veto applications. The formal rules alone cannot explain the extreme inefficiency of the proceedings. The informal procedures privilege the most powerful participants, compelling lesser powers to drop their objections to accessions that are preferred by the rest of the membership and preventing them from extracting non-germaine concessions, but allowing the most powerful trading powers to block accession indefinitely and to link it to political issues outside of international trade.

The WTO illustrates the ways in which informal influence is ubiquitous in international organizations, appearing even in the most formalized aspects of international trade politics. However, it also illustrates the variety of international organizations, where organizational forms can be chosen to minimize that influence. Unlike the IMF, the WTO was given a strong adjudicatory function that was legalized in order to guard it against excessive capture by powerful states.

6

The European Union

The European Union (EU), like the IMF and the WTO, combines elements of formal and informal governance, but the wider distribution of power in Europe and the high and rapidly increasing returns to European cooperation have shaped a different balance between formal and informal governance. The United States casts a long shadow over the EU, having deliberately encouraged many of its early steps towards integration, and having inadvertently incentivized many of the more recent developments, but the leading economic power's absence from EU membership is even more significant than its external influence. The model of informal governance focuses attention on the distribution of structural power, which in Europe is relatively flat: there are several countries that can compete for the role of leading power, and the power differentials among European countries are smaller than between European countries and the United States. In the absence of a single, overwhelmingly dominant state, several leading states are able to play the game of informal influence in Europe, which implies either low levels of cooperation or high levels of legalization. The history of European integration has seen both patterns, and legalization has been the only available solution to the dilemmas of sovereignty. Indeed, the contemporary EU is the most striking example of legislative and judicial delegation to an international organization.

There are striking similarities in the development of the GATT/WTO and the EU over time. Like the GATT, the predecessors to the European Union – the European Economic Community (EEC), created in 1957, and the European Communities (EC), created in 1967 – suffered from weak central institutions for the first thirty years of their existence. A significant breakthrough occurred only when common interests became so compelling and the costs of inaction so great that the leading states became willing to subject themselves to substantially formalized rules, beginning with the Single European Act of 1986. This followed a lengthy period in which European integration was blocked when the leading powers refused to surrender sovereignty. During the 1960s, French President Charles de Gaulle exercised a form of partial exit dubbed the "empty chair" tactic – boycotting summit meetings – to force a very restrictive interpretation of the Treaty of Rome. Under the resulting Luxembourg Compromise, any member state could invoke a unanimity voting rule by claiming that its fundamental interests were affected. Unanimity voting suited powerful countries, because it channeled decision making into informal intergovernmental bargaining, where they could most easily exercise their leverage. This restrictive voting rule prevented the integration process from progressing in ways that the member states anticipated would harm their interests, but tended to restrain European policy initiatives. When new policy issues came onto the agenda, innovations that enjoyed majority support were systematically blocked by the most conservative government on each dimension.

As the costs of Europe's disorganization in monetary and trade affairs escalated, countries became willing to surrender their veto rights in order to break deadlock. The turning point in French politics came in 1982, when it became clear to the Mitterand government that global capital markets had become too porous for a Keynesian policy of monetary expansion to work in one country, even behind the shelter of extensive capital controls. Mitterand conceived of his options in stark terms: socialism versus Europe. By casting his lot with Europe, he turned his back on generations of policies of the French left and paved the way for the neoliberal consensus embodied in the Single European Act of 1986.[1] In terms of the model of informal governance, an exogenous increase in the benefits of cooperation made a high-participation, formalized regime preferable, even for the leading states, to a low-participation, informal regime. Most of the milestones of European integration arose as efforts to coordinate domestic policies in order to maximize European bargaining leverage in world politics.

The common European trade policy serves as a prominent example.[2] Pascal Lamy labeled the European strategy "managing globalization," explicitly linking the priority for European integration to increased ability to manage the policy externalities originating outside of Europe. Pooling the bargaining power of European countries made it necessary to construct a single market that could make coordinated concessions, and this was one of the key arguments in favor of the Single European Act. With a common bargaining position, European countries were able to face the United States on equal terms in

[1] Abdelal 2007; Helleiner 1994; Moravcsik 1998.
[2] Meunier 2005.

trade, and this bilateral interaction set the agenda in the Uruguay GATT round[3] and subsequently in the WTO.[4]

Monetary policy provides a similar example. The European Monetary System (EMS) was developed as an effort to dampen the wild swings in exchange parities among European currencies that followed the demise of the Bretton Woods system of fixed exchange rates in 1971. Coordinating exchange rate and monetary policies was a way to reduce vulnerability to changes in US monetary policy.[5] The EMS regime had the consequence of transferring informal control over European monetary policy to the German Bundesbank, however, because Germany maintained trade surpluses and anti-inflationary monetary policies that forced the other countries to follow suit or abandon the EMS exchange rate corridor. From the point of view of several European governments, but most notably the French, the subsequent move to Economic and Monetary Union (EMU) traded a formalized regime in which they would share control for an informal one dominated by Germany.

Key departures in European politics are settled by informal intergovernmental bargaining.[6] Every major advance in European integration has been delayed, sometimes, as in the case of EMU, for decades; and every significant change in the rules has come about after high-stakes brinkmanship.[7] Decisions to deepen European integration have been made through bargaining among the leading states, and the key determinants of the outcomes have been the intensity of preferences, the quality of the players' outside options, and the credibility of threats to exclude laggards.

The Single European Act (SEA) of 1986 again serves as an example. The key parameters of the SEA were hammered out in private meetings between the leaders of Germany, France and Britain. Preferences over the European economic model had significantly converged, since French President François Mitterand had embraced a strategy of European integration based on deregulation and free movement of goods and capital, which mirrored the more conservative preferences of German Chancellor Helmut Kohl (CDU) and British Prime Minister Margaret Thatcher (Conservative). There remained, however,

[3] Grieco 1990.

[4] Barton *et al.* 2006.

[5] Henning 1998. US inflationary monetary policy exported inflation and shifted the exchange rates between European currencies because European countries chose different responses to the common external shock.

[6] While Moravcsik (1998) does not distinguish between formal and informal governance, he emphasizes that the process by which important decisions are made is intergovernmental bargaining that takes place outside of European institutions, and that the determinants of the outcomes are the intensity of preferences and the credibility of exit and exclusion threats rather than the voting rules.

[7] Schneider and Cederman 1994.

a significant divergence in preferences about European governance – Thatcher was very suspicious of supranational institutions, while Mitterand and Kohl argued that a significant deepening of integration could not take place without a substantial strengthening of European institutions. Thatcher had successfully forced her preferences through in the past by acting as a spoiler, blocking the adoption of the EC budget until Britain received a partial rebate of its net contribution to the Common Agricultural Policy (CAP), and she was prepared to do so again. This time, however, the constellations had changed. In a summit of the three leaders, Mitterand and Kohl confronted Thatcher with an ultimatum: agree to the governance reforms in the SEA, or Europe will move forward without Britain. Judging that the French-German threat was credible, Thatcher dropped her objections.[8]

The negotiations leading to EMU in the 1990s are another stark example of intergovernmental bargaining. German leaders preferred a set of clear convergence criteria for countries that sought to qualify for participation in the common currency, an independent central bank modeled on the Bundesbank, and a strict set of procedures to insure fiscal restraint after the common currency was adopted. French leaders, who chafed under strict German monetary policy, preferred a gradual transition to the common currency with fewer hurdles and a more malleable central bank. The Commission proposed a plan close to French preferences, which would have given substantial policy authority to the Commission and the Council. However, because Germany enjoyed the most attractive outside option to EMU in the 1990s, Germany prevailed on every major disagreement about the transition to the euro and the design of the European Central Bank. The reversion point in the event of no agreement was favorable to Germany, because the German Bundesbank effectively set European monetary policy under the EMS system. The construction of a common European currency without Germany was difficult to envisage, on the other hand, since the Deutsche Mark was the central European currency and the major currency with the strongest credibility. German leaders quietly refused to compromise, and the treaty on EMU eventually satisfied all of their preferences.[9]

The constitutional politics of the EU is a matter of intergovernmental bargaining. However, the successive rounds of institutionalization that have brought the EU to its current state of development have redirected increasing numbers of issues into formalized decision-making mechanisms. These procedures coexist with informal mechanisms, but the range of informal influence has gradually contracted as the importance of European policies has increased.

[8] Moravcsik 1998.
[9] Moravcsik 1998.

Legalization and the European Court of Justice

Legalization has gone further in the EU than in any other international organization. In contrast, IMF conditionality is not legally binding, and instead constitutes a gentlemen's agreement that is enforced only by the threat of withholding future disbursements. The only legally binding obligation entailed in borrowing from the Fund is the repayment of principal and interest. The WTO has an elaborate system of arbitration and appellate panels, but none of its decisions has the force of law enforceable in domestic courts. The European Court of Justice (ECJ), on the other hand, makes judgments that have direct effect upon the citizens of EU member countries, and which are acknowledged as superior to the rulings of domestic courts. The ECJ has competence over a wide-ranging and expanding set of issues.

Even in court, informal governance plays a role. Courts have to weigh the political implications of their decisions, since an unpopular decision can affect the careers of jurors, lead to legislation that overturns the decision, or lead to non-compliance that undermines the authority of the court. Although the ECJ has substantially expanded its powers in recent decades, it has done so by making canny strategic decisions that enhanced European integration in ways that the member states broadly supported. In the landmark *Cassis de Dijon* case that established the principle of mutual recognition of standards, for example, the ECJ chose a rule that solved problems for the member states and fit with the emerging effort to liberalize the internal market.[10] It is a matter of controversy whether the ECJ is more or less independent than domestic courts, and whether the most powerful EU member states have special influence over ECJ rulings.[11]

Nevertheless, it appears clear that legalization has solved important dilemmas for the member states of the EU and was a precondition for successful delegation. The ECJ emerged as the first powerful European institution. Delegation to a judicial process was less threatening to European states than delegation to an executive or a legislative authority, because it was less likely to be captured by powerful states. However imperfect it may be in practice, a judicial process has the advantages of relying on standards of fairness, being constrained by existing law and precedent, and deriving its authority from its reputation for impartiality. Furthermore, delegating decisions to a judicial process has some of the same advantages as holding elections as a way of sharing power:[12] the outcome of each case is uncertain, and it is unpredictable when

[10] Garrett and Weingast 1993.

[11] Tsebelis and Garrett 2001; Pollack 2003; Alter 2006; Carrubba *et al.* 2008.

[12] Przeworski 1991.

one will find oneself in the position of plaintiff or defendant. Delegation is preferable to the costly delays and externalities involved in resorting to informal bargaining on every possible dispute. Informal governance becomes less attractive as the number of countries capable of vying for informal influence increases, so it would likely be impossible to reach the high level of cooperation achieved in the EU without legalization.[13]

The prevailing approach to explaining legalization assumes that it is driven by transaction costs.[14] However, the pattern of legalization in the EU does not appear to be driven by transaction costs so much as by the distribution of interests. Legalization is controlled by EU legislation, which opens up new policy areas for adjudication and judicial review, or responds to ECJ activism by revising the law. There is no clear pattern relating EU legislation to the technical complexity of particular issue areas or to the need for credibility in particular circumstances, however, which are the leading hypotheses linking transaction costs to delegation.[15] EU legislation instead reflects a pattern of upside-down federalism, covering areas such as regulation and education that are typically left to sub-national levels of government, but directing less attention to areas such as justice, foreign policy and defense that are typically centralized. This seems to reflect the distribution of risks and rewards across issue areas: integration proceeds in the areas with the highest expected pay-offs and those that are least likely to embarrass national governments. Since the Maastricht Treaty of 1991, European law has gradually expanded to cover areas that were regarded as too sensitive in earlier eras.

European legislation

The EU delegates an unparalleled degree of legislative authority to its central organs, the Council of Ministers, the European Commission and the European Parliament. European legislation has the force of law, and often by-passes the requirement for ratification by national parliaments, so that European institutions transfer a substantial degree of legislative power to the chief executives of the member countries who form the Council and to supranational bodies. For example, the EMS was adopted in 1978 by vote of the Council in order to avoid the need to submit a treaty for ratification in Germany. According to the voting rules established in the Treaty of Rome, long disregarded, and subsequently amended and brought back in force by the SEA of 1986, formal

13 Franchino 2007.
14 Abbott and Snidal 2000.
15 Pollack 2006.

decision making in the Council on most issues is by qualified majority voting (QMV).

The European legislative process involves a substantial pooling of sovereignty, as European states delegate the power to create legal commitments to a collective body. Furthermore, as the process of European expansion has progressed and the club has expanded, the original members have gradually ceded shares of joint decision-making authority. Figure 6.1 presents the vote shares of the six original EC members and the United Kingdom as they have shifted over time. The decline in voting power is precipitous. Germany, France and Italy each held 23.5 percent of the vote from 1957 until 1973, so their combined votes were half of one percentage point short of the margin needed to pass legislation by qualified majority vote (71 percent). These shares dropped with each expansion round, to 17.2% in 1973, 15.9% in 1981, 13.2% in 1986 and 11.5% in 1995, so expansion traded off formal power within the institution for greater scope for integration. This trend was reversed in the draft European Constitution, and although the constitution was defeated in referenda in France and Denmark, the changes were incorporated into the Lisbon Treaty, which introduced a new double majority system. Henceforth EU legislation would require a 55 percent majority of the membership that also constituted a 65 percent majority of the population of Europe. The result was that the major powers in Europe were ceded a larger share of formal power to block decisions. Germany regained a formal vote share that it had not enjoyed since 1985, before the accession of Portugal and Spain.

As membership expanded in European institutions, the leading powers gradually ceded formal control in order to attract the participation of new members. However, they maintained a substantial degree of informal control, and in particular the ability to block new legislation that infringed on their core interests, until the legislative process became more formalized beginning in the 1980s. Despite these developments, Germany retained a *de facto* veto throughout the 1990s over the terms of transition to a common currency, which were the issues of most central concern to it, because introducing the euro required treaty revision and would be impossible without German participation. After the transition to the euro, however, German bargaining leverage declined precipitously. More dependent upon formal voting power to achieve its objectives, Germany began to insist on a revision of the QMV voting rule. Meanwhile, Germany's European partners were willing to cede a greater share of formal authority to Germany because its informal power was not so overwhelming. These patterns, and particularly the inverse relationship between formal and informal power, are broadly consistent with the model of informal governance.

Meanwhile, the process of European integration has gradually shifted

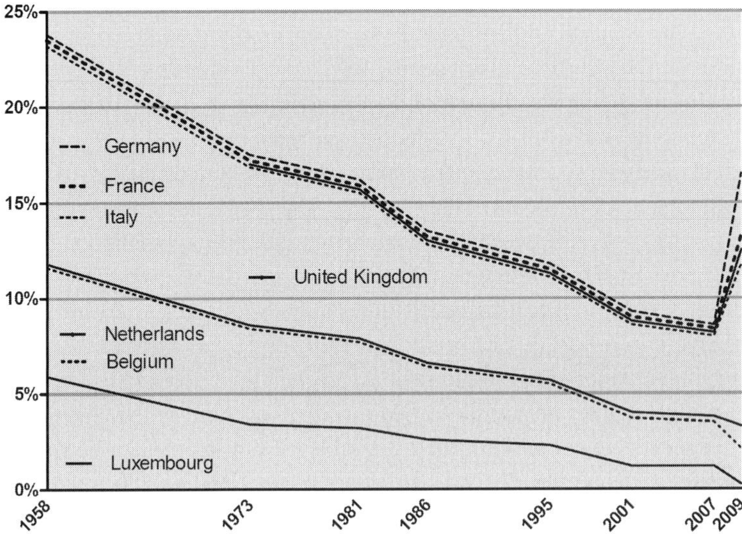

Figure 6.1 Vote shares in the Council of Ministers.

Source: Summary of the Treaty of Nice (europa.eu). Memo/03/23. 31/01/2003, accessed February 12, 2010; Madeleine O. Hosli. "Smaller States and the New Voting Weights in the Council." Clingendael: Netherlands Institute of International Relations (July 2000). Author's calculations.

legislative authority away from the member states and towards international bodies. Until the SEA, the Commission exercised little influence, and the European Parliament had no direct role in shaping legislation. With the reintroduction of QMV, the Commission's proposal power became substantively important, because it became possible to make a range of proposals that would pass with the support of different coalitions. The introduction of the cooperation procedure in the SEA gave the European Parliament an institutionalized role in the legislative process, although the Council could overrule it by voting unanimously. The co-decision procedure, under which the Parliament and the Council must come to agreement in order to pass certain types of legislation, was introduced in the Maastricht Treaty on European Union (1991) and extended in the Amsterdam Treaty (1997). Which procedure applies depends upon the treaty basis for the Council's legislative authority: for example, issues related to EMU are handled under the cooperation procedure, while those related to the CAP follow the older consultation procedure, which includes a largely symbolic role for the European Parliament.[16] While recent scholarly attention has focused on the implications of the co-decision procedure, which strengthened the European Parliament, only a small minority of European legislation actually follows this procedure.[17]

Quantitative studies of EU legislation have been hampered by the lack of a standard database, so that scholars make widely different estimates, for example, of the number of pieces of legislation.[18] The source documentation comes from two full-text resources maintained by the European Commission to track legislation, CELEX and PreLex. CELEX tracks legislative events, and several events may apply to the same piece of legislation, while PreLex documents the legislative process. Both data sources contain substantial amounts of missing data about variables of interest to scholars, such as which legislative procedure applied and whether unanimity or QMV voting was used in the Council, and where the data are not missing, there are substantial discrepancies between the two sources.[19] However, the two sources agree that since 1992 the co-decision procedure has been used in a small minority of legislative acts: 12.3 percent of legislative processes and 12.7 percent of legislative events, respectively.[20]

An extensive literature has arisen that focuses on these formal institutional details and how they structure legislative outcomes. The models generated by this approach, known as *procedural* models, explicitly treat the formal rules as the extensive form of the EU legislation game and use them to build extensive form games of complete information.[21] Holding expert opinions about the countries' preferences constant, different specifications of the formal rules lead to different predicted outcomes, and the fit of predicted to actual outcomes is used to evaluate the accuracy of the models. This approach implicitly assumes that the intensity of country preferences does not matter, that there are no informal interactions that overlap with the formal voting, and that the participants enjoy no outside options.[22] In fact, however, participant accounts reveal that most key decisions are made during informal bargaining sessions that precede formal meetings.

16 Borchardt 2000, 72.
17 König *et al.* 2006.
18 Alesina *et al.* (2005) use a CELEX search to code 25,472 pieces of legislation between 1986 and 1995, including regulations, directives and decisions, while König uses the same data source to identify 5,701 Commission proposals for binding legislation. The discrepancy appears to relate to complexities in interpreting the EU's full-text records and converting them into reliable data sets (König *et al.* 2006, 571, fn 2).
19 König *et al.* 2006.
20 Author's calculations using the König *et al.* (2006) dataset. The data are available at www.dhv-speyer.de/tkoenig/Downloads.htm.
21 Steunenberg and Selck 2006.
22 Achen 2006.

Even the scholars most committed to explaining outcomes in terms of formal procedural detail acknowledge that there is substantial scholarly disagreement about the details of European legislative procedures.[23] For example, it is a subject of controversy whether the Commission really exercises its *de jure* monopoly of proposal power. Article 149 of the Treaty of Rome that established the European Economic Community (EEC) gave the Commission the sole right to propose legislation and provided that its proposals could be amended only unanimously. In practice, however, proposals can originate in the Parliament or be raised by members of the Council, and it is doubtful that the Commission can really act as a gatekeeper if the membership wants action. Similarly, the implications of the revised co-decision procedure introduced by the Amsterdam Treaty of 1997 are subject to controversy. Crombez,[24] Steunenberg[25] and Pollack[26] argue that the Commission exercises agenda control under the co-decision procedure, while Tsebelis and Garrett[27] argue that the Commission is irrelevant under the Amsterdam rules because the final legislative product emerges from a conciliation committee representing the Council and the Parliament. Other scholars emphasize the proposal power of the Council presidency, which rotates among the members every six months.[28] Still others argue that the key decisions are made in informal discussions between the Commission, Council members and members of the European Parliament prior to the formal submission of a proposal by the Commission.[29] The procedure appears to be sufficiently malleable that the order of moves in the game – so critical to procedural accounts of agenda setting – is subject to informal negotiation.

The key feature that gives procedural models purchase is that a wide range of equilibria typically hold in multidimensional voting games, so that the power to set the agenda is substantively important because it determines which structurally-induced equilibrium will be played.[30] This reading of EU legislative rules is naïve, however, because the practice of European diplomacy is to avoid taking votes on controversial subjects. Instead, the would-be winners devote attention to building oversized coalitions and striving for the widest possible consensus.[31] As a result, instead of taking a series of close votes with strategically

[23] Steunenberg and Selck 2006.
[24] Crombez 2003, 110–11.
[25] Steunenberg 2001, 352–3.
[26] Pollack 2006, 177.
[27] Tsebelis and Garrett 2000, 2001.
[28] Tallberg 2003.
[29] Farrell and Hèritier 2003, 2004.
[30] Shepsle 1979.
[31] Hayes-Renshaw and Wallace 1997.

chosen minimum winning coalitions, the Council of Ministers generally votes unanimously even when QMV rules apply.[32] Voting in the EU is generally anti-climactic, because the vote is a formality that ratifies a deal that was struck previously.

Instead of voting on each issue strictly for unilateral advantage, EU states practice diffuse reciprocity. Legislation in the EU is a repeated game with variable stakes for each of the participants. The members recognize that it could be extremely costly to lose on some issues because of their specific constellations of domestic interests, and it is unpredictable when such costly issues may arise in the future. Consequently, an equilibrium in which all of the members refrain from pressing their short-term advantages when their partners are vulnerable to domestic pressures can be better for all of the participants in the long run than one in which they take issue-by-issue votes that pass with minimum winning coalitions.

European enlargement

As in the case of the WTO, the enlargement process stands out among the most highly formalized issue areas in European politics. The stakes of European enlargement are substantial and go far beyond admitting new members to a customs union, although enlargement has that effect. European enlargement has important distributional consequences, because new members place claims on the European CAP and Structural Funds, drawing resources away from other net recipients and increasing the demands on the budgets of net contributors. As the scope of European legislation has increased, admitting new members has taken on new implications for domestic visa, immigration and labor policies. Furthermore, enlargement has often been posed as an alternative to deepening integration, with the implication that rapid enlargement might make new initiatives unworkable. Meanwhile, the growing importance of European institutions has raised the stakes of the shifts that are caused in European governance when new members are admitted.

Given the stakes, it is unsurprising that EU members have opted to retain the unanimity voting rule for the enlargement process, under which any member can block the accession of any applicant. This formal rule is stricter than the informal consensus rule in the WTO, but its effects are similar, leading to lengthy delays in the accession negotiations and occasional bargaining failures that are inefficient for the membership as a whole. Most famously, Britain's

[32] Mattilla and Lane 2001.

accession was blocked by French President Charles de Gaulle throughout the 1960s, and after his resignation, President Georges Pompidou linked British accession to establishing a permanent financing arrangement for the CAP.[33] Norway's application was held up in the 1970s because of a dispute over fishing jurisdiction, and was finally blocked by referendum after Spain demanded and received fishing concessions. In the 1980s, Greece demanded special treatment in the distribution of Structural Funds in return for dropping its opposition to the membership of Spain and Portugal, and Germany agreed to increase its budget contribution in order to secure agreement.[34]

Accession negotiations are very one-sided, and the most common way to balance distributional demands from current members is to shift the burden to new members, often by temporarily suspending some of their membership privileges. Greece, Italy, Portugal and Spain threatened to derail the round of enlargement to the east that took place in 2004 because they anticipated losing aid in the form of structural funds and CAP payments. The compromise granted the east Europeans only 137 euros per capita in structural funds, compared to 231 euros per capita for the earlier members, and CAP subsidies would start at 25 percent of the west European level and phase in over ten years.[35]

Countries that join the EU derive substantial benefits, but in return they accept the obligation to adopt an extensive body of European legislation, the *acquis communautaire*, to honor all treaties to which the EU is a party, and to implement a series of accession criteria negotiated with the Commission. As a result, the accession process leads to an extraordinary temporary suppression of domestic politics. EU integration must be accepted or rejected by the legislative branch of the acceding country as a package deal, with very little opportunity for domestic political interests to influence the results. New members can influence the subsequent development of EU legislation, but supermajority voting and consensus decision making confer staying power on the status quo.

Indeed, the desire to manipulate the agenda by shaping the status quo is a prominent explanation for the pattern of sequential admission of new members. Downs *et al.* argue that the privileged position of insiders allows international institutions to choose consistently higher levels of cooperation by initially including only the most committed cooperators, and gradually broadening membership to include laggards.[36] In their model, late entrants prefer membership in an international institution such as the WTO or the EU to exclusion, even if

33 Moravcsik 1998, 181–93, 265.

34 Schneider 2009, 66.

35 Schneider 2009, 67.

36 Downs *et al.* 1998.

they must accept a high level of cooperation as the price of admission, and the level of cooperation within the institution is chosen by voting. By expanding membership sequentially, a group of intensive cooperators can assure a high level of cooperation, which then becomes the reversion point for future votes. A subsequent entrant is faced with a *fait accompli*: The status quo is more cooperative than it would prefer, and the pivotal voter, which likewise prefers more cooperation than the new entrant, will block any proposal that it does not prefer to the status quo. As new states enter, the intensity of cooperation is gradually diluted – there is a trade-off between the depth and breadth of cooperation – but cooperation remains consistently more intense than it would have been, had all states entered the arrangement simultaneously.

The necessary condition for this logic to work is that previous entrants prefer higher degrees of cooperation than subsequent entrants, which is plausible if cooperation occurs on only one dimension and highly motivated cooperators are most interested in joining institutions. Indeed, this story explains aspects of integration in the EU, as more committed cooperators gradually co-opted states that were initially reluctant. However, the EU also serves as a counterexample. Cooperation in the EU proceeds on numerous tracks that touch virtually every area of public policy, and these have gradually proliferated, so that the original cooperators could not anticipate all of the forms cooperation eventually took. On some of these dimensions the original cooperators have more conservative preferences than many of the countries that have joined more recently. To take a prominent example, Britain refused to sign the Treaty of Rome in 1957, and acceded to the EEC only in 1973, by which time the interpretation of the Common Market had become well established. Under a variety of Labour and Conservative governments, Britain consistently pushed for a more liberal trade regime in Europe; France was often able to block these proposals, relying upon its position as a veto player and the fact that the status quo was favorable to French interests. The impasse was finally broken only in 1986, when the SEA provided an opportunity to reopen the package deal of European integration. On other dimensions, of course, it was France rather than Britain that was in favor of deepening European cooperation in 1986, but this is the point: voting rules may favor deeper cooperation on some dimensions and shallower cooperation on others, depending upon which countries entered first.

Executive powers: the case of the Stability and Growth Pact

The model of informal governance makes two related predictions about executive powers. Because the distribution of power in the EU is relatively flat and the stakes of cooperation are high, a concentration of executive power in European institutions would be risky: it would represent a substantial temptation for European countries to attempt to manipulate common institutions. This implies, first, that European integration should primarily take the form of legalized mechanisms that are relatively difficult to manipulate, and that the capitals should retain the balance of legislative powers, as we have seen in previous sections. Delegation of discretionary executive powers should be minimal and closely circumscribed. Whenever possible, any executive agencies that are endowed with extensive discretion should be made legally independent of the members. Second, however, the model implies that when it nevertheless becomes necessary to delegate extensive executive powers to European institutions that the members control, governance will be informal rather than formal because the member countries' efforts to exert informal influence will become ubiquitous.

The EU has historically had few executive powers. For most of its history, the most important executive powers delegated to the Commission were to represent the members in foreign trade, to implement competition policy, and to disburse the common budget. However, the treaty on Economic and Monetary Union (EMU) delegated substantial authority to the new European Central Bank (ECB), and also created a mechanism for enforcing the accompanying Stability and Growth Pact. At the insistence of Germany, the ECB was created in the image of the Bundesbank, a highly independent monetary authority, and was insulated legally from interference by political authorities. German leaders expected the governments of historically weak-currency countries to continue to face incentives to manipulate monetary policy, so they refused to give up the stability of the Deutsche Mark without a legal guarantee of ECB independence. The ECB has subsequently proven its independence and commitment to anti-inflationary policies in the face of criticism from all quarters.

Fiscal policy has proven more difficult to regulate. The signatories recognized that a common currency without a common budget authority would create a collective action problem, because the members of the euro zone would retain control of fiscal policy and could export inflation to each other. Consequently, again at the insistence of Germany, they developed rules about fiscal policy, including strict ceilings for fiscal deficits (3% of GDP) and levels of public debt (60% of GDP), and stiff fines for violators that could amount to several percent of GDP. In order to enforce these rules, the treaty provided for a complex mechanism that delegated authority to the Commission and the Council of Economic and Finance Ministers (EcoFin), dubbed the European Stability and Growth Pact.[37] As Germany and France subsequently demonstrated, however, the rules of the Pact are difficult to enforce against powerful countries.

The failure of the EU to enforce the rules of the European Stability and Growth Pact against Germany and France in 2003 was widely hailed as a "disaster for Europe."[38] Austrian Finance Minister Karl-Heinz Grasser opined in 2004, "The future of the Stability Pact is a thing of the past."[39] This failure, however, should not have been surprising, and furthermore, was not devastating. Indeed, it had no immediate impact on financial markets, and the value of the euro steadily increased afterwards. It is consistent with the logic of informal governance that rules are enforced only when the powerful countries do not find them excessively inconvenient, and that executive powers are the easiest for powerful countries to suborn.

In early 2002 Germany appeared likely to violate the euro-area budget deficit ceiling, and a struggle broke out behind the scenes at the European Commission. The German General Director for Currency and Finance, Klaus Regling, had been a close advisor of the former CSU finance minister, Theo Waigel, during the negotiation of the Stability and Growth Pact, and he now pushed to see it enforced.[40] The Commission produced a "blue paper," a report that recommended opening a deficit reduction case against Germany and making cuts in the German deficit. When the report came before EcoFin, the German Finance Minister Hans Eichel (SPD) successfully organized a blocking coalition (see Figure 6.2, stage 3). However, when the annual budget reports for 2002 were presented it was clear that Germany's deficit of 3.5 percent of GDP was over the limit, as was the French deficit of 3.1 percent. Following the Commission's recommendation, EcoFin voted to open deficit cases against Germany and France, recommending substantial corrections in their budgets for 2003.

The dilemma was particularly acute for Germany's coalition of Social Democrats and Greens. Gerhard Schroeder had campaigned on a populist program in 2002, but then led his coalition into new territory in March 2003 with his Agenda 2010, a plan for wide-ranging reform of the social welfare state, labor market and tax structure. He now faced a revolt within his party, plummeting opinion polls and large-scale street protests. In an attempt to sweeten the pill

37 The phrase "... and growth" was added as a palliative at the insistence of France.

38 The departing president of the ECB, Wim Duisenberg, warning in his final speech in 2003 of an imminent collapse of the European Stability and Growth Pact.

39 "Österreich fordert neuen Stabilitätspakt." *Frankfurter Allgemeine Zeitung*. May 27, 2004.

40 "Der böse Bube in Bruessel kommt aus Berlin." *Die Welt*. November 19, 2003: 12.

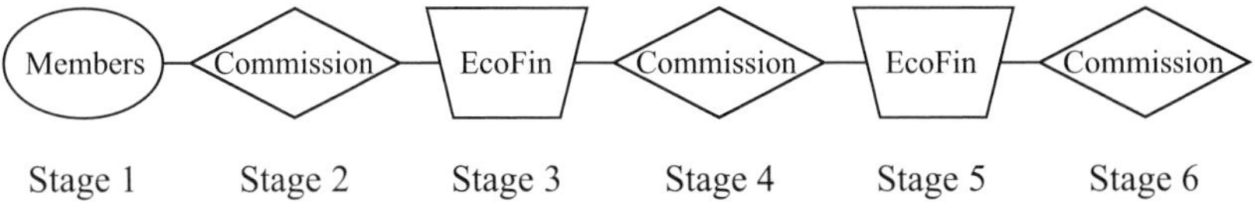

Stage 1 Stage 2 Stage 3 Stage 4 Stage 5 Stage 6

Stages in the Process:

1. Member countries report budget figures
2. Commission reports to EcoFin
3. EcoFin votes with a qualified majority to open a case and makes recommendations to reduce the deficit. Countries must adopt conditions within 4 months and reduce deficits within one year
4. Commission recommends a resolution that the necessary steps have not been implemented
5. EcoFin votes with a qualified two-thirds majority (excluding the affected state) to impose conditions to be implemented within two months under the threat of sanctions
6. Imposition of sanctions

Figure 6.2 The EMU Deficit Enforcement Mechanism.

of reform, Schroeder sought to hold fast to his old promise to lower German income tax rates in 2004, a decision expected to add 0.7% of GDP to the federal budget deficit. Schroeder later admitted that Germany "could have easily fulfilled" the Commission's conditions "if we had not moved up the tax cut."[41]

The vise tightened in the fall as new economic data forced the government to revise its projections for economic growth, and hence for budget revenue. At the EU level, the German government pushed for a "responsible interpretation" – a relaxation – of the rules.[42] As it became clearer that the leading countries were refusing to follow the rules, public diplomacy came to revolve around reinterpretations of the Stability and Growth Pact.

France became the next test case.[43] By fall it was clear that France was not going to meet the target. France was running a deficit of 4.2 percent of GDP in 2003, and the European Commission was projecting a deficit of 3.8 percent for 2004. The EU Commissioner for Economic and Monetary Policy, Pedro Solbes, announced that France was not in compliance with the Stability and Growth Pact criteria, and began the process of threatening to impose sanctions

41 "Rhetorische Pflichtübung." *Frankfurter Allgemeine Zeitung*. November 27, 2003: 3.

42 The term used was "verantwortungsvolle Auslegung." "Deutschland und Frankreich bringen die anderen Euro-Staaten gegen sich auf." *Frankfurter Allgemeine Zeitung*. November 11, 2003: 15.

43 Germany had delayed the timing of its own case again, this time by convincing the European Commission in the spring of 2003 that it was making progress towards bringing its deficit for 2003 under control. Consequently, its case did not advance to the next stage until November.

if it failed to bring its deficit under control. In October the European Commission recommended that EcoFin take the next step at its November meeting by ruling that France had not made significant steps towards meeting the target. This would leave France as little as three months away from the imposition of sanctions. The credibility of the process was jeopardized, however, by the fact that Germany was not expected to meet the criteria, either. When the French case came before EcoFin, German Finance Minister Eichel supported France, urging that the process be reversed. The Netherlands' Minister of Finance, Gerrit Zalm, complained that Eichel had joined "the other camp," declaring, "the Pact is no longer very much alive."

To the contrary, Eichel insisted, there was a consensus on maintaining the Pact and the possibility of imposing sanctions, "but the sanctions are only there for euro countries that do not cooperate."[44] The question then became how to define cooperation, if it does not consist of following the rules. For Solbes, Eichel's definition of cooperation fell far short. "If it were sufficient for a country to sit at the table and hold discussions in order to be considered cooperative and avoid sanctions," he argued, "that would be a different Pact."[45] His attention now turned to the other defector, Germany. Eichel argued that the German budget for 2004 would cut 0.6 percent of GDP from the structural deficit. However, the proposed budget was based on an optimistic economic forecast and assumed that several controversial tax reform proposals would pass the Parliament. Eichel himself admitted, "My fifth budget is the one with the greatest risks."[46] The CDU opposition threatened to block it in the Bundesrat (the upper house of parliament) on the grounds that it violated the constitutional requirement that the deficit not exceed the level of public investment. In November Solbes announced that he was initiating the next stage of Germany's deficit case (Figure 6.2, stage 4), requiring that Germany cut its proposed budget for 2004 by 6 billion euros, or 0.8% of GDP instead of 0.6%. Even this target fell short of bringing Germany's projected 2004 deficit of 3.9 percent of GDP under the 3 percent target, giving Germany until 2005 to reach the target level. The discussion had moved away from strict adherence to rules. The question now was how far to bend the rules, and how far below compliance the threshold for enforcement actually lay.

EcoFin had the next move. In effect, Solbes had challenged the Council of Ministers to support his ultimatum against Germany, which would also

44 "EU-Finanzminister vertagen Konflikt mit Frankreich." *Frankfurter Allgemeine Zeitung*. November 5, 2003: 11.

45 Andreas Middel and Cornelia Wolber. "Solbes will in Berlin mitregieren." *Die Welt*. November 19, 2003: 12.

46 "Eichels fünfter Haushalt ist mit zahlreichen Risiken behaftet." *Frankfurter Allgemeine Zeitung*. November 24, 2003: 13.

invoke a threat of sanctions ranging from 4 to 10 billion euros in the event of noncompliance. This was seen in the German press as "throwing down the gauntlet," and Eichel described it as a "caesura."[47] Germany's next diplomatic moves, however, made it clear that it regarded the Commission's sanctions as an empty threat. Eichel rejected further cuts in the week before the meeting, arguing that he did not want to endanger the shallow economic recovery expected for 2004 with a fiscal contraction. Meanwhile, the Ministry of Finance made no secret of the fact that it was not drawing up scenarios to meet the Commission's demands. A ministry spokesperson expressed confidence that EcoFin would support Eichel's position that further cuts would be counterproductive, and in the next sentence reaffirmed, "We are holding to the Growth and Stability Pact without reservation" – deliberately reversing the word order to emphasize growth over stability.[48]

As a practical matter, it required the votes of two large countries and one small one to block the imposition of sanctions – the affected country was not permitted to vote – and France, Italy and Luxembourg had signaled that they were willing to block sanctions against Germany. France was in the docket as a fellow accused, and Italy was likely to be a subsequent target of enforcement; Luxembourg, however, had strict preferences in favor of a strong interpretation of the Stability and Growth Pact. Nevertheless, Luxembourg provided the necessary third vote, because its leaders calculated that attempting to enforce the rules would lead to exit by Germany, which would be much more destructive to the regime than tolerating the deficit. Weak powers tolerate deviations by strong powers, because they value the externalities of the strong powers' participation. By the weekend before the EcoFin meeting the search for a compromise was in full swing, anonymous signals were leaking from Brussels that there was room for a tactical retreat, and the discussion was shifting to whether Germany and France would be required to meet the Maastricht criteria in 2005.[49] On the eve of the decisive meeting, the opposition CDU Shadow Finance Minister, Friedrich Merz, went so far as to say, "If Eichel's interpretation is adopted in Brussels on Tuesday, the Pact will be worthless on Wednesday."[50]

[47] Andreas Middel and Cornelia Wolber. "Solbes will in Berlin mitregieren." *Die Welt*. November 19, 2003: 12.

[48] "Eichel verschärft den Konflikt mit der EU-Kommission." *Frankfurter Allgemeine Zeitung*. November 20, 2003: 15.

[49] "Kompromiss im Defizitstreit zeichnet sich ab." *Frankfurter Allgemeine Zeitung*. November 24, 2003: 13.

[50] "Merz 'fassungslos' über Eichel." *Frankfurter Allgemeine Zeitung*. November 25, 2003: 1. Allowance has to be made for a bit of politically motivated exaggeration. The CDU was pushing the government to compromise on a series of fronts in the parliamentary reconciliation committee, and used its embarrassment over the deficit affair to score political

Solbes offered a compromise over the weekend: if Germany and France accepted the legitimacy of allowing the sanctions mechanism to proceed, he was willing to renegotiate the budget targets for 2004. By this point, however, Germany and France had counted the votes and were in no mood to compromise on Solbes' terms. Italy offered a compromise that the deficit countries found acceptable. On Tuesday they signed a non-binding declaration of intention to reduce their budget deficits – to the degree already foreseen in their respective budget proposals – but made their adherence to the 3 percent budget deficit target for 2005 conditional on their economic growth rates for 2004 and 2005. The deficit procedure was frozen, but could be reinitiated at any time. The majority in EcoFin accepted that this was the best compromise that could be achieved, and overrode Solbes' recommendation to take the deficit procedure to the next level.[51] The Irish and Portuguese finance ministers argued that this would lead to a desirable degree of flexibility in the pact; the Belgian that this was the only way to avoid a confrontation; only Spain, Austria, the Netherlands and Finland voted against the compromise proposal.[52]

"This is a defeat for Europe," announced Solbes, arguing that the EcoFin decision "corresponds to neither the spirit nor the rules of the Pact." An uproar followed in Berlin, where opposition politicians declared Hans Eichel the "grave-digger" of the Stability Pact.[53] Critics argued that if the sanctions mechanism allows for exceptions, this undermines the credibility of the EU's commitment to fiscal discipline, ultimately dooming the euro to the status of a weak currency.[54] The fact that the massive punishment foreseen by the EMU

points. At the same time, Merz hoped that internal critique would stiffen the Commission's back and that the Commission's pressure would weaken the government's internal bargaining position. Merz went on to argue that if the Commission compromised, it would be "another betrayal of the D-mark."

51 "Keine Strafe für die 'Sünder' – Solbes: Eine Niederlage für Europa." *Frankfurter Allgemeine Zeitung*. November 26, 2003: 1.

52 "Zerrissen in Europa." *Frankfurter Allgemeine Zeitung*. November 26, 2003: 15. When one of the major countries is affected its 10 votes do not count, so under the voting rules that prevailed at the time, the Council had a total of 60 votes. Consequently, two large countries (France, Italy and Germany had 10 votes each) plus any small country could form a coalition that could block the necessary two-thirds majority to proceed with a case. Portugal (5 votes), Ireland (3 votes) and Luxembourg (2 votes) opposed the Commission's proposal. When it became clear that a majority in support was not to be found, Belgium and Greece (5 votes each) voted for the Italian proposal.

53 "Keine Strafe für die 'Sünder' – Solbes: Eine Niederlage für Europa." *Frankfurter Allgemeine Zeitung*. November 26, 2003: 1.

54 Joachim Starbatty. "Menetekel über der Währungsunion: Die Europäische Währungsunion ist an einem Scheideweg angelangt." *Frankfurter Allgemeine Zeitung*. November 3, 2003: 15; Holger Steltzner. "Ein Pakt für Europa." *Frankfurter Allgemeine Zeitung*. November 25, 2003: 1.

treaty could easily be blocked by such large malefactors – or at the very least, delayed for years – did not hurt the critics' case.[55]

EU officials spoke of the need to reinforce the credibility of the regime, and of the danger that repeated violations could cause its norms to unravel. In calling on the finance ministers to "do their duty" on the eve of the November meeting, ECB President, Jean-Claude Trichet, expressed the hope "that we can not merely preserve the credibility of the monetary union, but also strengthen it once again."[56] This is not the way one would describe a dichotomous regime – one that either exists, because it is rigorously enforced, or does not, because it is not. Indeed, the "father" of the euro, Germany's Theo Waigel (CSU), emphasized on the day after the EcoFin meeting, "Naturally, the Pact is not dead."[57] Rather, officials in Brussels and Frankfurt seemed to recognize that the EMU regime was plastic from its inception and would continue to be problematic. The stock and foreign exchange markets seemed to support Waigel's interpretation of the Pact rather than Solbes': they did not react at all.

The violators argued repeatedly that the violations did not undermine the core principles of the regime, and maintained that their intentions were to make the Pact more flexible, or in French parlance, to "modernize" it. German Chancellor Gerhard Schroeder announced that he regarded the Pact as "capable of, and needing, interpretation."[58] On the other hand, defenders of the Pact sought to draw a clear line that could not be crossed, and pointed to the damage that the violations caused to the regime of financial discipline. The ECB, for example, reaffirmed that EcoFin had violated the spirit of the Pact, and ECB spokespeople emphasized that weakening the regime would lead to higher deficits, higher interest rates and lower growth.[59]

In January 2004 the Commission took the next step in attempting to defend a legal interpretation of the Pact by lodging a case against EcoFin before the ECJ. In oral arguments, the Commission's advocate described the failure to enforce the Pact as "a departure from the rule of law."[60] The ECJ disagreed, however, ruling in July that it was a Council prerogative to decide whether to

[55] On the other hand, the dramatic strengthening of the euro in 2003 could be seen as evidence that its credibility had not been severely impaired, but it was also driven by record-low interest rates in America and substantial covered interest differentials in favor of European investments.

[56] "Trichet wirbt für den Stabilitätspakt." *Frankfurter Allgemeine Zeitung*. November 21, 2003: 13.

[57] "Die 'Hüterin der Verträge' steht mit leeren Händen da." *Frankfurter Allgemeine Zeitung*. November 26, 2003: 3.

[58] "Schroeder: Die EU-Kommission ist nicht sakrosankt." *Frankfurter Allgemeine Zeitung*. November 27, 2003: 1.

[59] "EZB beklagt Bruch des Stabilitätspakts." *Frankfurter Allgemeine Zeitung*. November 26, 2003: 13.

[60] "Heftiger Schlagabtausch über EU-Pakt." *Financial Times Deutschland*. April 28, 2004.

approve the Commission's recommendations, although it could not suspend the deficit procedure. The effect of these rulings was to return initiative to the Commission, which now had to make another recommendation to the Council. The Commission began a tactical retreat: Pedro Solbes spoke openly of the need to relax the Stability and Growth Pact's requirements, but simultaneously advanced proposals for giving the enforcement procedure sharper teeth. The Commission preferred sharp rules that could be enforced unambiguously, but which would be easier to meet and would therefore present fewer challenges to its authority.

Debate swirled around these proposals for the rest of the year, but the idea of strengthening the Commission's enforcement powers was blocked at the June summit on the European Constitution. France proposed formal changes to make the deficit criteria conditional on the business cycle in order to allow countercyclical fiscal policies, and the new European Commission that came into office in August under Jose Manuel Barroso moved quickly to incorporate these changes into its reform proposals. The Commission proposed retaining the Maastricht targets of 3 percent deficits and 60 percent debt-to-GDP ratios, while loosening the interpretation of what "extraordinary circumstances" could be used to justify exceptions and conditioning the stringency of deficit enforcement on the overall level of government debt. While the Bundesbank, several other central banks and the ECB criticized these proposals for going too far, Schroeder and Chirac pushed for loosening them further. Germany proposed excluding investments in research and education from the deficit limits, and Italy proposed excluding payments into the EU budget. By November the apparent Italian goal was to eliminate the 3 percent deficit barrier and block proposals that would emphasize aggregate debt levels.[61]

In the end, the compromise solution was to reconcile the conflict between law and practice by codifying the status quo. Bowing to the inevitable, the Commission decided not to recommend reopening deficit proceedings against Germany or France in November 2004. In March, EcoFin approved a revision of the rules that left the main normative targets of 3 percent and 60 percent and the enforcement mechanism untouched, but created numerous loopholes – several of them custom-designed to fit the contours of the German budget – that effectively relaxed the fiscal rules and made the Pact less transparent. The effect was to reduce the emphasis on enforcement and move the deficit procedure out of the courtroom. However, the fiscal rules have not been rendered irrelevant; even participants who were critical of the outcome acknowledged that the compromise had saved the regime. "With this compromise," argued

[61] "Berlusconi stösst auf wenig Gegenliebe in der EU." *Frankfurter Allgemeine Zeitung*. November 25, 2004.

Wolfgang Schüssel, the Austrian Chancellor, "we have prevented deficits of 5 or 6 or 7 percent being considered tolerable."[62] What role was played by European rules is unclear, but the Merkel government reduced its deficits dramatically beginning in 2006 as Germany emerged from its long recession, and almost succeeded in balancing its budget in 2008.

Italy, the country that initially made the most impressive fiscal adjustments in order to qualify as a founding member of the euro zone, serves as an example both of the weakening of the regime and of its residual influence. Italy joined the euro zone with a government debt level of 110 percent of GDP, well above the 60 percent target. In order to compensate, Italy pledged to run a balanced budget after 2003 and a primary surplus (i.e. before accounting for debt service) of 5 percent of GDP. By 2003 these conditions still remained far from being fulfilled: the European Commission predicted a deficit of 2.6% of GDP for 2003 and 2.8% of GDP for 2004, while Italian Finance Minister Giulio Tremonti predicted 2.5% and 2.2%. Italy announced that it was putting off its target date for full implementation of its convergence commitments until 2007. However, the convergence process was not without influence over Italy's economic policies. Even as it postponed compliance, the government exerted substantial efforts and accepted political risks in 2003 to reduce its expenditures and reform the tax system. Italian politicians knew that their commitments were not strictly enforceable, but still acted as if they were constraining. Just how constraining the Stability and Growth Pact would turn out to be, however, depended on how other countries interpreted their own commitments, and the behavior of Germany and France did not go without notice. The Italian Prime Minister, Silvio Berlusconi, suggested that Italy could allow its deficit to go as high as 2.8 percent of GDP, if Germany and France were exceeding the three percent target.[63] Italy's diplomacy at the European level, meanwhile, was driven by the desire to prevent a total collapse of the regime, which could have had disastrous consequences for the interest rate on the Italian national debt.[64] By 2007, Italy had drastically reduced its deficit, although the impact of the global financial crisis caused deficits to shoot upwards again in 2008 and 2009.

An interesting question is what role the German and French deficits earlier in the decade played in the subsequent financial crisis in Greece, which unfolded in 2010. Greece qualified for entry into the euro zone in 2001 only after engaging in extensive off-balance sheet transactions intended to improve

[62] "Juncker achieves 'small miracle' as deal is rewritten." *Financial Times*. March 22, 2005: 6.

[63] "Deutschland und Frankreich bringen die anderen Euro-Staaten gegen sich auf." *Frankfurter Allgemeine Zeitung*. November 11, 2003: 15.

[64] "Italiens Rolle im Schurkenstück." *Frankfurter Allgemeine Zeitung*. November 26, 2003: 13.

the accounting of its debt. One such deal, named *Aeolos* after the ancient god of the wind, reduced the Greek official debt by selling future landing fees at Greek airports to Goldman Sachs; another, dubbed *Ariadne*, mortgaged the revenue stream of the national lottery. These transactions were not reported as loans, although they allowed the government to move income streams forward in time at what amounted to very disadvantageous interest rates.[65] Greek governments failed to come to terms with persistent deficits, pervasive tax noncompliance, and a level of debt that hovered around 100 percent of GDP, but the crisis broke when the new Socialist government unveiled the creative accounting of its predecessor in December 2009 and announced that the deficit for 2009 was 12.7 percent of GDP rather than the previously forecast level of 3.7 percent. The euro countries faced the dilemma that the Stability and Growth Pact had been designed to prevent: whether to rescue Greece, threatening price stability and weakening incentives for fiscal restraint, or to allow a damaging default – Greek foreign debt amounted to 300 billion dollars by 2010 – that would plunge global financial markets into turmoil and likely spread panic to the weaker euro zone members, including Portugal, Spain, Ireland and Italy. In spite of misgivings, the larger European countries agreed to mount an ambitious rescue of Greece using bilateral loans to supplement a record-setting 30 billion euro stand-by arrangement from the IMF. When this failed to calm markets and bond yields rose sharply in other southern European countries, the euro zone members announced a symbolic one-trillion euro commitment to support countries that might come under a speculative attack. The euro fell steadily in 2010 as the news about Greece worsened, from a high of $1.45 in January to a low of $1.21 in May.

The euro crisis of 2010 revealed the contradictions in the European macroeconomic compromise, which allowed states to retain fiscal authority while creating a common monetary authority. Without a set of enforceable fiscal policy rules, monetary stability was hostage to the weakest fiscal link. The alternative of allowing Greece to default was unavailable because a Greek default would have led to a banking crisis in the core euro countries. For years, the ECB had followed an ill-advised policy of accepting the sovereign bonds of all euro zone members as collateral for loans to euro zone commercial banks. This created a powerful incentive for French and German banks to buy the high-yield bonds of the weaker euro zone members and profit by arbitrage. As a result, the deficit countries were able to finance their deficits cheaply and

65 "Wall St. Helped Europe to Land Deeper in Debt." *New York Times*. February 14, 2010: 1, cont. 16. Greece paid Goldman Sachs $300 million in fees to arrange the *Aeolos* transaction in 2001.

amass debts that would become unsustainable if interest rates rose, and the financial system of the whole euro zone became vulnerable to a default.

The lack of an effective central authority in Europe delayed a coordinated response to the Greek crisis for several months, which caused the crisis to deepen as market confidence declined. As late as March 2010, European governments, the ECB and the IMF busily denied that Greece was contemplating an IMF program or that there would be any need for an international rescue operation.[66] Domestic politics in Germany played a key role. The German press dwelt on the excesses of Greek fiscal policy with a mixture of *Schadenfreude* and genuine outrage, and public opinion strongly opposed a bail-out that might further weaken the euro. With a key state election approaching in Nordrhein-Westphalen, Germany's largest state, Chancellor Angela Merkel tried to delay the unpopular decision to extend loans to Greece. At the same time, Germany worked behind the scenes at the IMF to assure that the conditions attached to its assistance would be rigorous. As I show in Chapter 8, countries with substantial financial ties to the borrower usually lobby for gentle conditionality, and this influence is generally monopolized by the United States. Greece, however, is a rare case in which the Europeans controlled the negotiations and those most directly interested insisted on harsh terms. The reason was to deflect domestic criticism in Germany, and the effect was to create such a draconian program that it seemed incredible that Greece could meet its terms.[67]

At each stage, the Greek crisis underscored the inadequacy of European monetary and fiscal instruments: European institutions were unable to limit the deficits of member countries, to contain the financial imbalances they created, or to move swiftly to limit the damage when market confidence declined. While none of this was surprising, it created a new impulse for institutional innovation, and at this writing it is unclear what its consequences will be. Similarly, the fact that European institutions lacked the autonomy to enforce the rules of the Stability and Growth pact in 2003 against Germany – much less, against Germany and France simultaneously – should not have come as a surprise. Indeed, the fact that the episode did not move asset prices suggests that it did not surprise well-informed insiders. The Pact was not designed to meet such a rigorous test. Its designers assumed that Germany would never violate its deficit criteria, so it would remain solidly on the side of the enforcers, and that the only test the Commission was likely to face was enforcing the rules

66 "IMF Help For Greece is a Risky Prospect." *New York Times*. March 5, 2010.

67 The program included long-term fiscal adjustments, including reductions followed by three-year freezes in public sector wages, reductions in pensions, and an increase in the retirement age, an 11% of GDP reduction in the budget deficit over three years, and numerous structural conditions. This ran counter to announced IMF policies of reducing conditionality, particularly in the structural area.

against weak countries. Just as in the case of the IMF, credibility problems are greatest when the interests of powerful countries are affected; international institutions can only lend credibility to weak countries. As in the IMF, however, the powerful countries in the euro area can inherit the credibility problems of the weak countries if their own financial interests become deeply involved. The stability of the euro zone and the attractiveness of the euro as a reserve currency will depend on how these dilemmas are resolved.

Conclusions

Like the WTO and its predecessor, the GATT, the EU and its predecessor organizations illustrate the ubiquity of informal governance. Deviations from the formal rules vary as much as the form of the rules and the substance of the issues they are meant to coordinate, but neither of these organizations, any more than the IMF, can be understood accurately by reading its treaty articles. Both institutions consistently rely on consensus decision making even when the formal rules would allow more expeditious procedures that would benefit the pivotal voter. Both institutions tolerate inefficient delays as a result, particularly in their accession procedures for new members. In both organizations, informality systematically privileges the interests of the most powerful members. In the EU, furthermore, we witness a striking parallel to the IMF's credibility problems when European institutions attempt to insert themselves into the most sensitive of domestic policies, fiscal policy. In both cases, credibility problems are greatest when the interests of the strongest states are affected.

As striking as these parallels are, the differences in the forms of informal governance across the three organizations do more to illustrate the usefulness of the model of informal governance. The model predicts variation in governance structure as a function of the distribution of power and the expected frequency of conflict. In both the WTO and the EU, where competing leading powers had incentives to manipulate central institutions and the opportunities for conflicting interests were legion, the model predicts minimal creation of executive powers, retention of the key legislative powers by states, and legalization. Both the WTO and the EU retained weak executive institutions but created powerful judicial agencies to adjudicate disputes, and have developed extensive libraries of case law. Resolving disputes through courts rather than through diplomacy has served to mute the ability of powerful states to exercise informal influence, which has made delegation tolerable.

Like the trade regime, European institutions have developed over time in a way that reflects the trade-offs between formal and informal governance.

The early EEC was paralyzed by the threat of exit by one of its leading powers, and adopted a consensus rule that blocked steps towards integration. The logjam was broken only when the costs of disorganization became so intolerable that countries became willing to sacrifice elements of formal sovereignty. Progress in delegating powers to the European level was accompanied by a formalization of governance, as institutional reforms made European politics more transparent and embodied international commitments in legal texts that were enforceable in court. Meanwhile, the degree of conflict across issue areas was reflected in the degree of formalization. European legislation has opened up wide scope for judicial activism in the area of the common market, but national policies in justice and foreign affairs have remained much more independent. Meanwhile, although the judicial processes in the EU have become highly legalized, the legislative process remains informal and consensual in practice rather than majoritarian.

The most striking form of executive delegation in European politics is EMU, which delegated monetary policy to a supranational ECB and created a formal mechanism to regulate fiscal policy. Some member countries, of course, chose not to participate in EMU for this reason. The failure to enforce the Stability and Growth Pact in 2003–04, however, when its provisions were violated by its two most important members, demonstrated the limits of formal governance. It is evident that the rules were not intended to apply strictly to the most powerful members, and that credibility is available only to weak countries. As the case of Greece demonstrated in 2010, even small members may be able to operate outside the rules if the financial interests of the leading powers are deeply implicated.

PART THREE

HYPOTHESES

7

Access to IMF resources

Part Two presented three international organizations as case studies to illustrate the logic of the model of informal governance and to assess its broad applicability. Part Three is more rigorous, and turns to empirical hypothesis testing. This is the first of three chapters that turn up the power on the microscope and study the behavior of the IMF quantitatively. The empirical strategy is to investigate the stages of the IMF product cycle in detail, moving from the initiation of IMF programs to their design and ultimate implementation. The current chapter focuses on the initiation stage, in which countries request to participate in an IMF program, and the Fund makes a portion of its resources available to support the country's adjustment plans. The key dependent variable in this chapter will be the degree of access granted to Fund resources.

In this chapter and the ones that follow, the quantitative analysis will be supplemented with illustrations drawn from five prominent financial crises that I have studied in detail: Mexico (1994–5), Korea (1997), Indonesia (1997), Russia (1998) and Argentina (2001). The cases were selected for their systemic importance, and there is no intention to claim that they are a representative sample of IMF lending or of financial crises; the generality of the results rests on the quantitative analysis, not on the cases. However, the cases perform two important functions that the quantitative analysis alone could not. First, they present possibility results that make it possible to interpret statistical findings: they demonstrate that the mechanism posited to explain a particular correlation can operate in an empirical example. Second, they make it possible to probe aspects of the formal argument that are not amenable to quantitative measurement and statistical testing. I do not attempt to tell the full story behind the cases. I simply draw upon them as they are helpful to illustrate particular points.

The theory of informal governance generates testable hypotheses about the conditions under which the United States should exercise its influence and how this influence should modify IMF lending practices. First, exercising informal power is costly, so it is used only sparingly, when the returns outweigh the risks. This implies that US influence will be used only when US interests are strongly engaged. Second, informal influence is used to suspend the ordinary rules of procedure, so it is applied in order to secure exceptions to rules. In the case of IMF lending, exceptions are valuable to the borrowers. These expectations combine to predict an interactive effect, in which the United States exercises its influence to waive IMF rules only when a country that is inherently important in terms of US interests finds that it has a compelling need for IMF support. Exceptions are made when a country that has a lot of chips needs IMF financing enough to be willing to cash them in.

These expectations about informal governance apply generally across institutional settings, but the model predicts a pattern of variation across and within institutions that depends on the distribution of issue-specific power and the degree of conflict in particular issue areas. Among the institutions investigated in this study, informal governance is expected to be most pronounced in the IMF. However, informal governance is also expected to be most pronounced in IMF activities that involve the most substantial degree of executive delegation. We have already seen in Chapter 3 that within the IMF, general policy issues are much less subject to informal influence than particular country-specific matters. Similarly, I expect to see less informal governance at the earliest stage of program initiation than at the stages of program design and enforcement. Nevertheless, I find evidence of informal governance in the size of loans. The evidence becomes stronger and the tests more robust in the subsequent chapters.

Dependent variable: access to Fund resources

An extensive literature seeks to explain the pattern of participation in IMF programs, usually as a preamble to correcting estimates of their effects for the distorting influence of sample selection.[1] This literature has had to cope with a number of difficulties, however, which make program participation far from an ideal dependent variable for this study. Program participation depends at least as much on decisions by borrowing country governments as on those of the IMF, and the estimated effects of covariates are joint effects on both

1 This literature is reviewed in Steinwand and Stone 2008. Participation equations are typically used in an effort to counter the effects of selection bias (Heckman 1979). Since countries typically call upon the IMF in reaction to economic crises, the sample of countries under IMF tutelage is systematically different from the overall population of states, and statistical analyses that do not correct for this self-selection are in danger of producing biased results.

decisions, so it is difficult to attribute effects to one agent or the other. It is possible to estimate separate equations for government and IMF decisions using partial observability models, but the results depend on the validity of the assumptions used to identify the models.[2] Partial observability models have poor convergence properties, and the results are not generally robust to specification changes. Using the data set for this study and a range of specifications, convergence could not be achieved using models that included the interaction terms required by the theory.

However, the loan commitment amount is a theoretically appropriate dependent variable that should be more subject to informal influence than the pattern of participation. The initiation of IMF programs is determined through a formalized process that is governed by the provisions of the IMF's Articles of Agreement, and in principle every IMF member has the right to participate in a program when it has balance of payments difficulties. The initiative to apply for IMF support comes from the member country that requests it, and moves through a standard series of bureaucratic channels. A mission brief is drawn up and circulated for interdepartmental review, an IMF mission is dispatched to the member capital, a letter of intent is drafted by IMF staff and negotiated with the member country, a staff report is prepared for the Executive Board and reviewed by various departments, and management presents a proposal to the Executive Board for approval. The process is summarized in Figure 7.1. Along the way, there are opportunities for the shareholders to use informal participation to influence the staff's bargaining position over conditionality, which may block or ease the way to agreement, and the United States can almost always prevent a proposal from coming to the board.[3] Intervening in the initiation of a program is more public and transparent than influencing the substance of the negotiations over conditionality or its subsequent enforcement, however, so this is a more costly and less effective way to exert informal influence. In extraordinary cases, such as those of Mexico and Korea discussed below, the process of program preparation may be rushed, but this is rare and raises objections even on the normally quiescent Executive Board. Even in those cases, the element of controversy surrounded the amount of Fund resources committed to a particular country rather than the initiation of a program.

[2] Przeworski and Vreeland 2000, 2002; Vreeland 2003.

[3] In at least one case, that of India in 1981, the United States was apparently unable to prevent a program from going forward that it opposed (Gould 2006). The US position was that India already had access to private capital markets, although this is not generally an argument against eligibility for an IMF program. A more convincing objection was that the Reagan administration was suspicious of Indira Gandhi's ties to the Soviet Union. On the other hand, in 2008 Britain was able to delay approval of a facility for Iceland until Iceland agreed to refund British deposits in Icelandic banks.

Before an IMF program can be approved by the Executive Board, a series of documents must be prepared and a number of officials of the Fund must be consulted, in a process that ordinarily would take a minimum of three months.

Preparation of the Mission Brief by the Chief of Mission	Two weeks
Area Department Front Office Approval of the Brief	2–3 days
Interdepartmental Review (PDR, FAD, Research, etc.)	3 days
Management Approval	2–3 days
Mission visits the program country and reports back	Two weeks
Preparation of the Staff Report	Two weeks
Department Approval of the Staff Report	2–3 days
Interdepartmental Review (PDR, FAD, Research, etc.)	One week
Management Approval	3–5 days
Circulation to the Executive Board and Meeting	Two weeks
Total:	Twelve weeks

The process often takes much longer because negotiations are extended and multiple missions are necessary, but most programs are approved within 3–12 months. In urgent crises, this timeline can be dramatically compressed. In the case of Korea's first program in 1997, for example, the authorities approached the Fund with a request for a program on November 21, the mission arrived in Seoul on November 26, and the letter of intent was signed on December 3 and approved by the board on December 4.

Figure 7.1 Timing of IMF program preparation.

IMF lending is covered by a series of rules that are analogous to credit limits and prudential requirements for private borrowers. On one hand, these rules limit access to Fund resources, and on the other, they require that the borrower's balance of payments be adequately financed in order to limit risks. Credit limits are determined by IMF quotas, which correspond to country contributions to IMF capital and determine vote shares. Cumulative access to Fund resources is ordinarily limited to 300 percent of a country's quota. During urgent crises in systemically important countries, however, the formal regulations are frequently waived and replaced by a non-transparent process of informal bargaining.[4] In some cases, it is difficult to reconstruct exactly how the degree of access was finally decided. The amount of access is one of the most intensely political decisions in these cases, because the probability that the program succeeds in stemming a crisis is generally an increasing function of the IMF resources committed, and the amount of policy adjustment required of the borrower in the short run is a decreasing function of the IMF commitment. The leading shareholders want to restrain contagion, which argues in favor of

[4] The Fund introduced the Extraordinary Access Framework in response to the experience of the Asian crisis in 1997, and these rules were loosened further in response to the global financial crisis of 2008.

making larger loans, but they are also interested in maintaining the pressure for reform, which argues in favor of smaller ones, and they are wary of creating precedents that will lead to moral hazard on the part of investors and governments. Disagreements arise among the leading shareholders in particularly prominent cases when their interests are engaged to different degrees.

According to IMF procedure, the amount of financing should be determined by calculations performed by the Fund to determine the size of the financing gap between probable foreign-currency expenditures and receipts. These calculations are performed for every program, and they play an important role in IMF staff reports presented to the board. However, the calculations are based on a number of uncertain assumptions, and the degree of financing required depends upon the amount of adjustment required in the program, the amount of official support forthcoming from other sources (the World Bank, member countries, regional development banks, debt rescheduling, etc.), and the reaction of private capital flows. Private capital flows are a particularly important variable in emerging markets, and the effect of IMF programs on capital flight, the roll-over of short-term debt, and portfolio investment depends on the credibility of the program.[5] In essence, these projections are judgments about what is politically feasible, and it is telling that in major crises the answer is generally a round figure either when expressed in billions of dollars, in Special Drawing Rights (SDRs), or as a percentage of quota.

Informal input into the process arises at several points. First, the country seeking assistance requests a figure that it believes politically feasible. For example, the augmentation of Argentina's program in September 2001 by $8 billion followed the figure proposed by Argentina. However, US Treasury Undersecretary John Taylor was in Buenos Aires negotiating with Argentine Finance Minister Cavallo in early August, and the figure was floated to him before it was proposed to the IMF.[6] The United States was reluctant in this case, and only accepted the $8 billion augmentation when it was agreed that $3 billion of it would be earmarked for a debt rescheduling operation.[7] Other members of the G-7 were more skeptical, and agreed to go along only after the United States pushed for the augmentation in a conference call involving the G-7 deputy finance ministers.[8]

In the end, the size of financing in crises is determined by informal consul-

[5] IMF estimates of the reaction of capital flows were much too optimistic in the Asian financial crisis. As we shall see below, some of those estimates were in turn driven by constraints imposed by leading shareholders.

[6] Taylor 2007, 83–87.

[7] This proviso was insisted upon by US Treasury Secretary O'Neill, and was vigorously opposed by IMF management. IEO interviews and interviews with IMF staff.

[8] John Taylor describes the Argentine case in detail (2007, 87).

tations with the leading shareholders – a conference call by the G-7 deputies is usually involved – and in systemically important crises the United States has played the central role.

Measuring informal influence

The concept of informal influence is very general, as the United States could exert its influence on behalf of any country in which it perceives a critical interest, and the model does not define what those critical interests may be. Indeed, the model assumes that these interests change substantially over time, and are not fully predictable: they are modeled as a random variable. Consequently, my empirical strategy in this chapter and the two that follow is to focus attention on five independent variables that represent a broad range of possible measures of US motivations to intervene on behalf of particular countries: US foreign aid, US bank exposure, US exports, voting in the United Nations, and alliance portfolios. A number of studies have already linked IMF program participation to US aid, US bank exposure, and UN voting.[9] Although measures and results vary, the cumulative effect of these studies is to suggest that the preferences of the leading shareholders, and particularly the United States, have a potent influence on IMF lending practices.

Foreign aid was the variable I used to measure US interests in my previous studies of enforcement of conditionality in post-Communist countries[10] and in Africa,[11] and of the scope of conditionality.[12] In the last study, in addition, I found it to be a strong predictor of IMF decisions to approve the initiation of programs, and Eichengreen *et al.* similarly link US foreign aid to IMF financing.[13] Aid is a diffuse measure of influence because donors give aid for a variety of reasons, but it has the virtues of being a policy instrument that the United States controls directly, and of being a monetary measure with budgetary consequences. The distribution of aid across countries reflects the relative priority that donors attach to them, and it can vary substantially as these priorities shift. Aid is not particularly effective at promoting goals such as economic or human development, which is consistent with the interpretation that the aid is tied to other agendas besides promoting development.[14] In the analysis that follows, I assume that foreign aid is an investment in a relationship with a leader or

9 Steinwand and Stone 2008.
10 Stone 2002.
11 Stone 2004.
12 Stone 2008.
13 Eichengreen *et al.* 2006.
14 See, for example, Burnside and Dollar 2000; Dollar and Pritchett 1998; Knack 2001.

regime, representing a direct monetary measure of the importance of a particular recipient to a particular donor. Aid is measured in millions of US dollars – not normalized by GDP – because it is used as a measure of US interests expressed by aid, rather than the degree of the recipient's dependence.

The next two measures, bank exposure and exports, provide straightforward measures of economic interests as they relate to international finance and trade. A number of the countries that have been at the epicenter of international financial crises, such as Mexico, Brazil, Argentina and South Korea, are important to the United States because they are at the center of webs of financial transactions that can imperil American financial institutions during crises. However, much of this debt is held by individuals and dispersed institutions in the form of securities, and bondholders have weak incentives to organize collectively, so aggregate debt is a poor instrument for US financial interests. Banks, on the other hand, organize collectively, cooperate with national regulatory agents in refinancing debt, and represent concentrated interests, as well as playing a critical role as financial intermediaries at home. Consequently, bank exposure is the best available measure of politically relevant financial interests.[15] Broz and Hawes find that high credit exposure of US and German banks increases the scale of IMF lending.[16] Copelovitch finds that high average levels of bank exposure of the major shareholders increases the size of IMF loans, but that high variance in exposure across the major shareholders reduces this effect.[17] In this book, bank exposure is calculated as the proportion of total US bank lending to foreign countries and institutions owed by a particular country.

Exports represent the commercial stake of the United States economy in prosperity abroad. Financial crises abroad reduce demand for US products, and this is of greater concern to policy makers if the countries involved are major US trade partners. Aggregate exports do not capture the ability of particular industries to organize collectively, however, so the effect of trade exposure is expected to be primarily a function of preemptive action by policymakers rather than a response to lobbying. Exports are measured in millions of US dollars to provide a common metric of the relative importance of alternative export markets to US producers.

A growing number of studies relates IMF lending to the political affinity of countries for potential foreign patrons by using measures of the similarity of their votes in the UN General Assembly.[18] Barro and Lee find that IMF loans

[15] Copelovitch 2010.
[16] Broz and Hawes 2006.
[17] Copelovitch 2010.
[18] Barro and Lee 2005; Oatley and Yackee 2000; Thacker 1999.

are associated with similarity to US voting patterns in the UN.[19] Thacker finds that increasing this congruence over time is associated with a higher probability of IMF lending.[20] Pop-Eleches finds the same effect, but only in post-Communist countries in the 1990s, and not in Latin America.[21] On the other hand, Eichengreen *et al.* report that similarity to US voting patterns in the UN decreases the chance of receiving IMF loans, after controlling for receipt of US foreign aid.[22]

From the perspective of informal governance, two alternative effects of political affinity are possible: it may be the case that countries that vote in accord with the United States are rewarded; alternatively, it may be the case that habitual US opponents in the UN are favored because the United States uses IMF loans as a way to buy support from skeptical countries during crises. The informal governance model does not speak to this question, since its prediction is about the intensity of US interests, which varies over time, rather than about the source of these interests. If US interests primarily relate to saving sympathetic regimes from the political consequences of financial crises, the former effect should predominate – the United States will lend its influence to prop up the fortunes of like-minded leaders. The examples of Zaire and the Philippines during the Cold War come to mind. On the other hand, if US objectives primarily concern the construction of ad hoc "coalitions of the willing" to achieve particular objectives, the latter effect should be more important, because countries with policy preferences close to those of the United States will be less likely to demand compensation in return for their cooperation. The examples of Russia, Pakistan and Egypt after the Cold War fit this pattern, and it is likely that the pattern shifted with the end of the Cold War, as the stakes of supporting client regimes declined. Either effect is consistent with the theoretical argument, because there is no reason other than political manipulation to expect to find a correlation between UN voting and IMF lending. In either case, however, the theory predicts a conditional effect, so the hypothesis will be disconfirmed if the effect of affinity is not conditional on vulnerability to withdrawal of external financing. Political affinity is measured as an S-score, which summarizes the similarity between two voting profiles as the length of a line segment connecting two points in a multidimensional issue space, normalized to $[-1, 1]$.[23]

Finally, alliance patterns measure a sharper dimension of alignment than

[19] Barro and Lee 2005.
[20] Thacker 1999.
[21] Pop-Eleches 2009.
[22] Eichengreen *et al.* 2006.
[23] Signorino and Ritter 1999; Gartzke *et al.* 1999.

UN voting, capturing formal military commitments. Countries located near the center of the web of US military and strategic commitments can call upon the United States for support when they get into financial difficulties because issues that affect allies are associated with intense US preferences. As US allies or allies of close US allies, their critical concerns become important national security issues. Furthermore, because of the military and diplomatic implications of formal alliances, US allies have entree into levels of the United States government that other countries cannot reach, and have counterparts in the State and Defense Departments who can be called upon to argue their cases with the officials in Treasury who deal with the IMF. The similarity of each country's alliance portfolio to that of the United States is measured by an S-score that ranges from –1 (most dissimilar) to 1 (most similar).

Across each of these five measures, the theory of informal governance predicts stronger effects when the participating country urgently needs IMF support, because urgent financial need makes countries willing to make greater concessions to US objectives. Consequently, the analyses that follow present the effects of these variables interacted with three variables that represent the borrowing country's vulnerability to sudden loss of external financing.[24] *Trade/GDP* measures the openness of the economy; relatively closed economies are insulated from external shocks and less dramatically affected by currency or financial crises. *Debt service/exports* captures the severity of a country's debt burden, which is often a leading indicator of a financial crisis. *Short-term debt* measures the percentage of debt held in instruments with a maturity of one year or less, which represents roll-over risk, or a country's vulnerability to the risk that creditors will refuse to extend additional credit. Maturities typically shorten as a crisis becomes acute. These three variables work in tandem to increase the risk of sudden reversals of capital flows: open economies that are highly leveraged and dependent on rolling over short-term debt are at significant risk.

Results

I use five independent variables to test hypotheses about informal governance – US aid, US bank exposure, US exports, UN voting and alliance portfolios – and interact each with trade/GDP, debt service/exports and short-term debt. The quantity of interest is the ratio of the total amount committed when a new

[24] Stone 2008.

commitment is made to the recipient country's quota in the IMF.[25] IMF quotas are country-specific limits that regulate the amount of access to IMF resources that is allowed under the formal rules. Normalizing commitments by dividing them by IMF quotas, therefore, focuses attention on variations that arise outside of the formal rules. In particular, this focuses attention on the political determinants of short-term exceptions to rules, rather than upon the political determinants of the rules themselves. The dependent variable for these analyses is the natural logarithm of the ratio, because I expect to find non-linear effects, and the natural log is normally distributed and therefore appropriate for Ordinary Least Squares (OLS) analysis. Table 7.1 presents the results of these analyses for the quantities of interest. Control variables are not displayed, but the full table is available in Appendix A as Table A.7.1. Significant controls include debt service/exports, total debt, budget balance/GDP, time under IMF programs and polity, and insignificant controls include foreign debt/GDP, reserves/GDP, GDP per capita, devaluation and missing data.

The results indicate that none of the five measures of US interests is associated with increases in the size of IMF loans when country vulnerability reaches its lower bound of zero: all of the coefficients are negative. In addition, 11 of the 15 interactive terms take the expected positive sign, indicating that the effects of US influence increase as country vulnerability increases. In order to evaluate the significance of the interactive effects, it is necessary to compute the size of the coefficients at various levels of country vulnerability.[26] These results are presented in Table 7.2.

The interactive results indicate that two measures of influence, US bank exposure and US exports, have statistically significant effects on the size of IMF loans when recipient countries are vulnerable to sudden reversals of international financing. Vulnerable in this case means one standard deviation above the mean in terms of trade openness, debt service and short-term debt. Furthermore, these effects disappear as country vulnerability drops to merely average levels: in the case of bank exposure, the effect becomes insignificant, and in the case of exports it reverses sign.

These results are substantively quite significant. Recall that the dependent variable is the natural logarithm of the ratio of commitments to quotas, so the effects of the coefficients on the ratio of commitments to quotas are exponen-

[25] A new observation occurs when a new program is initiated or there is an increase in the amount of outstanding IMF commitments to a recipient country (e.g. an existing facility is augmented, or a second facility is created). The appropriate focus of interest is the total amount committed because formal IMF rules of access relate to totals, not to particular commitments.

[26] Braumoeller 2004.

Table 7.1 *Effects of US influence on commitments of IMF resources.*

	US aid		Bank Exposure		Exports		UN Voting		Alliances	
	Coef. *Std. Err.*	*p*	*Coef.* *Std. Err.*	*p*	*Coef.* *Std. Err.*	*p*	*Coef.* *Std. Err.*	*p*	*Coef.* *Std. Err.*	*p*
US Influence	−0.0011	0.14	−25.01	0.01	−0.0022	0.00	−0.0959	0.76	−0.3743	0.59
	0.0007		*9.52*		*0.0006*		*0.3099*		*0.6973*	
Interactions with:										
Trade/GDP	1.2×10^{-5}	0.29	0.2618	0.01	1.1×10^{-5}	0.08	−0.0028	0.40	−0.0094	0.21
	$\mathit{1.2 \times 10^{-5}}$		*0.1021*		$\mathit{6.4 \times 10^{-6}}$		*0.0033*		*0.0074*	
Debt Service/ Exports	-9.3×10^{-6}	0.31	0.2601	0.09	1.5×10^{-5}	0.04	0.0152	0.09	0.0230	0.02
	$\mathit{9.2 \times 10^{-6}}$		*0.1545*		$\mathit{7.0 \times 10^{-6}}$		*0.0089*		*0.0100*	
Short-term Debt	2.2×10^{-5}	0.57	0.7245	0.03	7.3×10^{-5}	0.00	−0.0018	0.87	0.0124	0.58
	$\mathit{3.8 \times 10^{-5}}$		*0.3246*		$\mathit{1.2 \times 10^{-5}}$		*0.0108*		*0.0225*	
Control variables...										
Observations	351		351		351		350		351	
R^2	0.31		0.36		0.38		0.30		0.31	

Note: The dependent variable is the natural logarithm of the ratio of IMF commitments to IMF quotas. OLS estimates. Standard errors in italics. The full table is reported in Appendix 1 as table A.7.1.

Table 7.2 *Interactive effects of US influence on IMF commitments.*

	US aid		Bank Exposure		Exports		UN Voting		Alliances	
	Coef. *Std. Err.*	p	*Coef.* *Std. Err.*	p	*Coef.* *Std. Err.*	p	*Coef.* *Std. Err.*	p	*Coef.* *Std. Err.*	p
Vulnerability:										
High	0.0003	0.64	24.87	0.00	0.0009	0.00	0.0663	0.79	−0.3577	0.45
	0.0006		*6.60*		*0.0003*		*0.2436*		*0.4696*	
Mean	−0.0003	0.15	4.26	0.37	−0.0004	0.00	−0.0177	0.88	−0.4389	0.09
	0.0002		*4.76*		*0.0001*		*0.1199*		*0.2597*	
Low	−0.0008	0.11	−16.36	0.04	−0.0018	0.00	−0.1018	0.65	−0.5201	0.32
	0.0005		*7.99*		*0.0004*		*0.2265*		*0.5265*	

Note: The dependent variable is the natural logorithm of the ratio of IMF commitments to IMF quotas. OLS estimates. Standard errors in italics. "High" and "Low" vulnerability are one standard deviation above and below the mean, respectively, in terms of Trade/GDP, Debt service/Exports and Short-term Debt.

tial.[27] At high levels of vulnerability, a one standard deviation increase in the exposure of US banks, which corresponds to an increase in the exposure to a particular country of 1.9 percent of total US foreign lending, increases IMF commitments by 79 percent of quota. These effects accelerate rapidly, so an increase in bank exposure of two standard deviations raises IMF commitments by 219 percent of quota. Figure 7.2 uses three-dimensional graphs to illustrate how the effects depend upon various dimensions of country vulnerability, while holding the other dimensions of vulnerability and all of the other covariates at their mean values. The vertical axis of each graph is the ratio of IMF commitments to quotas. Bank exposure ranges along the x-axis. The mean value in the data is 0.005, and the maximum – Mexico in February 1995 – is 0.18. Each graph varies one of the vulnerability measures along the y-axis. The graphs indicate that bank exposure has essentially no effect on loan size when vulnerability is low according to one of the three measures and average on the other two. The mean level of trade/GDP is 62 percent, of debt service/exports is 22 percent, and of short-term debt is 10.5 percent. However, bank exposure begins to have effects when vulnerability is average on all three measures, and the effects rise rapidly (and become statistically significant) as vulnerability increases on each dimension.

The effects of US exports are substantively significant as well. When countries are highly vulnerable to changes in capital flows, a one standard deviation increase in monthly US exports, or $491 million, increases IMF commitments by 57 percent of quota, and a two-standard deviation increase raises commitments by 231 percent of quota. Figure 7.3 illustrates these effects in three dimensions while varying vulnerability. The vertical axis again represents IMF loan commitments/IMF quotas. The x-axis is now occupied by US exports in millions of dollars per month, which has a mean in the sample of 122 million dollars, and a maximum, again represented by Mexico, of 7.04 billion dollars. Mexican imports from the United States increased rapidly during the 1990s in the wake of the NAFTA treaty, from 3.1 billion dollars per month in 1992 to 10.4 billion in 2001. The y-axes in the three graphs, respectively, represent trade/GDP, debt service/exports, and short-term debt. The three graphs indicate that US exports are estimated to have a negative effect on the size of IMF loans when vulnerability is low on one dimension and average on the others. This effect reverses as vulnerability increases on any dimension, however, and the effect of US exports on the size of IMF loans becomes an increasing exponential function of vulnerability. The flatter appearance of these graphs compared to those for bank exposure is due to the narrow range of US exports

[27] Since $\ln(y) = X\beta$, $y = e^{X\beta}$, which implies that the effect of x on y is an exponential function of x, and that these effects depend upon the values of all of the other covariates.

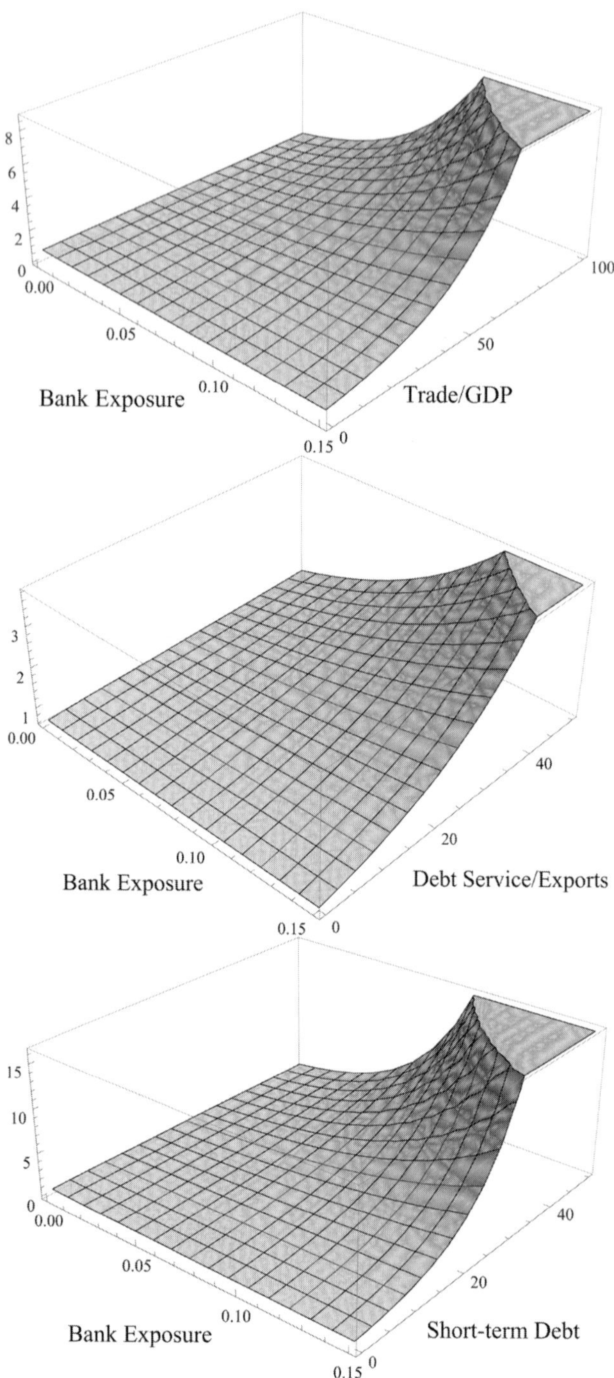

Figure 7.2 IMF commitments/quota and US bank exposure.

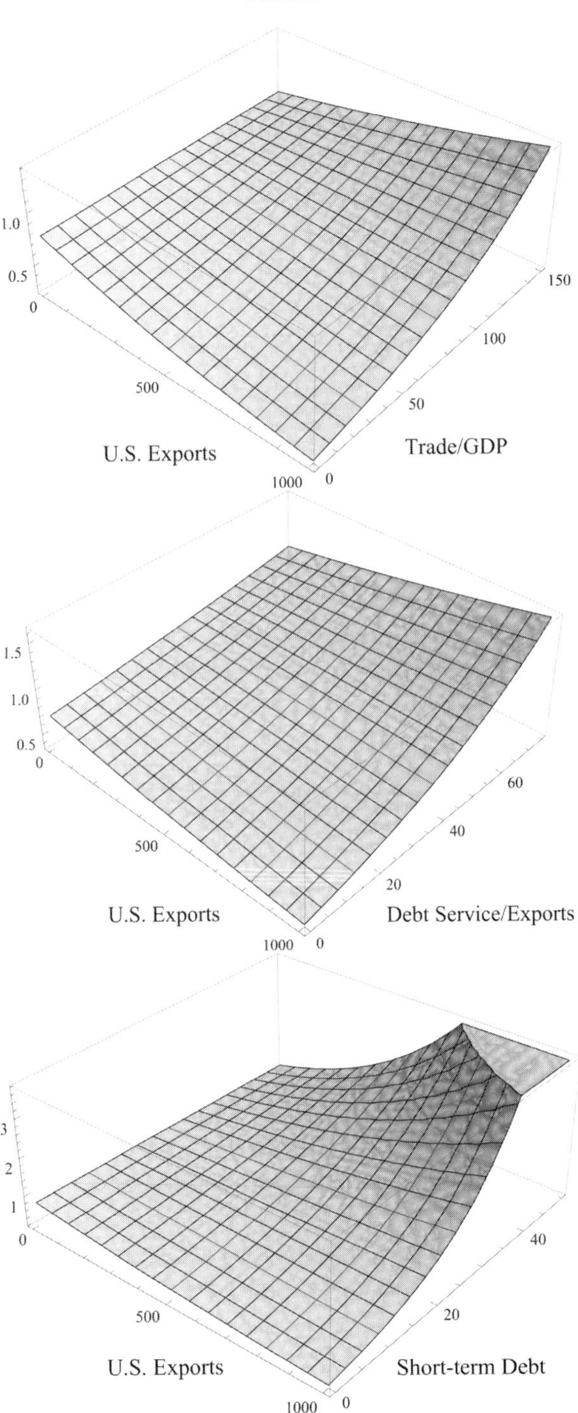

Figure 7.3 IMF commitments/quota and US exports.

used to compute them, which was chosen in order to highlight the fact that US exports have non-monotonic effects. If US exports are allowed to range up to their sample maximum of $7 billion, the graphs take on the familiar upward slope to the right.

These findings are consistent with interpretations of IMF policy making that emphasize US domestic economic interests. As Broz and Hawes show, US Congressmen who represent districts containing major money center banks are more likely to support IMF quota replenishments, and countries that borrow substantially from US banks receive more IMF support.[28] Copelovitch demonstrates that countries that borrow heavily from the banks of major shareholders receive larger loans.[29] Similarly, Gould shows that banks are able to influence the terms of conditionality when they provide substantial financing, which usually happens when a major debt rescheduling event occurs.[30] The chapters that follow find evidence of effects of all five influence variables on the pattern of conditionality and enforcement, indicating that informal governance has a wide range of motivations.

The results reported above indicate that informal influence leaves a broad footprint on the allocation of IMF resources. When US preferences are intense, as measured by the exposure of US banks and important export markets, IMF loans become markedly larger – but only when the borrowers are unusually vulnerable to sudden reversals of international capital flows. Countries with open economies that are heavily indebted and dependent upon rolling over short-term credits to stave off default have strong incentives to draw upon their influence with the United States to secure more generous terms. Those that are not vulnerable in these ways might also have been able to obtain larger loans in return for corresponding concessions, but their need for financing is not so urgent, so they have weaker incentives to make concessions. The quantitative results provide a basis for broad generalization, but only hint at the mechanisms involved. The next section explores the logic of these inferences by examining two empirical examples and tracing the process by which loan sizes were determined in crises.

Cases: Mexico 1995 and Korea 1997

Political approval for access to Fund resources is secured before a program comes to the board, but this is nevertheless the most controversial point in

28 Broz and Hawes 2006.
29 Copelovitch 2010.
30 Gould 2006.

Board discussions, and the one most likely to lead to abstentions. The premier case was the extraordinary financing provided to Mexico in February 1995. The background was a controversial election, the assassination of the leading presidential candidate, Luis Donaldo Colosio, and the outbreak of rebellion in Chiapas. The Mexican government decided to float the peso in December 1994 after resident capital flight led to a sharp decline in official reserves. For several weeks in January President Clinton sought Congressional approval for a $40 billion loan-guarantee plan to help with the conversion of Mexican short-term peso-denominated but dollar-indexed debt, or *Tesobonos*. In addition, the IMF was asked to offer a $7.8 billion Stand-By Arrangement (SBA) to be available immediately. There were several informal Board meetings to prepare for the SBA proposal and a two-day board seminar, and the proposal was on track for smooth approval. The US guarantee package collapsed because of Congressional opposition, however, and the administration was compelled to improvise. Treasury Secretary Rubin created a $20 billion loan-and-guarantee facility using the Treasury's Exchange Stabilization Fund, and the IMF increased its support for Mexico to unprecedented levels to make up the difference, expanding the package with an additional $10 billion facility. How this figure was arrived at is an interesting illustration of the ambiguity and informality of decision making at this level. Three people were in the room with IMF Managing Director, Michel Camdessus, and they all agree with his account that the $10 billion figure arose at his initiative; the ambiguity arises because they only heard half of the conversation, and he was on the telephone at the time with the US Treasury Secretary, Robert Rubin.[31] It is clear that the United States welcomed the large scale of the IMF package, and that Fund officials thought it was essential because the market had already adjusted to the announced scale of the US guarantee. European officials were dismayed by the size of the IMF package, which they regarded as an investor bailout that should be provided by the United States or not at all.

The board meeting that followed on February 1 featured an emotional clash of views that stood out as unique in the memory of long-term Fund officials. The meeting lasted past midnight, and there was constant activity in the anteroom as directors called their capitals for instructions.[32] The usual style of consensus building broke down because there had been no time to clear the increase in the size of the loan by $10 billion at the G-7 level. According to the British ED's statement for the record, the staff report was not presented until an hour before the meeting on February 1 to approve the arrangement,

[31] Inverviews with IMF staff, senior staff, and management.
[32] Interview with IMF senior staff.

and the $10 billion increase in the amount of the requested commitment was announced at the same time.

Several board members disputed the essence of the case made by the Mexican representative and IMF staff that the crisis was a liquidity crisis rather than a case of fundamental market disequilibrium caused by unsound macroeconomic policies. In the former case, a large-scale loan would not be particularly risky; but if the crisis revealed fundamental economic mismanagement, the risks could be substantial. In addition, some EDs disapproved of the proposal to make the first $7.8 billion available immediately, and at least one ED who voted in favor of the proposal nevertheless argued that the Fund's support should be tranched, or spread out over time. More fundamentally, however, EDs complained about the timing and process of the management proposal, which gave them insufficient time to evaluate the staff report and consult with their capitals. One ED, Jarle Bergo of Norway, who represented a constituency of Scandinavian countries, indicated that he was abstaining because his authorities held conflicting views and they had not had time to arrive at a common position. Several objected in principle to the practice of making important, precedent-setting decisions without adequate opportunity for their authorities to weigh in. German ED Stefan Schoenberg argued that the crisis was not so urgent that two days could not be allowed for consultation, in view of the public discussion that had been going on in Washington for several weeks.[33] Officials were further angered that President Clinton announced the size of the IMF program before the Executive Board had a chance to discuss it. A German finance official is reported to have blustered, "President Clinton goes to the press and says the IMF will do this and that. It was just not acceptable. We are not banana republics."[34] In the event, the decision to approve the program was adopted in spite of five abstentions, including Huw Evans of the United Kingdom and Stefan Schoenberg of Germany.[35] This was the first case in which G-7 members had abstained in a vote on the board since a controversial program for Egypt in the 1980s, and it has not been repeated subsequently.

The dispute over the use of Fund resources in the Mexican case led to the close consultation among the G-7 deputies that subsequently became the norm in crises.[36] While this improved the smoothness of decision making, the degree

[33] Executive Board Minutes. EBM 95/11: 65.

[34] "Mexican Rescue: Bitter Legacy of the Battle to Bail out Mexico." *Financial Times*. February 16, 1995. Cited in Copelovitch 2010, 121.

[35] The other abstentions came from Oleh Havrylyshyn (Ukraine), representing a multi-country constituency including the Netherlands and several post-Communist countries, Jarle Bergo (Norway), representing Scandinavian countries, and Stefan Link (Poland), representing Switzerland and several countries of the former Soviet Union (EBM 95/11: 114).

[36] Interview with IMF senior staff.

of access permitted to Fund resources remained a political issue, and was not always regarded as adequate by staff. The case of Korea is instructive. When it turned to the Fund in November 1997, Korea faced an acute liquidity crisis on a scale the IMF had not yet confronted. The initial mission brief estimated the financing gap at $25 billion, which it acknowledged was substantially larger than the amount that the Fund would be able to offer, although the amount of Fund resources was left to be filled in subsequently.[37] In his comments, First Deputy Managing Director Stanley Fischer noted, "The analysis of financing needs is obviously preliminary. But given the supposed high levels of external exposure of Korean firms, and the ongoing loss of confidence, it is likely that the estimates here are much too small."[38] Indeed, the brief estimated Korean short-term debt at $60–70 billion, and the subsequent staff paper put the figure at $65 billion, including approximately $40 billion in loans to Korean banks. IMF estimates of usable Korean reserves had to be revised during the mission as the Korean authorities revealed the true scale of their predicament, and Fund staff revised their estimate of the financing gap in the staff report to $55 billion.[39] The G-7 deputies and their superiors, however, were not willing to authorize a multilateral loan package of that magnitude or to provide bilateral support to Korea to make up the difference.[40] Instead, they agreed to put up a "second line of defense" composed of a series of non-binding bilateral commitments, which was intended to mollify markets but was not expected to be used.[41] The staff report indicated that the Fund would provide up to $21 billion over three years, but only 6.7 billion SDRs would be available in December and another 1.5 billion in January. In addition, the World Bank would disburse "up to $10 billion" and the Asian Development Bank $4 billion. The commitment to the second line of defense was left deliberately vague:

> In addition, in the event that circumstances warrant, a number of countries – including at this stage, Australia, Canada, France, Germany, Italy, Japan, the United Kingdom, and the United States – are prepared, to provide supplemental financing in support of Korea's

37 IMF – Korea. *Briefing Paper for Negotiation of a Stand-By Arrangement.* Prepared by the Asia and Pacific Department (in consultation with other departments). Approved by Wanda Tseng and Joaquin Ferran. November 21, 1997: 15.

38 Fischer, Stanley. "Korea draft mission brief." Office Memorandum to Mr. Aghevli. November 15, 1997: 1.

39 *Korea: Request for Stand-By Arrangement.* Prepared by the Asia and Pacific Department (in consultation with other departments). Approved by Hubert Neiss and Joaquin Ferran. December 3, 1997: 12.

40 Blustein 2001, 178–180.

41 The conditions for the SLOD were negotiated bilaterally with the creditors, and the United States insisted on a non-negotiable set of conditions for disbursement that were unlikely to be met. Goldsbrough, David. "Korea: Managing Director's Meeting with Deputy Prime Minister Lim." Memorandum for Files. January 12, 1998.

> program with the Fund. This second line of defense is expected to be in excess of $20 billion.[42]

It was clear to Fund staff that the program was underfinanced, and it could only be successful without drawing on the second line of defense if it generated a significant psychological turnaround in the market. The second line of defense was needed in order to restore market confidence, but the creditors were unwilling to approve a program that committed them to disbursing it. The IEO report on this crisis concluded that staff received instructions to rewrite their projections of Korean debt roll-over in order to show the program to be fully financed without relying on the second line of defense, and found that "the program as presented was clearly underfinanced, although this fact was not explicitly acknowledged."[43]

The markets never believed in the second line of defense. The drain of reserves continued as banks continued to refuse to roll-over their credits as they came due, and during December the IMF's Wanda Tseng wrote daily memos to Management that appear in the files detailing the deterioration of Korean markets and the need either to arrange a substantial infusion of financing or minimize the damage by organizing an orderly default. Korea was compelled to appeal for an augmentation of the program three weeks later. Throughout the crisis, US policy makers had resisted Japanese and European proposals for a state-led restructuring of commercial debt held by banks on the model of Mexico in 1982, but when it became clear that the December 4 program had failed to reverse market sentiment and the alternative was default, the New York Federal Reserve helped to lead a multilateral effort to encourage money-center banks to participate, and this effort stemmed the tide. The speed of the subsequent recovery suggests that the main shortcoming of the December 4 program was the central one that staff had identified: it did not provide enough liquidity to solve the short-term financing problem. A report issued by the IMF's IEO identified the same problem of under-financing in the programs for Indonesia in 1997 and Brazil in 1998, but concluded that the failure to restore market confidence was primarily attributable to insufficient financing only in the Korean case.[44]

The cases of Mexico and Korea illustrate the range of the positive and

[42] *Korea: Request for Stand-By Arrangement.* Prepared by the Asia and Pacific Department (in consultation with other departments). Approved by Hubert Neiss and Joaquin Ferran. December 3, 1997: 12.

[43] IEO 2003, 19, 37, 112–13.

[44] In the interdepartmental review of the Brazil program, the Research Department argued that the program was underfinanced (IEO 2003, 136). The December 2000 program for Argentina likewise assumed official financing that was insufficient to cover the financing gap (IEO 2004, 41).

negative influence the United States can exert over the size of IMF loans. Neither country's participation in an IMF program was controversial. Controversy arose about the size of the loans, however, because they critically affected the prospects to successfully contain the crisis and prevent damage to financial institutions abroad. Primarily US trade and financial institutions were exposed in Mexico; in Korea the net was cast more widely, with significant exposure of European and Japanese trade and institutions. In the first case, the United States appears to have driven the agenda, although it acted through the IMF managing director, and an IMF loan for Mexico was approved of unprecedented size, over the objections of the Europeans. In the second case, the United States put a brake on the size of the financial package for Korea, and US hesitation sufficiently delayed the effort to organize a private sector rescheduling to allow the crisis to deepen. Within weeks, both a larger loan and a US-led effort to coerce private lenders into rolling over their loans became necessary.

Conclusions

A combination of quantitative and qualitative evidence indicates that the United States exerts substantial informal influence over the amount of support offered to countries that participate in IMF programs. These quantitative results join a growing literature that acknowledges that US influence is a critical determinant of IMF lending practices. In addition, they present a critical test of the theory of informal governance because the theory specifically predicts an interactive effect between measures of US interests and measures of borrower vulnerability. The results presented here are not robust across all measures of US interests. However, there are strong quantitative results that point to a general pattern of US influence being exerted when client states are particularly vulnerable to a sudden reversal of international financing.

The cases of Mexico and Korea illustrate the range of US influence, which serves to increase access to IMF support dramatically in some cases, while limiting it in others. The cases go on to elucidate the means by which US influence is exerted. US decision makers have a unique degree of access to IMF management. They are consulted routinely before important proposals are tabled, and they have an opportunity to shape those proposals. In many cases, they initiate the proposals. Ordinarily, major IMF programs are discussed multilaterally by the G-7 deputies as well, so that EDs have clear instructions before they arrive at the Executive Board. If contentious issues have to be resolved, therefore, there is time to do so in private and without involving the broader membership of the Fund.

8

Conditionality under IMF programs

Conditionality, the practice of requiring policy reform as a condition for receiving IMF support, is not stipulated in the IMF's Articles of Agreement and was originally instituted at the insistence of the United States and over the objections of the rest of the membership. After the collapse of the Bretton Woods system of fixed exchange rates the Fund reinvented itself as an agency with extensive involvement in the politics of development, and a broad consensus emerged on the Executive Board that managing conditionality should become a more important part of its mandate. As late as the 1970s, only 26 percent of IMF loan disbursements involved substantial conditionality, but the Latin American debt crisis in the 1980s and the expansion of lending to Africa increased this figure to 66 percent by the end of the 1980s.[1] The number of conditions specified in an IMF program steadily climbed in the subsequent decade as the Fund sought to manage the transition from state planning to the market in former Communist countries and grappled with financial sector issues in the East Asian crisis. At the same time, the scope of conditionality ventured into areas of domestic economic structure and policies outside the Fund's traditional purview and competence.

The Executive Board does not play a direct role in designing the conditionality in individual programs. As a practical matter, by the time a program reaches the board it has been thoroughly analyzed by the staff, negotiated with the authorities of the borrowing member country, and approved by management and the shareholders that choose to participate. The board does not have the option of rewriting the program on the spot, and it never exercises the theoretical options that it has of rejecting the program or sending it back for revision and renegotiation. In an interview, one ED indicated that this was a serious shortcoming of IMF governance.

[1] Boughton 2001, 561.

The fact that the board does not formally amend conditionality does not mean that it exerts no influence, of course, since potential objections can be anticipated. Management assures itself that a program enjoys a comfortable majority through informal contacts before bringing it to the board, which means in practice that management consults with the G-7. In addition, EDs comment on program design during board discussions in order to influence conditionality in the future, and staff members try to avoid controversy and criticism at the Executive Board, so they take careful note of these comments. However, the fact that programs are adopted as proposed means that it is possible for the United States to exert decisive influence behind the scenes in particular cases by shaping the management proposal before it goes to the board.

In contrast to the Executive Board, individual EDs do play an important role in shaping conditionality in programs, but they do so in their capacity as representatives of important countries, and they do so informally. EDs have direct access to the staff, and a few of them take advantage of this when they are interested in particular countries. The intensive consultations that staff holds with the US ED with regard to Latin American countries and countries with systemic importance, and with the French ED with regard to francophone African countries, offer ample opportunity to influence the Fund's bargaining position and monitor the progress of negotiations.[2] When systemically important countries become involved in crises, however, the locus of decision making moves up the chain of command, and the EDs find themselves out of the loop. The US Undersecretary of the Treasury for International Affairs and his assistants are frequently involved in the negotiations in important cases, and sometimes the Treasury Secretary becomes directly involved.

Both the degree and type of informal influence over conditionality is idiosyncratic. US influence over conditionality was at its apex in Mexico in 1995, because the conditionality that it had negotiated bilaterally in return for extending a credit in December 1994 was used as the basis for designing the IMF program in January.[3] This program included a number of trade and investment items that were in fact leftover business from the NAFTA negotiations. Interviews and discussions with staff indicate that US informal influence over conditionality was also extraordinarily pronounced in the cases of Korea, where the United States insisted upon concessions to liberalize banking rules that it had failed to obtain during Korea's OECD accession, and Indonesia, where it insisted upon a number of trade reforms.[4] These examples are consistent with the view that US intervention in the design of conditionality takes a form

2 Interviews with IMF staff.
3 Interview with IMF senior staff.
4 IEO 2003; interviews for IEO 2003; Blustein 2001.

similar to trade policy, and that narrow, well-organized private sector interests lobby to insert conditions into programs. On the other hand, the major shareholders may plead for more lenient conditionality for particular countries, as Japan did in Korea and Indonesia.

The model of informal governance predicts that the predominant motive for intervention should be to soften the terms of IMF conditionality.[5] IMF conditionality already embodies principles that advance US long-term interests in promoting liberalization and prudent financial management in developing countries. Private sector interests in developed countries are generally well-served by the default option of allowing the Fund to develop policy autonomously, so groups representing US business interests have weak incentives to organize and lobby. On the other hand, if the incentive to participate in the process is to accommodate the interests of an important client, US influence should be exercised to reduce conditionality, rather than to expand it. The United States participates when its security or broader strategic interests become involved, because these interests are not ordinarily represented in IMF objectives.

The US motive for intervening in the Fund's operations is to respond to a client state's request for support. Consequently, the model predicts an interaction between US interests and the interests of IMF borrowers: US participation in program design should be skewed towards countries that are important to the United States, but these strategic interests only become operative when securing IMF financing becomes a high priority for the borrower. From the U.S perspective, using informal influence to roll back conditionality is costly because it overrides long-term US economic interests and because it undermines the legitimacy of the IMF. Consequently, it will only be done on behalf of important countries, when foreign policy objectives override economic analysis. From the borrower's perspective, influence with the United States is a valuable resource, which should only be drawn down when the stakes are high. Thus, the effects of the borrower's strategic importance should be conditional on the borrower's external vulnerability. Together, the hypotheses that US influence should be used selectively, that it should reduce conditionality, that it should only be available to important countries and that it should only be used when those countries are vulnerable make possible a sharp test of the informal governance model.

[5] This is consistent with the quantitative and case study evidence presented in Gould 2003, 2006. See also De Gregorio *et al.* 1999.

Data

The data are extracted from the IMF's Monitoring of Agreements Database (MONA), which covers the 99 countries that participated in IMF programs between 1992 and 2002, organized in terms of country-month units. I code IMF conditionality in nineteen categories, representing the most frequently applied types, ranging from fiscal and monetary policy to exchange rate restrictions and structural reforms.[6]

The data measure quantitative macroeconomic performance criteria and structural benchmarks, which are the key yardsticks of compliance with conditionality. Performance criteria are formal conditions that must be met by a corresponding test date, or officially be waived by the Executive Board in the event of non-compliance, in order for scheduled disbursements to be made under IMF programs. Benchmarks are more specific structural reforms, such as privatization, deregulation and tax reform, that are used to determine a country's compliance with a program but do not automatically call for suspending IMF support in the event of non-fulfillment. Information about prior actions, which are conditions that must be met before the Executive Board approves a program, is not available unless they are subsequently covered in a review. The data measure the elements of conditionality that a country promises to implement in the future when it contracts with the Fund, rather than policy changes that have been implemented in order to obtain a program.

Six and a half categories of conditions were subject to test in an average review; about two-thirds of the time, at least two and no more than ten types of conditions were under review. Figure 8.1 illustrates the variation in the number of categories of conditionality applied.[7] For the statistical analysis of conditionality reported below, I include only observations that fall on test dates to avoid inflating the number of observations.

Table 8.1 illustrates the substantive variation in IMF conditionality. The scope of conditionality varies across types of IMF programs. Stand-by facilities (SBAs) are typically one- to two-year programs offered to middle-income borrowers, and they test an average of 6.3 categories of conditions; Extended Fund Facilities (EFFs) are typically three-year arrangements with more ambitious goals, and they average 7.6 test categories. Enhanced Structural Adjustment Facilities (ESAFs) and Poverty Reduction and Growth Facilities (PRGFs) are low-interest lending facilities for poor countries, with average levels of

[6] MONA data have recently been made available on the IMF web site going back to 2002. The earlier data used for this study were extracted and compiled by Adrian de la Garza.

[7] The unit of analysis is the test date, which includes formal program reviews, disbursement dates and planned disbursement dates. A version of this figure that used program months as the unit of analysis appeared in Stone 2008.

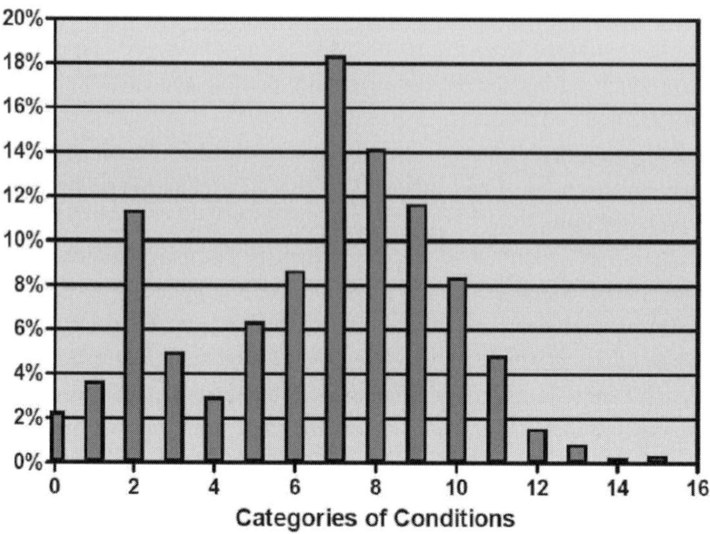

Figure 8.1 Conditionality in IMF programs.

conditionality intermediate between the other two, which place heavier emphasis on structural conditions and debt arrears. The replacement of the ESAF program by the PRGF ushered in new poverty-reduction targets, reduced the emphasis on privatization and increased the emphasis on debt arrears, but otherwise followed the pattern of conditionality established under the ESAF.

Some aspects of IMF conditionality are very consistent: domestic credit is constrained and reserve targets are set for about three-quarters of test dates in SBA and EFF programs and about half the time in the concessional lending programs, and there is almost always some limit on public debt or government spending, although the forms of those restrictions vary. Some programs involve extensive regulation of public spending, taxation, borrowing, and the maturity structure of domestic and foreign debt, while others simply set deficit targets. There is a strong emphasis on avoiding foreign debt arrears. However, the frequent criticism that the IMF systematically promoted fixed exchange rate regimes in the 1990s is not supported by the data on conditionality.[8] To the contrary, the data support a different criticism: the Fund is too neutral with respect to exchange rate policy, and allows itself to be captured by country authorities that are determined to defend overvalued exchange rates, as happened

[8] Hills *et al.* 1999; Meltzer 2000; Stiglitz 2002.

Table 8.1 *Coverage of conditions under IMF programs, 1990–2002.*

	All programs	SBA	EFF	ESAF	PRGF
Monetary policy:					
Domestic credit	61.9%	71.6%	73.9%	56.7%	48.6%
BOP reserve test	62.3%	75.7%	82.1%	49.1%	49.1%
Fiscal policy:					
Fiscal deficit	43.6%	50.9%	64.3%	30.9%	37.1%
Private credit to government	52.2%	44.6%	52.9%	65.2%	56.3%
Domestic public debt	37.8%	33.2%	35.2%	45.4%	41.8%
Long-term foreign debt ceiling	72.2%	77.2%	84.0%	69.0%	64.1%
Long-term for. debt sub-ceiling	55.1%	54.1%	69.8%	52.4%	56.3%
Short-term debt	68.0%	71.4%	82.4%	64.2%	66.6%
Fiscal actions	41.5%	34.7%	52.4%	46.3%	48.9%
Debt service:					
External arrears limit	21.3%	19.2%	16.1%	30.3%	11.3%
No new external arrears	66.8%	49.3%	68.3%	80.3%	97.3%
Exchange rates:					
Exchange rates	7.0%	10.3%	11.3%	2.8%	2.1%
Foreign exchange operations	3.1%	5.5%	2.2%	1.3%	3.4%
Structural reforms:					
Public sector reform	12.2%	4.1%	9.1%	22.1%	26.1%
Banking	21.1%	22.2%	29.9%	23.7%	22.9%
Privatization	8.7%	3.0%	3.4%	18.0%	11.6%
Price controls	6.7%	0.9%	12.4%	13.6%	11.4%
Trade actions	2.2%	0.7%	1.6%	4.6%	5.2%
Others	7.1%	4.7%	3.5%	11.1%	11.1%
Observations	3345	1278	733	1173	560

Note: Observations are defined on test dates, which include program reviews, scheduled disbursements and disbursements.

in Russia in 1998, Brazil in 1999 and Argentina in 2001.[9] Although structural conditions of some sort are being tested 44 percent of the time, even this coarse breakdown of structural reforms into six categories indicates that structural conditionality varies enormously across countries. In fact, aggregating the data in this way understates the variation, because a six-fold categorization of structural reforms exaggerates the similarity of conditions across countries.

The dependent variable of interest is the number of categories of conditions subject to test in a particular review. This measure of conditionality captures the scope – or, to the Fund's critics, the intrusiveness – of conditionality. This definition of conditionality focuses on the range of obligations that constrain country authorities at any given point in time, and has advantages over

[9] Blustein 2001; IEO 2003, 2004; Mussa 1998.

Table 8.2 *Correlations among measures of US interests.*

	US aid	Bank exposure	US exports	UN voting	Alliances
US aid	1.00				
Bank exposure	−0.02	1.00			
US exports	0.004	0.60	1.00		
UN voting	−0.08	−0.11	−0.10	1.00	
Alliances	−0.03	0.36	0.26	−0.02	1.00

Correlations calculated for countries under IMF programs, 7,053 observations.

assessments of conditionality that depend on letters of intent.[10] Conditionality evolves over the course of a program in response to country policies and unanticipated events, so the scope of a program contained in a letter of intent may give a misleading snapshot of what is really a moving target.[11]

The dependent variable ranges from 0 to 19, and I use a negative binomial event count model to analyze variation in the scope of conditionality.[12] Observations are defined whenever new information about conditionality appears in the dataset: when a new program is initiated, when a program review occurs, and when a disbursement is scheduled or actually takes place.

Independent variables

As I explained in Chapter 7, I use a range of measures of US economic, political and military interests as my key explanatory variables: US foreign aid, the exposure of US banks, US exports, affinity in voting in the UN General Assembly, and similarity in military alliance profiles. These five dimensions measure distinct reasons for the United States to have intense interests in a particular country, and they are not strongly correlated. The correlations for the set of countries that participated in IMF programs are presented in Table 8.2.

These measures represent distinct reasons for the United States to have strong interests in a particular country, rather than alternative measures of the same latent variable. The bivariate correlations among the measures within the

10 Gould 2003; Dreher and Jensen 2007; Copelovitch 2004.

11 Mussa and Savastano 1999.

12 Negative binomial regression is a generalization of the Poisson event count model that allows the rate of occurrence to vary across the events that generate an observation. For example, additional conditions may become more likely when a number of other conditions are imposed.

sample are quite low. US bank exposure is correlated with US exports (0.60), and US alliance portfolios are modestly correlated with bank exposure (0.36) and exports (0.26), but the other seven bivariate correlations are negligible. The results will be robust, and therefore persuasive, to the extent that a range of subjectively valid measures that are not highly correlated perform similarly. As in the previous chapter, the hypothesis to be tested is that these measures of US interests are associated with exceptions to rules – in this chapter, with reductions in the scope of conditionality – when they interact with high levels of borrower vulnerability to sudden reversals of international capital flows.

Control variables

The publication of letters of intent on the IMF web page and the opening of the IMF archives has recently encouraged quantitative studies of conditionality. Ivanova *et al.*,[13] Dreher,[14] Dreher and Vaubel[15] and Copelovitch[16] investigate the number of conditions the IMF imposes, while Gould distinguishes among types of conditions,[17] and Stone analyzes the scope of conditionality.[18] These studies suggest a number of control variables to include in the present analysis. Each study finds an upward trend in conditionality over time, for example, which is also consistently found in the models presented in this chapter. In contrast to Ivanova *et al.* and Dreher, however, which find no evidence that domestic political variables affect the pattern of conditionality, the models presented here find substantial effects of domestic political constraints.

The effects of domestic political conditions and state capacity suggest that bargaining strength derives from domestic constraints.[19] Countries with democratic institutions receive markedly fewer conditions: an increase of one standard deviation on the polity scale, or 5.5 points on a 21-point scale, results in a decrease in the number of conditions that ranges from 7.3 to 9.8 percent. It may be that the Fund is sensitive to the criticism that its conditionality endangers the fragile, new democracies in many borrowing countries. Alternatively, it could be that democratic governments insist on more lenient programs because they face more domestic policy making constraints than authoritarian governments. In either case, the IMF apparently accommodates the constraints

13 Ivanova *et al.* 2003.
14 Dreher 2004.
15 Dreher and Vaubel 2004.
16 Copelovitch 2005, 2010.
17 Gould 2003, 2006.
18 Stone 2008.
19 Stone 2008.

of democratic politics. Controlling for the degree of democracy, presidential systems receive fewer conditions than parliamentary democracies. This effect, which ranges from 7.2 to 9.2 percent in the models in Table 8.3, is consistent with a two-level bargaining interpretation: presidents lack some of the institutional advantages for legislating reform that prime ministers enjoy, and domestic weakness is associated with international bargaining power.[20]

Fragmentation of governing coalitions substantially constrains the scope of conditionality. Each additional party added to a coalition government reduces the breadth of conditionality by 2.1 to 2.7 percent. In addition, governments with leftist ideologies receive less expansive reform programs. I find no evidence that left-wing governments are particularly anxious to adopt extensive conditionality in order to establish credibility or to avoid the policy consequences of populist electoral mandates.[21] To the contrary, governments of the left are more resistant to expansive proposals for sweeping reform. Moving one point to the left on the seven-point left-right scale reduces the incidence of conditionality by 1.1 to 1.5 percent.

Some of the state capacity variables have effects consistent with the hypothesis that domestic constraints represent bargaining advantages. Controlling for per capita income levels, the weak states in sub-Saharan Africa received 19.5 to 21.9 percent fewer conditions. In addition, weak administrative capacity, as measured by the propensity for data to be missing, is associated with reduced conditionality. The size of this effect and its statistical significance varies substantially depending upon which measure of US interests is included in the model. The strongest result, which is significant at the 0.06 level, indicates that countries with one standard deviation lower administrative capacity than the mean received 19.6 percent fewer conditions. This may indicate that IMF staff prefer narrower programs because more ambitious ones would be likely to fail, or it may indicate that countries with weak states leverage their weaknesses into bargaining strength. In either case, weak states bargain for reduced conditionality rather than using the IMF as a cover to implement expansive reforms.

Informal governance

The informal governance model implies that the United States is able to control IMF policies in extraordinary cases, and exercises its influence on behalf of important borrowers when they are sufficiently motivated to appeal for aid.

[20] Putnam 1988; Mansfield *et al.* 2000; Martin 2000.
[21] Milesi-Ferretti 1995; Cukierman and Tommasi 1998.

This generates the prediction that there should be an interactive effect between measures of US interests and measures of borrower-country vulnerability to sudden reversals of international financial flows. Table 8.3 presents the results of the analysis. The table presents models that use the same five measures of US interests employed in the previous chapter, each of which is interacted with the same three variables representing the borrowing country's vulnerability to sudden loss of external financing. Trade/GDP represents the degree of openness of the national economy, which increases the risks involved in a currency or financial crisis. Debt service/exports represents the long-term sustainability of the country's debt burden, which provides a metric for the need for official financing. Short-term debt, the percentage of debt held in instruments with a maturity of one year or less, represents roll-over risk, which captures the acuteness of a crisis.

Each model uses a common set of controls, which are not reported in the table. (The full table of results is available in the Appendix as Table A.8.3.) Table 8.3 indicates that the interaction terms are generally in the expected direction – US interests reduce conditionality more when countries are vulnerable – and significant. The predicted values are a non-linear function of the coefficients and the hypothesis tests of the variables of interest depend on the values of the interacted variables, so additional analysis is necessary to evaluate the hypotheses. In particular, the signs, size and hypothesis tests for the coefficients of measures of US interests are only valid when trade/GDP, debt service/exports and short-term debt take the value zero. The results of tests of the joint significance of the coefficients of interest and their interactions, evaluated at mean levels of vulnerability and at one standard deviation above and below the mean, are presented in Table 8.4.

The results strongly support the informal governance model. US foreign aid, the exposure of US banks, US exports, UN voting patterns and alliance portfolios are all strongly associated with reduced conditionality when countries are vulnerable to reversals of external financing. Furthermore, these results weaken sharply when vulnerability drops to average levels, and in the case of bank exposure and UN voting become statistically indistinguishable from zero. When vulnerability drops to the bottom third of the sample, all of these effects are either insignificant or reversed. The effects are substantively important. One standard deviation of US aid, or $173 million, is associated with a 27 percent drop in conditionality when a country is highly vulnerable, but with only a 9 percent drop when a country is no more vulnerable than the average IMF borrower.[22] The effect of bank exposure is weaker, but still substantial. A one-

[22] The results of additional models that are not reported here confirm that the unconditional

Table 8.3 *US influence over the scope of conditionality.*

	Coef. *Std. Err.*	p	*Coef.* *Std. Err.*	p	*Coef.* *Std. Err.*	p	*Coef.* *Std. Err.*	p	*Coef.* *Std. Err.*	p
US aid	0.0009	0.00								
	0.0003									
US bank exposure			5.4161	0.04						
			2.6731							
US exports					0.0006	0.00				
					0.0002					
UN voting (S-US)							−0.2886	0.00		
							0.0979			
US alliance portfolio									0.4642	0.03
									0.2169	
Interactions with:										
Trade/GDP	-9.1×10^{-6}	0.01	−0.1040	0.00	-6.8×10^{-6}	0.00	0.0011	0.22	−0.0087	0.00
	3.5×10^{-6}		*0.0294*		2.0×10^{-6}		*0.0009*		*0.0021*	
Debt service/exports	-2.5×10^{-5}	0.00	−0.0821	0.01	-6.1×10^{-6}	0.00	0.0125	0.00	−0.0171	0.00
	8.3×10^{-6}		*0.0326*		1.7×10^{-6}		*0.0030*		*0.0032*	
Short-term debt	-3.6×10^{-5}	0.03	0.1586	0.12	-4.8×10^{-7}	0.88	0.0036	0.46	0.0150	0.04
	1.6×10^{-5}		*0.1016*		3.1×10^{-6}		*0.0048*		*0.0073*	
Control variables…										
Observations	2823		2823		2823		2794		2823	

Negative binomial regression. Note: Standard errors in italics.

Table 8.4 *Effects of US interests on conditionality.*

	Vulnerability	Effect	p
US foreign aid	High	−26.7%	0.00
	Mean	−8.8%	0.00
US bank exposure	High	−1.9%	0.01
	Mean	−1.3%	0.33
US exports	High	−17.0%	0.00
	Mean	3.0%	0.06
UN voting	High	−10.8%	0.00
	Mean	−1.6%	0.23
Alliances	High	−9.3%	0.00
	Mean	−4.3%	0.00

Note: Effect of a one-standard deviation increase in the left column variable conditional on vulnerability. "High" is one standard deviation above the sample mean on trade/GDP, debt service/exports, and short-term debt.

standard deviation increase raises US bank exposure from the average level of 0.5 to 2.4% of US foreign loans outstanding, and results in only a 1.9% drop in conditionality. However, these effects were substantial for the countries in the sample with the highest shares of US lending, which reached peaks of 8.8% in Argentina, 14.6% in Brazil, and 18.5% in Mexico. Economic ties represented by US exports also have substantial effects. A country that absorbs one standard deviation more than the average level of US exports – $709 million as compared to $125 million – is subject to 17 percent narrower conditionality.

A one-standard deviation shift in S-scores for UN voting is associated with a 10.8 percent decrease in conditionality when countries are highly vulnerable. These effects occur, perhaps surprisingly, when countries oppose rather than support US votes in the UN. That is, the United States appears to reward recalcitrant regimes by intervening on their behalf – but only when they are vulnerable to financial crises. The same pattern appears in the enforcement of IMF programs (Chapter 9). To put this finding in perspective, consider the

effect of aid is to reduce conditionality. The simple correlation between US foreign aid and conditionality is positive. However, the relationship becomes negative and significant when we control for variables that strongly influence both US foreign aid and conditionality, and remains robust in regressions that include or exclude numerous other variables. A negative relationship emerges between US foreign aid and conditionality when we control for democracy and whether the borrower is in sub-Saharan Africa, both of which are associated with significantly lower levels of conditionality. Controlling for institutional weakness, the left–right partisanship of governments and whether the program is extended over more than 12 months, whether the program is in a category designed for low-income borrowers and for the time trend further strengthens the effect. When aid is interacted with the borrower's financial vulnerability, however, all of these effects vanish when vulnerability is low.

identities of some of the countries that play important roles in US foreign policy but generally vote against the United States in the UN General Assembly. The average UN S-score in the sample is −0.085 on a scale of −1 to 1 (the United States votes in the minority much more often than in the majority on substantive issues, but many procedural votes are uncontested), and drops to −0.11 among IMF program participants. The standard deviations are 0.37 for all countries and 0.31 for IMF program recipients. Pakistan, which has been an important recipient of US foreign aid and a key partner in US security policy, votes consistently against the United States on issues involving the Middle East, and is approximately one standard deviation more oppositional than the average country with an average score of −0.41 (varying over time from a minimum of −0.52 to a maximum of −0.25). There can be little doubt that Pakistan's close cooperation with the United States on security issues has been achieved in spite of, rather than because of, the general foreign policy preferences of both its elected and military leaders – and this cooperation has often been smoothed when the United States interceded on Pakistan's behalf with the Fund.

A similar example is Egypt, which has an average S-score of −0.37 (minimum −0.56, maximum −0.18), and frequently opposes the United States on votes involving Israel. Egypt has been a mainstay of American foreign policy in the Middle East, however, and was explicitly promised US aid in return for peace with Israel in the Camp David Accords. Egyptian troops played a prominent psychological role in the first Gulf War in 1991, and Egypt was rewarded with a dramatic debt reduction package and briefly became the leading recipient of US foreign aid. In contrast, there are two groups of countries that receive IMF programs and are one standard deviation more supportive than average of US positions in the UN: small former Communist countries, and small, poor countries in sub-Saharan Africa. Most of these countries have no particular political weight and occupy no strategic position that could allow them to extract favors from US policy makers.

Alliances are strongly associated with narrower conditionality when countries are vulnerable to external shocks. A country that is one standard deviation closer than the mean to the network of US alliance commitments receives 9.3 percent narrower conditionality. Allies have a constant claim on US policymakers' attention, and issues of critical concern to them can be interpreted as national security concerns in Washington. US allies have direct access to US policy makers, and they can access officials in the State and Defense Departments that can lobby on their behalf with Treasury officials. In addition, allies of US allies have been known to call upon their friends to help lobby the United States.

The pattern is robust across measures of US interests that range from the most general, such as foreign aid, to narrow economic interests in the stability of the United States banking system and in promoting exports, to broad foreign policy orientations revealed in patterns of UN voting and to specific military and defense commitments. The conclusion is that it does not matter precisely why your country is important to the United States; if it is important to US policy makers for some reason, it is possible to use that leverage to significantly shape the deals that you make with the IMF.

The conditionality-reducing effects of each of the measures of US interests are contingent upon the vulnerability of the borrower. When vulnerability to external financial shocks drops to the bottom third of the distribution, all of the effects are reversed. Very low vulnerability is a rare state of affairs, so the average effect of measures of US interests is to decrease conditionality. However, it is significant that these interests have no restraining effect on conditionality unless the borrower's vulnerability to reversals of external financing rises above a certain threshold. It appears that below that threshold, the United States typically does not interfere in the design of conditionality, and the IMF exercises autonomy to design conditionality according to its own technical objectives. This is consistent with the interpretation that countries that are not particularly vulnerable to reversals of external financing do not place a high priority on their relations with the IMF, so they choose not to draw on their stores of influence with the United States in order to get a better deal from the Fund. These results hold in the simplest versions of the interactive model, and they are robust to the inclusion of numerous control variables.

Discrimination

The results to this point present a strikingly robust pattern that is consistent with the informal governance model, but so far they have not probed whether the pattern is really one of monopolistic control by the United States or one of collective informal governance by the Fund's leading shareholders. This calls for additional analysis. First, aggregate measures of interests of the other four G-5 members – Japan, Germany, Great Britain and France – are substituted for the US interest measures where such aggregates are meaningful: total aid for US aid, average bank exposure for US exposure, and total exports for US exports. Aggregating S-scores in this way is not meaningful, however, so in the subsequent stage of the analysis the results for UN voting and alliances are replicated country-by-country.

The full table of results for aggregate measures of G-5 interests is presented

Table 8.5 *Effects of G-5 interests on conditionality.*

	Effect	p
Foreign aid (total)	1.0%	0.66
Bank exposure (average)	−0.7%	0.00
Exports (total)	−7.2%	0.00

Negative binomial regression. Note: Effect of a one-standard deviation increase in the left column variable conditional on high vulnerability (one standard deviation above the sample mean on trade/GDP, debt service/exports, and short-term debt).

in the Appendix as Table A.8.5. As indicated above, tables of coefficients such as this do not in themselves answer the question of whether the interactive effects pass hypothesis tests. Table 8.5 presents the substantive effects of the measures of G-5 interests at various levels of borrower vulnerability and the corresponding results of joint tests of statistical significance. The results indicate that the substantive effects of measures of G-5 interests are much weaker than those of measures of US interests when countries are vulnerable to reversals of capital flows. The effects of foreign aid from the other G-5 countries are statistically insignificant. The effects of bank exposure and exports are significant, but are substantially weaker for G-5 interests than for US interests. The effect of a standard deviation of bank exposure drops by two-thirds, from 2.1 percent reductions of conditionality for US bank exposure to 0.7 percent for exposure of other G-5 banks. The effect of a similar increment of exports drops by almost two-thirds, from almost 20 percent reductions of conditionality for US exports to 7.2 percent reductions for other G-5 exports. These effects remain significant, however. Since bank exposure and exports are more highly correlated among the G-5 countries than aid, aid provides a more discriminating comparative test, and the results favor the hypothesis of US influence rather than collective influence.

Tables A.8.7 and A.8.8 in the Appendix present the results of country-by-country negative binomial regressions that examine the effects of UN voting and alliances, respectively, of the United Kingdom, France, Germany and Japan. Table 8.6 presents the substantive effects and corresponding hypothesis tests for the effects of UN voting and alliances at a high level of borrower vulnerability. S-scores measuring UN voting similarity with Britain are insignificant, and with Japan are marginally significant, but for France and Germany are highly significant and substantively important. The effect of UN voting with other G-5 members is consistent with the effect observed for the United

Table 8.6 *Effects of G-5 interests on conditionality (UN voting and alliances).*

	UN Voting		Alliance portfolios	
	Effect	p	Effect	p
United Kingdom	−2.0%	0.39	1.0%	0.79
France	−7.5%	0.00	0.9%	0.81
Germany	−10.8%	0.00	0.9%	0.81
Japan	−5.0%	0.08	8.5%	0.01

Negative binomial regression. Note: Effect of a one-standard deviation increase in the UN voting/increase in alliances conditional on high vulnerability (one standard deviation above the sample mean on trade/GDP, debt service/exports, and short-term debt).

States: intervention occurs on behalf of troublesome states that can be useful for achieving particular objectives.

In contrast, military alliance patterns provide a comparative test of the US influence and collective influence hypotheses that neatly comes down in favor of US influence. None of the other G-5 alliance portfolios is associated with reduced conditionality. The results for Britain, France and Germany are insignificant and substantively close to zero. The coefficient for the Japanese alliance portfolio is significant in the opposite direction, so a similarity with the Japanese pattern of alliances is associated with an increase in conditionality. The interpretation of this result is unclear, but it rejects the hypothesis that Japan uses its influence in the IMF to secure IMF funding on soft terms for its allies.[23]

In sum, tests that attempt to discriminate between the effect of US influence and influence by other G-5 countries provide stronger support for the hypothesis of US influence than for the competing hypothesis, but there is evidence consistent with G-5 influence as well. Two broad measures of interests, foreign aid and military alliances, provide strong support for the hypothesis of US influence and no support for the hypothesis of G-5 influence. Bank exposure and exports provide evidence supportive of both hypotheses, but the estimated effects of measures of US economic interests are much stronger than those of the other G-5 countries. UN voting patterns provide support for both hypotheses. The measures that provide the most discriminating tests, because they are least highly correlated between the United States and the other G-5 countries, reject the hypothesis of G-5 collective influence.

[23] The apparent effect may be an artifact of the opposite US portfolio effect, since Japan has very limited alliances and the United States has the widest range of alliance commitments (the correlation is −0.64).

The case of Indonesia in 1997: slamming the door on Japan

The case of Indonesia in 1997 is useful for discriminating between the effects of US influence and broader G-5 influence. As we will see, it is difficult to disentangle the substantive impact of US influence from the policy preferences of IMF management in this case. However, the sharp divergence between US and Japanese preferences in Indonesia makes it possible to assess the limits of Japanese influence, because Japanese efforts to exert informal influence were thwarted. Indeed, the peremptory style with which US policy makers rebuffed Japanese advances in Indonesia and the contemporaneous case of Korea strained relations within the G-7 and undermined Japan's commitment to the IMF as the key institution for managing international financial turmoil.

The extensive structural conditionality imposed upon Indonesia in 1997 has been widely criticized as excessive in the wake of the social upheaval that followed. The United States expressed a strong preference for sweeping reform, including the closure of insolvent banks, liberalization of state-run monopolies, and measures to combat corruption. In a popular account, *Washington Post* correspondent Paul Blustein argues that the original IMF mission brief did not include a detailed blueprint for conditionality, and the extensive conditionality subsequently included in the program came about because of US pressure.[24] There is no question that the mission in Jakarta steadily escalated its demands for structural reform in October 1997 – the mission brief was leaked to the *New York Times*[25] – or that the United States was pressing at every level for extensive reform of the crony system in Indonesia; however, the degree of US influence is hard to gauge in this case because US preferences aligned so closely with the objectives of IMF management.

While the mission brief was not specific about which structural reforms the mission should focus on, it did indicate that structural reform would be important to establishing a credible program that would restore confidence in the Indonesian economy. The brief was written under time pressure, and it was also vague on many other fronts, including such traditional areas of Fund strength as foreign exchange intervention (which was specified in a supplement a few days after the draft brief appeared) and fiscal policy.[26] The lack of specifics on structural reform was singled out by the Director of the Policy Development and Review Department (PDR), Jack Boorman:

24 Blustein 2001, 101–2.

25 Neiss, Hubert. "Indonesia – Secrecy." Office Memorandum To the Indonesia Team. October 7, 1997.

26 *Indonesia: Briefing Paper for Discussions on a Stand-By Arrangement*. Prepared by the Asia and Pacific Department (in consultation with other departments). Approved by Bijan B. Aghevli and Jack Boorman. October 7, 1997.

> We believe the evaporation of market confidence in Indonesia is not unrelated to long-standing governance issues. When the government recently announced the abandonment and/or postponement of several public sector projects, it was noticeable that some of the most egregiously unproductive (e.g. the "national car" project) were left untouched. For the program to have credibility, targeting such unproductive spending will be essential.[27]

It is interesting that Boorman specifically raised the objective of dismantling the national car project, which in retrospect appeared to be a concession to the Japanese car industry. Boorman's view of the importance of structural conditions was by no means the minority view in the Fund, and it was echoed in Deputy Managing Director Stanley Fischer's instructions to the team, which emphasized that although the Fund did not have a detailed list going in, the mission was expected to develop one. In particular, the program should address restrictions on imports and should attempt to dismantle some of the "less sensible" investment projects that the regime had pursued. Conditionality was expected to be a work in progress, and the Mission was encouraged to take the initiative.

> The economic team is itself anxious to deal with some of these problems, and the mission could in the first instance be guided by them. But the mission should not be confined by the views of the team: it will have to formulate its own views, and push them in the negotiations. Successes will be beneficial for the business climate; in any case, we will have to be ready to explain to the Board that these issues were addressed by the mission.[28]

Fischer saw structural reform as substantively important, symbolically important, and politically important in order to garner support for the program from the major shareholders.

In the Executive Board meeting to approve the program, the main concern raised was that structural reform did not go far enough. The US ED, Karin Lissakers, stated the US case clearly:

> On structural measures, we attach great importance to producing a detailed schedule of reforms in time for the first review of the program... We are faced with an audience that is both weary of promises for future reform and increasingly sophisticated in reading Fund-supported programs... We expect to see a clear plan of early action incorporated in the first review.[29]

27 Boorman, Jack. "Indonesia – Draft Briefing Ppaer for Discussions on Stand-By Arrangement." Office Memorandum to Mr. Aghevli. October 7, 1997: p. 2.

28 Fischer, Stanley. "Indonesia briefing papers." Office Memorandum to Mr. Neiss. October 10, 1997: 2–3.

29 Executive Board Minutes. EBM/97/109/R-5-11/5/97 (Restricted session): 16.

A number of the other EDs echoed Lissaker's statement. Bernd Esdar, the German ED, was more ambitious, urging a "more ambitious timetable," and "abolishing obstacles for foreign investment."[30]

The significant opposition to the Fund's approach to conditionality in Indonesia, as in Korea, came from Japan. Japan opposed the high level of interest rates called for in both programs and the substantial expansion of conditionality into microeconomic structural issues. Japanese officials were deeply concerned that the combination of rapid economic reform with the disruption caused by the accelerating financial crisis could destabilize the Indonesian political regime, which in fact occurred. Indonesia was regarded by Japan as a key economic partner and an important strategic ally. Relations with the Suharto regime were very close. Indonesia received $197 million in foreign aid from Japan in 1997. In comparison, an average recipient of Japanese aid received $55 million, and the standard deviation in the sample of IMF program participants was $130 million. The S-score relating Japan's and Indonesia's alliance portfolios is 0.96 on a scale from −1 to 1, compared to a mean of 0.84 and a standard deviation of 0.13. In addition, Japanese economic ties to Indonesia were substantial and stronger than the ties of any other G-7 country. Japanese bank exposure to Indonesia was 5.7 percent of total Japanese overseas bank exposure in 1997, compared to a mean for the sample of IMF program participants of 0.2 percent and a standard deviation of 0.8 percent. Japan's exports to Indonesia amounted to $849 million in 1997, compared to a sample mean of $50 million and standard deviation of $190 million. Furthermore, Japan considered Indonesia, as well as Korea, to be countries within its legitimate sphere of interest because of their geographic proximity and intense economic ties, and it put a high priority on being perceived by these countries as a supportive regional partner during the crisis.

Japanese opposition was sufficiently intense to lead the Japanese Deputy Finance Minister, Eisuke Sakakibara, to fly to Jakarta to launch a counter-intervention in Indonesia and argue with the IMF Chief of Mission, Hubert Neiss.[31] EDs also recall opposition from the Japanese ED, although it was much more muted at that level. ED Yoshimura spoke appreciatively at the board of the structural reforms Indonesia had undertaken: "As for structural policy, it is commendable that progress has been made in addressing governance issues... I call to mind, especially... the local content program for motor vehicles... and..., the National Car project..."[32] His agenda seems to have been to deflect calls for further expansion of the program. Japan ran into a

30 Executive Board Minutes. EBM/97/109/R-5-11/5/97 (Restricted session): 24.
31 Blustein 2001, 102.
32 Executive Board Minutes. EBM/97/109/R-5-11/5/97 (Restricted session): 11.

solid wall of opposition, however, which included all of the European EDs as well as the United States.

The informal intervention in the design of conditionality declined after the Asian crisis, and was much more muted in subsequent cases. The direct role of member countries receded at about the same time that the crisis led to a reassessment of the role of the IMF and increased skepticism within the Fund about the effectiveness of including large numbers of structural conditions in programs. The handling of the Asian crisis created a widespread perception that IMF conditionality was excessively intrusive and directed from Washington, however, which led Asian countries to develop economic policies designed to limit their exposure to financial crises – and their dependence on the IMF – in the years to come.

Africa: a special case?

Africa represents an important caveat to the generalizations made above about the relative weight of US interests and those of the other G-5 countries in determining the policies of the IMF. France and Britain were the major colonial powers in Africa, and have sufficient weight as contributors to IMF resources to appoint their own EDs. France remains the largest single provider of aid to Africa, frequently uses its military forces to intervene in African affairs, and has the most active foreign economic policy in the region. Britain also maintains significant ties to its former colonies in Africa, although its military commitments are much more limited. The United States, in contrast, did not perceive any vital interests in Africa throughout most of the 1990s. My previous study of the IMF's role in Africa found patterns of French and British influence that rivaled those of the United States.[33]

Britain and France maintain extensive contacts with their former colonies and treat the cultivation of post-colonial international institutions as the centerpiece of their respective foreign policies in Africa. Britain promotes the Commonwealth of Nations, a loose regime that has gradually evolved into a "good governance" club. For example, South Africa was readmitted to the Commonwealth after the end of apartheid, and Zimbabwe was expelled after its president, Robert Mugabe, came under severe criticism for confiscating land holdings and inciting conflict targeted at white landowners. Britain subsequently expanded its humanitarian foreign aid to Zimbabwe substantially, but channeled it through NGOs. Members of the Commonwealth are expected

[33] Stone 2004.

to respect human rights and pursue recommended economic policies, and in return they receive benefits in terms of foreign aid. The correlation between Commonwealth membership and British aid is 0.49. In addition, Commonwealth countries granted each other trade preferences that were recognized under the GATT/WTO Generalized System of Preferences, accorded one another special diplomatic status, and attended multilateral summit meetings. There is substantial anecdotal evidence that Britain plays an important role in IMF policy making towards its former colonies in East Africa. For example, IMF officials have indicated that British intervention secured loan facilities for Kenya during the 1990s.

France has pursued the most consistent and vigorous policy of nurturing its ties with its former African colonies, and has applied an explicit carrot-and-stick approach combining foreign aid, trade and monetary policy, and military intervention. The centerpiece of this policy has been the promotion of the CFA Franc Zone, a regional currency union tied to the French currency.[34] Membership in the CFA Franc Zone represented a substantial degree of continuity with the colonial past: it meant adopting a common currency that was guaranteed by France, accepting French control of monetary policy, and holding national foreign currency reserves in French francs (now euros) at the French Treasury. France has formal military agreements with most CFA Franc Zone members, has stationed troops in the capitals of several of them to deter coup attempts, and frequently intervenes in times of civil unrest.[35] France maintains strong precedents for ostracizing uncooperative former colonies, which go back to Charles de Gaulle, who cut off aid and preferential trade arrangements with Guinea when it failed to pass his referendum reorganizing French relations with its former colonies.[36] Similarly, Mali lost access to French import preferences when it withdrew from the CFA Franc Zone in 1962, effectively closing

[34] The CFA Franc Zone was created in 1945 and currently consists of fourteen members. The acronym originally stood for Franc des Colonies Françaises d'Afrique (Franc of the French Colonies of Africa). In 1958 it became Franc de la Communauté Française d'Afrique (Franc of the French Community of Africa). Currently, the CFA Franc is a common currency for two different currency areas, each with its own central bank, and each with its own interpretation of the acronym. For members of the West African Economic and Monetary Union (WAEMU) it now means franc de la Communauté Financière d'Afrique (Franc of the African Financial Community), and for members of the Central African Economic and Monetary Community (CEMAC) it means franc de la Coopération Financière en Afrique Centrale (Franc of Financial Cooperation in Central Africa). The CFA franc was pegged to the French franc until France's accession to EMU, and has since been pegged to the euro. Its convertibility is guaranteed by the French Ministry of Finance.

[35] Stasavage (2003) notes that France scaled back its military commitments to CFA Franc Zone members in the 1990s, closing bases in Chad and the Central African Republic. While it maintained garrisons in Gabon, Ivory Coast and Senegal, it did not intervene in the 1999 coup in Ivory Coast, which he argues may undermine the value of CFA Franc Zone membership.

[36] Abdelal 2007.

the French market to its major export crops; economic pressure and hyperinflation forced it to negotiate its reintegration into the Franc Zone on French terms in 1966.[37] Countries like Senegal and Ivory Coast, which cooperated with France and remained loyal, received trade preferences and disproportional shares of French aid. Anecdotal evidence and conversations at the Fund suggest that France has played an active role in promoting its clients' interests when their cases came before the IMF.[38]

Fund officials report that France plays much the same sort of hands-on role in developing programs in francophone Africa that the United States plays in Latin America and other areas of strong US interest, and that the Fund has developed standing procedures that accommodate this special interest. When IMF missions visit countries in francophone Africa to negotiate or monitor programs, they routinely stop in Paris to brief the French Treasury before visiting African capitals or on their return trip, or both. French officials are not privy to the mission's briefing documents, but extensive conversations ensure that they are kept fully informed. Fund officials indicate that the exchange of information flows both ways, and these meetings are very useful because the French Treasury maintains an unparalleled staff to monitor African events. This superior information and preferential access to the negotiators in real time clearly represent an opportunity for France to inject its preferences into the Fund policy-making process, however. Since France is the only leading shareholder with strong interests in most of these countries and the United States has tacitly ceded this region as a sphere of French influence, Fund management closely follows French preferences here.

To investigate the effects of French influence over conditionality quantitatively, I replicate the analysis reported above, substituting French interest variables (aid, bank exposure, exports, UN voting and alliances) and interaction terms with vulnerability measures (trade/GDP, debt service/exports, percentage of debt that is short-term) for the corresponding US measures. The specification of the control variables is the same as in Table 8.3. The model is estimated once for a sample including only former French colonies and other countries in sub-Saharan Africa, and again for a global sample excluding those countries. Table 8.7 summarizes the substantive results of this analysis. Effects of aid, bank exposure and exports are not reported because the effects in the two samples are statistically indistinguishable: French aid is insignificant in both samples, and the economic measures are qualitatively indistinguishable from the effects of US bank exposure and exports. As noted earlier, it is generally difficult to disentangle the effects of G-5 economic interests, since they

[37] Kirshner 1995, 151–154.
[38] Stasavage 1997.

Table 8.7 *Effects of French interests.*

	Colonies & Sub-Saharan Africa		Rest of the World	
	Substantive effect	p	Substantive effect	p
UN voting	−42.7%	0.02	−15.1%	0.00
Alliances	−8.9%	0.15	6.1%	0.03

Note: Effect of changing x by one standard deviation, conditional on trade/GDP, debt service/exports and short-term debt one standard deviation above the mean.

are highly correlated. The results for the measures of the most political reasons for French interests, however, are quite revealing.

The results support the view that French political interests play a much more potent role in the development of IMF conditionality in sub-Saharan Africa and in its other former colonies than in the rest of the world. The association between French votes and African countries' votes in the UN has a significant effect in both samples, but the substantive effect is almost three times larger in the sample of sub-Saharan countries and former colonies than in the rest of the world. The effect of alliances also shifts between the two samples. As noted above, none of the G-5 countries' alliances patterns, aside from those of the United States, are associated with reduced conditionality in the global sample. In the sample covering the countries that are neither in sub-Saharan Africa nor former French colonies, French alliance patterns are significantly associated with increased conditionality, which rejects the hypothesis of French informal influence to grant concessions to favored regimes. On the other hand, in the sample of former colonies and sub-Saharan countries, alliance portfolios are associated with a substantial reduction of conditionality. The negative effect is only marginally significant ($p = 0.15$) and the estimate of its size is imprecise, ranging from a 12.3 percent decrease to a 6.6 percent increase in conditionality with 95 percent confidence. Nevertheless, these results support the interpretation that France is much more likely to intervene to relax conditionality for countries with which it has military alliance commitments if those countries are African countries or former colonies.

The qualitative evidence suggests that French and British influence over the application of conditionality is very substantial in Africa, but is largely limited to their respective former colonies on that continent. France has made much more substantial investments in African political regimes and economic management than any other country. Besides the United States, only France systematically enjoys privileged access to information about IMF decision making during negotiations, and France enjoys that privileged access only in Africa. Quantitative analysis fails to fully disentangle the effects of French and US influence, but provides some support for the interpretation that the French role in influencing conditionality is concentrated in Africa and its former colonies.

Conclusions

This analysis supports three specific hypotheses derived from a model of informal governance. US intervention should reduce, rather than increase, conditionality; intervention should only be offered to countries in which the United States perceives an important influence; and intervention should be limited to countries that are sufficiently vulnerable to prioritize their relations with the IMF in their foreign policy. Countries that enjoy the strong support of the IMF's largest shareholder, the United States, enjoy a substantial bargaining advantage because the IMF cannot credibly threaten to withhold support from them. A battery of tests using a range of measures of US interests confirms this interpretation: countries that play an important role in US policy are subject to fewer categories of conditions, but only when they are sufficiently vulnerable to sudden reversals of international financial flows to be willing to exert their potential leverage. The pattern holds for US foreign aid, bank exposure, exports, UN voting and alliance portfolios.

Associations between variables are susceptible to multiple interpretations, so conditional hypotheses provide tighter tests of models. The model implies that countries are reluctant to draw on their reserves of influence with the United States when their need for financing is not urgent, leaving the IMF free to negotiate conditionality according to its own objectives. This hypothesis is confirmed by the result that US interests only constrain conditionality when the borrowing country is relatively vulnerable to international shocks compared to the sample of program participants.

The evidence broadly supports the interpretation of US informal influence over IMF conditionality rather than the competing hypothesis that the G-5 countries share governance of the Fund more or less equally. The policies that determine the general outlines of the IMF's strategy of designing conditionality are consensual, and with minor differences of emphasis, all of the major shareholders support them. When it comes to making exceptions to these general rules for reasons of national policy, however, disagreements are much more likely. Foreign aid and alliance patterns provide sharp tests that discriminate between the hypotheses of US and G-5 influence, because aid and alliance patterns are not highly correlated between the United States and the other G-5 countries, and these tests reject G-5 effects. Bank exposure, exports and UN voting provide weaker discrimination, but again the effects of US influence are stronger than those of other G-5 countries.

The cases of Indonesia and Africa provide qualitative evidence that illustrates the limits of the influence of other G-5 countries. In Indonesia the IMF's second largest shareholder, Japan, perceived critical interests and launched a concerted intervention to reduce the scope of IMF conditionality in 1997. Its efforts were rebuffed, however, and the Indonesian program became one of the IMF's most ambitious. This is consistent with quantitative results that suggest that informal influence is largely monopolized by the United States. Africa provides a different sort of example, because this is an area in which France, and to a lesser degree Britain, have carved out traditional spheres of influence and in which the United States generally perceives very limited interests. Both France and Britain have intervened on behalf of their former colonies to help them to secure IMF support, and France enjoys privileged access to IMF negotiators on their way to and from francophone Africa. Quantitative evidence suggests that French influence over conditionality is heavily concentrated in sub-Saharan Africa and former French colonies.

This chapter presents a picture of substantial US influence over the content of conditionality, but this is subject to a critical caveat. While the United States enjoys the influence to moderate conditionality in a variety of countries and circumstances, it exercises that authority much less frequently. Countries receive the benefits of US influence only when they are particularly important to US policy in some way and they are highly vulnerable to external financial shocks. This intersection of countries with influence to spend and the incentive to spend it is relatively limited. In all other countries, including many that play an important role in US policy but are not particularly vulnerable, and many that are vulnerable but possess no leverage over the United States, the IMF develops its conditionality relatively autonomously. Outside of Africa, furthermore, the other G-5 countries do not appear to substantially influence conditionality. This evidence, therefore, is consistent with the view that the IMF enjoys a wide range of delegated authority. The major shareholders agree on the broad outlines of the policy reforms that they seek to promote in countries that draw on IMF resources, and they trust their agent sufficiently to allow it a wide range of discretion to negotiate reform programs with the member countries.

9

Enforcement

The IMF enforces the conditionality attached to its lending facilities by suspending disbursement of loan installments, or tranches, if borrowing countries fail to implement the associated conditions. The IMF Executive Board formally approves all disbursements of Fund resources. When a performance criterion is not implemented by its review date, this provokes an automatic suspension of the corresponding disbursement unless the board decides to issue a waiver or modify the conditions. According to staff, the requirement to seek Executive Board approval for changes to conditionality can constrain management's discretion and consequently reinforce its bargaining position with country authorities. However, management has discretion to recommend waivers or modifications to the board or to adjust the schedule of reviews and disbursements, and in practice its recommendations are not overruled. Because of the combination of management discretion and consensus decision making, it is easy for major shareholders to use their informal influence to urge management to propose waivers for favored client states. Since the status quo outcome is that the program is suspended until every performance criterion is met, shareholders' informal influence has the effect of relaxing the enforcement of conditionality.

Management's dilemma is as follows. After a program goes off track, it is generally optimal to modify it, because the original macroeconomic forecast is no longer valid and key performance indicators may no longer be achievable. Furthermore, even when a program goes off track because the government has made political decisions not to implement its conditions, it is optimal *ex post* to renegotiate in order to give the government incentives to modify its policies when the original set of targets is no longer realistic. The problem is that governments know that it is optimal for management to renegotiate *ex post*, and this creates moral hazard: governments have weak incentives to implement conditionality if they anticipate that they will be rewarded with weaker conditionality when they renege on their commitments. The IMF management tries to ameliorate the moral hazard problem by developing a reputation for enforcing conditionality rigorously, and resists efforts by shareholders to undermine its reputation; but it is ultimately understood by all of the participants that different rules, and a different reputation, apply to countries that have substantial influence in Washington.[1]

The key argument of *Lending Credibility* was that the IMF's reputation is built on differentiated strategies for enforcing reputation once a program goes off track.[2] Some countries face rigorous enforcement: no modifications or waivers; disbursements are delayed until the corresponding conditions are implemented. Other countries are subject to a fluid set of conditions that are renegotiated periodically as the targets are missed. The first set of countries should miss their targets less frequently, but face lengthier program suspensions when they fail to implement their conditions. The second group of countries receives more waivers and faces shorter program suspensions, because there is pressure on the IMF management to renegotiate their targets in order to bring them back on track. As a result, they have weak incentives to implement conditions, and they face frequent program suspensions.

The United States has used informal contacts to obtain waivers for a number of countries that play important roles in US foreign policy, including Zaire and the Philippines in the 1980s, Egypt in the early 1990s and subsequently Pakistan and Turkey. Among the post-Communist countries, Russia and Ukraine have frequently received waivers because of direct contacts by US officials, which have sometimes occurred at the highest level. My previous study of 26 post-Communist countries found that countries that received substantial amounts of US foreign aid were subject to much shorter program suspensions when their programs went off track. They received waivers or their conditions were modified so that they could quickly get back into good standing. As a result of the weak incentives that they faced, their economic policies were more inflationary, and they failed to implement conditions and went off-track more frequently.[3] Another study of 53 African countries revealed a similar pattern with respect to US foreign aid, and also found that countries with close ties to France and Britain received similar treatment.[4] Using different samples, Edwards finds that US aid decreases the probability of program interruptions,[5] and Pop-Eleches finds that states with voting patterns similar to the United

1 Stone 2002, 2004.
2 Stone 2002.
3 Stone 2002.
4 Stone 2004.
5 Edwards 2005.

States in the UN General Assembly have a lower probability of program interruptions.[6]

This chapter extends and revises these findings in several respects. First, it takes advantage of the data on conditionality in the MONA database to refine its statistical tests, as explained below. Second, it uses the theoretical model of informal governance to generate more precise hypotheses. As the previous chapter explained, the informal governance model predicts a conditional effect of measures of US interests on IMF policies: US intervention should only be observed when the borrowing country is important to the United States and has an intense need for IMF support. Third, this chapter explores the robustness of these findings by using the same five measures of US interests as in the previous two chapters: foreign aid, bank exposure, exports, UN voting affinities, and military alliance patterns. These measures are only weakly correlated and capture different dimensions of US foreign policy interests, so effects that are robust across measures are persuasive evidence of a pattern of deliberate intervention.

In addition, this chapter explores the collective governance of the Fund by examining the evidence of US control as opposed to more widely shared influence by the G-5 – the United States, Japan, Germany, the United Kingdom, and France – which are the largest IMF shareholders and the only countries to appoint (rather than elect) their own EDs. The model of informal governance is consistent with informal control either by a single leading state or by a group of leading states, and other international organizations demonstrate each pattern, but I have argued that the IMF is an example of unusually strong US control. An advantage of using multiple measures of US interests is that some of the measures, particularly foreign aid and alliances, are weakly correlated with the corresponding measures for the other G-5 countries and consequently provide strong tests of US vs. G-5 effects.

To foreshadow, the chapter finds strong evidence of US influence over the enforcement of conditionality that is robust across measures, and confirms that this influence is invoked only when countries are vulnerable to sudden reversals of international financial flows. Consistent with the model in *Lending Credibility*, this influence is exerted after a disbursement is suspended and affects the duration of the suspension. Where comparative tests are possible, the evidence points to US influence rather than collective governance by the G-5, although some of the results are inconclusive in this respect. The argument is illustrated with two case studies, Russia (1996–8) and Argentina (2000–01), which represent distinct reasons for urgent US intervention.

[6] Pop-Eleches 2009.

Data

The data cover 99 countries that participated in IMF programs between 1992 and 2002. During this period, 92 of the 99 countries experienced at least one program suspension, for a total of 752 program interruptions. In this set, 78 countries experienced short program interruptions of one or two months in duration an average of 4.7 times; 77 countries experienced suspensions of 3 to 8 months an average of 3 times; 67 countries experienced suspensions of 9 months or more an average of 1.6 times; and ten countries experienced very long interruptions of 24 months or longer.

The MONA data make it possible to overcome some important data limitations of previous studies of IMF program enforcement. First, previous work has had to rely on interpolation to determine when an IMF program was suspended. The IMF does not announce when a program goes off track, it simply suspends the next scheduled tranche of a loan facility. Thus, the only available measure of program suspensions was an interruption in the pattern of loan disbursements; but it was not always clear when the next scheduled disbursement was supposed to occur, or when disbursements were cancelled at the request of country authorities (as happened in Poland in 1994, for example) rather than because of non-compliance. The MONA data include the schedule of disbursements and its subsequent modifications, so it is possible to fix the exact date of program suspensions.

Second, previous studies had no independent measure of program compliance. Non-compliance was inferred when programs were suspended, and often the undisbursed portion of a facility was used as a proxy for partial compliance, but it was impossible to observe non-compliance that was not accompanied by a program suspension. The MONA data include the content of conditionality being tested at each review date and indicate which conditions were judged by the IMF to have been implemented, so it is possible to measure compliance with conditionality independently from enforcement. This avoids serious problems of inference. For example, if we observed in a previous study that democracies were subject to less lengthy program suspensions,[7] we could not be certain whether this occurred because democracies implemented their programs better and got back on track more quickly than autocracies, or because the IMF was less rigorous in punishing democracies.[8] More broadly, because studies of implementation and enforcement used the same dependent variables, it was impossible to determine whether any of the effects found were due to

[7] Stone 2002, 2004.

[8] The results of the analysis reported below indicate that the rigor of enforcement does not depend upon polity scores, which suggests that these effects had been correctly attributed to variations in implementation in these earlier studies.

variations in implementation or to variations in enforcement – or whether non-findings were due to contradictory effects that cancelled each other out. Using independent measures of compliance and suspension makes it possible to resolve these issues.

Third, previous studies were unable to control for variations in conditionality that might affect compliance and enforcement. As we saw in the previous chapter, the substantive scope of conditionality varies substantially, and there is no reason to expect it to be equally difficult to achieve compliance with narrowly defined programs and with sweeping reform plans, which typically involve many more structural benchmarks. In addition, it is reasonable to expect the IMF to take the difficulty of compliance into account when determining whether to declare a program off track. As we will see below, the number of categories of conditions that have not been implemented is a strong predictor of the duration of program suspensions, while the number of categories of conditions being tested is strongly associated with leniency. Controlling for conditionality and implementation removes an important source of heterogeneity in the data, and also makes it unnecessary to control for domestic political factors that are related to implementation when we study enforcement.

As in previous chapters, five key explanatory variables are used to measure a range of US economic, political and military interests: US foreign aid, the exposure of US banks, US exports, affinity in voting in the UN General Assembly, and similarity in military alliance profiles. Foreign aid is a monetary measure of how much importance the donor attaches to a particular country or regime, but says nothing about why particular countries are important. Bank exposure and exports, on the other hand, measure narrow economic interests that motivate US intervention on behalf of particular countries. Votes in the UN General Assembly capture the similarity of two countries' foreign policies. Alliance portfolios represent military commitments for mutual defense, which are associated with intense national security concerns. These five dimensions of US interests represent distinct reasons for the United States to have intense interests in a particular country. Taken together, these variables offer a nuanced view of the politics of enforcing IMF conditionality programs.

The analysis proceeds as follows. The key dependent variable is the duration of suspension episodes. The logic of *Lending Credibility* was that board members exert influence after a program has been suspended to shorten the duration of suspensions.[9] They do this by lobbying for waivers of conditionality or modification of its terms, which makes it easier and less politically costly to get programs back on track.[10] In addition, the MONA data allow me to take

9 Stone 2002.

10 It is possible in principle to lobby for waivers before a program is suspended, but I have not

a closer look at the substantive implications of lax enforcement by analyzing the number of waivers that are granted when a suspended program comes back into good standing. This provides a second check on the logic of the argument. If it is true that informal influence over enforcement operates through the manipulation of management's discretion about whether to seek waivers, this discreet influence should leave traces in the pattern of waivers.

Duration of program suspensions

The primary means for shareholders to exert influence on behalf of a borrowing country is to contact Fund management after a program has been suspended. This should have the effect of reducing the duration of program suspensions. The dependent variable for tests of this hypothesis, therefore, is the duration of program suspensions in months. As discussed above, the theory does not pin down which measures of US preferences should be associated with intense motivations to influence conditionality, so my approach is to use a range of subjectively plausible indicators that are weakly correlated with each other and that capture a variety of motivations. The theory of informal governance does make a precise conditional prediction, however: influence should be exerted when there is a combination of latent US interest in the borrowing country and intense need for IMF financing on the part of the borrowing country. Consequently, each of the models that follow uses interaction terms between measures of US interests and the same measures of borrower-country vulnerability to sudden reversals of external financing: trade/GDP, debt service/exports, and the percentage of debt held in short-term instruments.

I want to separate the rigor of enforcement from the government's record of implementing conditionality, so in the models that follow I control for the number of categories of conditionality in which the borrower has failed to implement conditions. I also control for the number of categories of conditions covered in the current review, on the assumption that management makes allowances for the scope of conditionality when assessing country performance. Both of these measures are robustly significant across models: countries that have missed more categories of conditions have longer program suspensions, while countries that were required to implement more conditions have shorter ones. Because I control for conditionality and implementation, I do not have to control for political factors that might affect program suspensions through

found systematic evidence that this occurs. In practice, suspensions are almost automatic because the institutional default is to suspend a tranche when a performance criterion is not met.

effects on conditionality or implementation. (It is better to control for the intervening variables.) However, I also control for the possibility that the rigor of IMF enforcement of conditionality systematically depends upon factors such as political regime, GDP per capita, or government capacity. Similarly, central bank reserves in months of imports is used to assess the possibility that bargaining power affects the rigor of enforcement. I find no systematic evidence that these variables affect enforcement once we control for the scope of conditionality and program implementation, although they have substantial effects on conditionality and implementation.

The full tables of results of models testing for interactive effects of US aid, US bank exposure, US exports, UN voting affinity and alliance patterns are reported in the Appendix as Table A.9.1. The models are parametric duration models using the Weibull distribution.[11] The table in the Appendix is mainly useful for researchers, who can use it to understand how the models were specified and replicate the results. In order to conduct meaningful hypothesis tests or to understand the substantive significance of the results – whether they are big or small – we have to calculate predicted probabilities or marginal effects. Since the quantities of interest in this case are interactions between variables, the hypothesis tests represented by the significance levels reported in the table in the appendix are not particularly informative. The significance test for the coefficient for US aid, for example, is only valid when trade/GDP, debt service/exports, and short-term debt are equal to zero. In order to test the hypothesis that US aid has a significant effect when countries are vulnerable to disruptions on international financial markets, I test the joint effect of the coefficient of US aid and the coefficients of its interactions with trade/GDP, debt service/exports and short-term debt, evaluated at the desired levels of vulnerability. These are the hypothesis tests reported in Table 9.1.

Table 9.1 reports the substantive effects calculated from the models reported in Appendix Table A.9.1. In each case, the effects shown are for a one standard deviation change in the values of the measures of US interests. "High" levels of vulnerability to external financial shocks are one standard deviation above the sample means, respectively, on each of the three vulnerability measures. When all variables are held at their means, the median predicted duration of a program suspension is 5.8 months. When US foreign aid is increased by one standard deviation and vulnerability measures are at their mean, there is only a small decrease in the predicted duration, to 5.4 months, and the effect is not statistically significant. As the borrower crosses into the top third of the

[11] The Weibull model estimates a monotonically changing hazard rate (which may be increasing or decreasing) with time-varying covariates. Observations of suspensions that had not ended by the end of 2002 are right-censored.

Table 9.1 *Duration of program suspensions: substantive effects.*

	Vulnerability	Median duration (months)	Change in duration (months)	Percentage change	p
Baseline		5.8			
US aid	High	3.4	−2.4	−41.4%	0.03
	Mean	5.4	−0.4	−6.9%	0.97
US lending	High	4.2	−1.6	−27.6%	0.05
	Mean	4.2	−1.6	−27.6%	0.00
US exports	High	3.8	−2.0	−34.5%	0.15
	Mean	6.2	0.4	6.9%	0.52
UN voting	High	3.4	−2.4	−41.4%	0.00
	Mean	5.0	−0.8	−13.8%	0.02
Alliances	High	3.4	−2.4	−41.4%	0.05
	Mean	5.0	−0.8	−13.8%	0.09

Note: Effect on the predicted median duration of increasing the variable in the left column by one standard deviation, conditional on the levels of trade/GDP, debt service/exports and short-term debt. High vulnerability signifies one standard deviation above the mean.

vulnerability distribution, however, the effect of US foreign aid becomes statistically significant, and the expected duration drops 41 percent to 3.4 months. The patterns across the other measures of US interests are broadly similar.

Increasing US bank exposure to a single country by one standard deviation – about 2 percent of total foreign exposure of US banks – decreases the median suspension duration by 27.6 percent to 4.2 months. For the sake of comparison, this represents a quadrupling of the average level of US bank exposure to a particular country, but is substantially lower than the peak levels of exposure in the sample to Argentina (8.8%), Brazil (14.6%) and Mexico (18.5%). The effect of bank exposure on suspensions reported in the table does not appear to vary significantly as external vulnerability changes, but this is due to aggregating contradictory effects. The pattern is consistent with the broader pattern when vulnerability is measured in terms of trade/GDP and debt service/exports – interactions with these variables strengthen the effects of bank exposure that reduce the length of suspensions – but the pattern reverses for short-term debt. Short-term debt weakens the effect of bank exposure and counteracts the effects of the other two vulnerability variables, so the combined effect of increasing all three is insignificant. A possible interpretation of this result is that banks have weaker incentives to lobby when debt is held in short-term instruments.[12]

12 When bank exposure to a developing country takes the form of short-term debt, the banks are substantially protected against the risk of default, because they can refuse to roll-over their

Table 9.2 *Substantive effects of bank exposure.*

	Predicted duration (months)	Decrease (months)	Percentage decrease	p
All variables at mean	5.8			
Effect of bank exposure:				
Trade, debt service & short-term debt high	4.2	1.6	27.6	0.05
Trade, debt service & short-term debt low	4.2	1.6	27.6	0.00
Trade & debt service high	3.8	2.0	34.5	0.02
Short-term debt high	5.0	0.8	13.8	0.02

Note: Effect of an increase in US bank exposure by 2.1% (one standard deviation). Predicted median duration. High and Low indicate one standard deviation above or below the mean; all other variables held at their means.

The other measures of vulnerability have the familiar effect of strengthening the effect of bank exposure on duration. The expected duration falls by two months, or almost 35 percent, when bank exposure and vulnerability are high and all other variables are at their means. These results are presented in Table 9.2.

The effect of US exports has only marginal statistical significance, even at high levels of external vulnerability, but this is not because the estimated effects are small – in fact, the effects of a standard deviation of exports are comparable to those of a standard deviation of foreign aid, reducing the median duration 34.5 percent, to 3.8 months. Rather, the weak significance is due to the very large standard errors around the estimated effect. The correct interpretation of this result is not that the effect is near zero, but rather that the effect is probably quite large, but cannot be estimated with enough precision to rule out the possibility that it is zero. The estimated effects increase substantially as the level of vulnerability rises, but so do the standard errors, so that significance levels improve slowly.

UN voting has a strong association with the duration of punishment, and it varies sharply with vulnerability. When borrowers have average exposure

loans or demand higher interest rates if the risks change. This should weaken banks' incentives to coordinate their actions or to lobby their governments to bail out their debtors. Therefore, the assumption that short-term debt, or roll-over risk, affects only the intensity of borrower interests and not US interests may not hold for the case of bank exposure, although it does hold for the other measures of US interests.

to external shocks, the effect of (the preferences reflected in) UN voting is to reduce the length of suspensions modestly, by less than one month; when external vulnerability increases by one standard deviation, however, expected suspensions shorten by 41.4 percent, to 3.4 months. As vulnerability drops below the mean, the effect of UN voting becomes insignificant, and when vulnerability drops to very low levels the effect switches signs and significantly extends the length of suspensions. As we found in the previous chapter, these effects occur when countries oppose rather than support US votes in the UN. The United States intervenes on behalf of countries that generally oppose its preferences in the UN, but only when they are vulnerable to financial crises. Recalcitrant regimes that are not vulnerable to sudden reversals of external financing do not benefit from US patronage, and in fact have substantially longer than average program suspensions. For countries that are not vulnerable that oppose the United States in the UN General Assembly one standard deviation more than average, the expected suspension duration is two months longer than average, an increase of almost 35 percent (significant at $p = 0.01$).

Pakistan and Egypt are examples of countries that frequently oppose the United States in the UN, and both have called upon the United States to intercede on their behalf with the IMF. Pakistan has repeatedly failed to fulfill the conditions attached to its programs, and has turned to the United States for help managing the Fund on numerous occasions. Its programs were interrupted for non-compliance seventeen times between 1990 and 2002, or roughly 1.5 times per program year, and the length of those interruptions ranged from very short – 1 to 2 months eight times – to two very long suspensions. The last long suspension from IMF and World Bank financing occurred while the Clinton administration was punishing Pakistan for developing nuclear weapons, and was brought to a close when the Bush administration required Pakistan's assistance in the 2001 war against Afghanistan. Similarly, Egypt supports US initiatives in spite of, rather than because of, the inclinations of its leaders and the pressures of public opinion, and Egypt has been a stark example of the failure to enforce IMF conditionality. US intervention on behalf of Egypt became a prominent example of the IMF's credibility problem during the 1980s and early 1990s.

Alliance patterns show a strong substantive effect: US allies and countries that share allies with the United States have program suspensions that are sharply reduced in length. A country one standard deviation closer than average to the US alliance network has an expected duration that is reduced by over 40 percent to 3.4 months. This effect, again, depends upon vulnerability. The duration rises to five months and the effect of alliance portfolios becomes only marginally significant when vulnerability to external shocks drops to mean values, and durations continue to rise while the effects of alliances become ever more insignificant as vulnerability falls below the mean. These results are easy to interpret. US allies have a constant claim on US attention. Security issues demand high priority, and allies can rely on their counterparts in the United States defense and foreign policy bureaucracies to interpret their needs to Treasury. These ties and relationships are not drawn on lightly, however, so they only have a practical influence on IMF enforcement of conditionality when the borrowing country is sufficiently vulnerable to reverses of international capital flows to prioritize its interactions with the IMF in its foreign policy.

Robustness and discrimination

Statistical results are convincing to the extent that results are robust to alternative specifications and tests discriminate effectively between alternative theories. Robustness can be thought of in three ways: measurement robustness, specification robustness and methodological robustness.

Measurement robustness is important in cases where there exists no single, obvious measure of the quantity of interest. In this case, the intensity of US interests in a particular country has no obvious metric, and can be expected to vary over time and across countries with respect to different issues. Some countries are important because of their economic ties and others because of their strategic military locations, and the balance between these sources of US interests shifts over time with the salience of security and economic crises. The results presented above demonstrate an impressive degree of measurement robustness.

A second form of robustness check is specification robustness. The results have been subjected to a range of alternative specifications, and they are broadly consistent across specifications. First, I have experimented with dropping control variables and including additional control variables related to the domestic politics of borrowing countries, and while significance levels and substantive effects vary, the qualitative effects do not change. Robustness appears to be provided by the strong anchoring effect of controlling for conditionality and implementation, which soaks up the effects of domestic politics on the duration of suspensions. Second, I have nested these models in larger models that include all of the measures of US interests and their interactions or subsets of them, and the results are consistent with those presented above for US foreign aid, bank exposure, UN voting and exports. The effect of alliances becomes statistically insignificant in models that include US aid, but the pattern of increasing effects with increasing vulnerability remains. Here, robustness appears to be provided by the low correlations among most of the measures of US interests, which suggests that they really capture distinct reasons for the United States to have strong interests in particular countries rather than simply representing different measures of the same underlying latent variable.

A third kind of robustness check is methodological. The results presented here are produced by a parametric Weibull duration model, and alternative methods for analyzing the data are possible. The Weibull model estimates a parameter that determines how rapidly the baseline hazard rate increases or decreases over time, but assumes a monotonic rate of change. The exponential model, for example, is a special case where the hazard rate does not change as a function of time, and the Weibull is more general. A parametric hazard model is appropriate if we have prior beliefs about the shape of the hazard. In this case, I expect a monotonically decreasing hazard, because unobserved variation in the difficulty of implementing conditionality across countries should screen the sample of programs that are off track until only the hard cases are left, and this is consistent with the estimated results.

The results using a non-parametric Cox model instead of Weibull are qualitatively the same, but significance levels drop: US aid and bank exposure are only marginally significant, exports and alliances become insignificant, and only UN voting remains strongly significant. There is, unfortunately, no direct test of the hypothesis that the Weibull results fit the data better than the Cox results, or vice versa, because the likelihood functions computed by the models are not conformable.[13] A possible explanation for the differences between the Weibull and the Cox models is that the Cox model allows for a very flexible and non-monotonic hazard function, so if some countries consistently have longer durations than others – which is the essence of the argument made here – the Cox model may attribute these cross-sectional variations to the shape of the hazard function rather than to the independent variables.

Another form of methodological robustness check is to include fixed effects. Country-specific fixed effects are impractical because there is not enough variation in the dependent variable to calculate all of the country coefficients, and in any case country fixed effects would absorb all of the cross-sectional variation in the importance of particular countries, which are the quantities of interest, into theoretically uninformative country effects. However, the results are robust to the inclusion of a variety of specifications of regional fixed

[13] They effectively treat the definition of observations differently, so their likelihoods cannot be compared meaningfully. This rules out comparisons based on the Akaike information criterion or the Bayesian information criterion, and also rules out tests of non-nested model fit such as the Vuong test or the Clarke test.

effects, and the results reported include controls for the most important regional effects – sub-Saharan Africa, Latin America and the countries of the former Soviet Union.

Another approach is to estimate a frailty model. Parametric hazard models such as the Weibull model make a proportional hazards assumption, which is analogous to the OLS assumption of no omitted variables: if there is unmeasured heterogeneity in the data this assumption does not hold and the results are biased. Of course, there is always unmeasured heterogeneity in the data, so a common approach is to estimate a frailty model, which estimates an additional parameter to correct for the resulting bias. All of the results are robust to estimation of a frailty model with shared regional parameters over nine regions.[14]

In summary, the results are very robust to alternative measures, alternative specifications, and alternative models. Every measure is not statistically significant in every specification of every model, but this is nearly the case. UN voting is significant across the board, and US aid and bank exposure are almost always significant and always at least marginally significant. The pattern holds across the board that measures of US interests have substantially stronger effects when countries are highly vulnerable to external financial shocks, and in most cases those effects are only significant when countries are in the top third of the distribution on at least one dimension of vulnerability.

Waiver of conditionality

A further test of the robustness of the results is to generate additional testable implications of the model that predict effects on additional dependent variables. An alternative way to measure lax enforcement of conditionality is to count the substantive concessions, or waivers, that the IMF grants to countries when their programs come back on track after a suspension. When program suspensions are cut short because of informal influence, this should show up in adjustments to conditionality, which may take the form of waiving performance criteria. The measure used here is derived from the MONA dataset and counts the number of types of conditions, ranging from zero to a possible maximum of 19, on which waivers were granted in a particular review. Observations are recorded when a program suspension ends. The dataset contains 688 instances when a suspended program came back on track after a successful

[14] The nine regions, coded by Przeworski *et al.* (2000), are Latin America, the Caribbean, sub-Saharan Africa, North Africa and the Middle East, South Asia, South-East Asia, East Asia, Eastern Europe and the former Soviet Union and Oceania.

Table 9.3 *Effects of US influence on waivers.*

	High vulnerability		Mean vulnerability	
	Substantive Effect	p	Substantive Effect	p
US Foreign Aid	46.3%	0.03	14.9%	0.21
US Exports	65.3%	0.02	−2.4%	0.91

Negative binomial regressions. Vulnerability measures with significant interaction effects are one standard deviation above the mean, all other variables are at mean values.

review, and in 35 percent of those cases the Executive Board granted at least one waiver, for a total of 546 waivers. Two or more waivers were granted in 21 percent of program resumptions, three or more were granted in 12 percent of cases, and four or more were granted in 6 percent of cases. The maximum number of waivers granted in a single successful review was eight, which occurred in Russia in 1998 and in Zambia in 1999.

Since the dependent variable is an event count and I expect to observe over-dispersion – countries that receive one waiver in a given review are more likely to receive additional waivers – the appropriate statistical model is a negative binomial count model. The hypothesis of over-dispersion is confirmed in the analysis to a high degree of confidence. The regressors specified in the models are identical to those for the duration models presented in the previous section. The full results of the analysis are presented in Table A.9.3 in the Appendix.

The analysis of waivers provides additional support for the hypothesis of informal governance, although the results are positive for only two of the five measures of US interests: foreign aid and exports. Joint tests of significance for these variables and the interactive measures of vulnerability, with all other variables held at their means, are presented in Table 9.3.

Table 9.3 introduces additional evidence that US informal influence reduces the enforcement of conditionality. US foreign aid and US exports have significant effects that increase the incidence of waivers. The substantive effects of these measures of US interests on the incidence of waivers are substantial when countries are highly vulnerable to sudden reversals of external financing. A one-standard deviation increase in US aid, or $137 million in the set of IMF program participants, increases the incidence of waivers by about 46% (the 95% confidence interval ranges from 6% to 87%). Increasing US exports by one standard deviation, or by $584 million in the set of countries under IMF programs, increases the incidence of waivers by an estimated 65% (the confidence interval ranges from 11 to 119%). Each of these effects appears only in

Table 9.4 *Correlations of measures of US and G-5 interests.*

	Foreign Aid	Bank Exposure	Exports	UN Voting	Alliances
United Kingdom	0.12	0.96	0.36	0.82	−0.55
France	0.29	0.72	0.36	0.84	−0.56
Germany	0.15	0.47	0.34	0.78	−0.56
Japan	0.15	0.36	0.38	0.76	−0.64

Sample: country-months under program suspensions, 3,724 observations.

the presence of high vulnerability; at mean levels of vulnerability the effects are insignificant.

Discrimination

A final consideration is discrimination among alternative theories. The results have two significant advantages in terms of theory discrimination. First, the specification of an interactive effect between measures of US interests and measures of borrowing country vulnerability to external financial shocks is consistent with the theory of informal governance, but seems too specific to be subject to ad hoc explanations or explained by omitted variables. Second, only the theory of informal governance explains a common pattern of interactive effects across variables that measure US economic, political and strategic interests.

A separate question is how well the results discriminate between the hypothesis of US informal control of the IMF and collective control by the G-5, and this calls for additional analysis. Up to this point, all of the hypotheses tested have measured US interests. The measures that are most likely to discriminate among US preferences and those of other G-5 countries are those that are not highly correlated across countries. Measures that are highly correlated are less able to provide sharp tests. The correlations across measures are presented in Table 9.4.

As noted in the previous chapter, bank exposure and UN voting provide weak discrimination among national interests because they are so highly correlated among the G-5 countries. Replications of the analysis of the duration of program suspensions using average bank exposure rates and average UN voting scores for the G-5 countries other than the United States – Japan, Germany, the United Kingdom and France – are qualitatively identical to the results presented above using US measures. Because the other G-5 countries vote

Table 9.5 *Effects of US vs. G-5 aid.*

	Substantive Effect	p
US Aid	−35.5%	0.03
Other G5 Aid	–	0.21

Dependent variable: Duration of program suspensions. Note: Change in the probability that a suspension continues for an additional month, with vulnerability one standard deviation above the mean and other variables at their means.

similarly to the United States, countries that vote similarly to the United States must also vote similarly to the other G-5 countries. Bank exposure to particular countries varies quantitatively across G-5 countries, but the other G-5 countries' banks are highly exposed to most of the same countries as US banks. There are some important regional variations, however: French banks are more highly invested in Africa, and Japanese banks are more highly invested in East Asia.

Foreign aid and alliances provide strong comparative tests of US versus G-5 control. Foreign aid correlations within the sample are quite low: the correlation with US foreign aid ranges from 0.12 for Britain to 0.29 for France. Replications substituting total aid from other G-5 countries for US aid find that the predicted pattern does not hold for aid donors other than the United States. The results are reported in Table 9.5. As noted above, US foreign aid has no statistically significant effect at average levels of vulnerability, but program suspensions shorten as aid recipients become more vulnerable to external financial shocks, and this effect is highly significant for the top third of the distribution of vulnerability. In contrast, aid from other G-5 countries is associated with a substantively marginal but statistically significant decrease in the length of program suspensions at average levels of vulnerability, but this effect becomes insignificant as vulnerability increases. Aid from other G-5 countries does not reduce the duration of program suspensions for the countries that have the strongest incentives to ask their patrons to lobby the Fund, which suggests that informal influence is generally limited to the United States.

Alliances reveal a similar pattern. As Table 9.4 indicated, S-scores for alliances with the United States are negatively correlated with S-scores for alliances with the other G-5 countries. The United States is allied with the other G-5 countries, of course, but the correlations reflect the fact that US alliance commitments are flung widely around the world, and do not generally coincide with those of even its closest allies. Results of replications of earlier models that substitute alliance portfolios of other G-5 countries for those of the United

Table 9.6 *Effects of US and G-5 alliances.*

	Substantive Effect	p
US Ally	−14.0%	0.04
UK Ally	−3.6%	0.67
French Ally	−3.1%	0.72
German Ally	−3.6%	0.67
Japanese Ally	50.0%	0.06

Dependent variable: Duration of program suspensions. Note: Vulnerability one standard deviation above the mean.

States are reported in Table 9.6. Table 9.6 reports the results of tests of the joint significance of alliance portfolios and their interactions with trade/GPD, debt service/exports, and short-term debt, evaluated at the means of the three vulnerability levels and at one standard deviation above the mean. The results for US alliances are calculated from the model reported in Table A.9.1, and the other results are calculated from analogous models that substitute the alliance portfolio of a different G-5 country and its interactions for the corresponding US variables. Only the US variables are statistically significant in the predicted direction. US alliances are marginally associated with reduced length of program suspensions at mean levels of financial vulnerability, and the effects become stronger and highly significant as vulnerability increases. In contrast, none of the other alliance portfolio measures is significantly associated with reduced duration of program suspensions. British, French and German alliance portfolios, furthermore, have weaker and less significant effects as vulnerability increases. Only Japanese alliance portfolios have any discernible effect, and their effect takes the opposite of the predicted direction.[15]

Discrimination between the hypotheses of US influence and G-5 influence becomes sharper when we turn to the analysis of waivers. Replications of the analysis of the number of waivers granted when programs are allowed to come back on track indicate that none of the statistically significant results survive when measures of US interests are replaced by analogous measures for the other G-5 countries. The results are summarized in Table 9.7.

In each case, the results presented replicate the models presented above, which also represent the ones that are most favorable for the hypothesis of G-5 influence. The models substituting total aid from Britain, France, Germany

[15] Since the Japanese alliance portfolio is sparse, and the US alliance portfolio is wide-ranging, the positive effect of Japanese alliances may simply be the mirror image of the US effect. Japanese and US alliance portfolios are correlated at −0.64.

Table 9.7 *Effects of Other G-5 interests on waivers.*

	High vulnerability		Mean vulnerability	
	Substantive Effect	p	Substantive Effect	p
G-5 Foreign Aid	−13.8%	0.40	−17.1%	0.03
G-5 Exports	16.7%	0.06	−4.0%	0.65

Negative binomial regressions. Vulnerability measures with positive interaction effects are one standard deviation above the mean, all other variables are at mean values. This is the case with the strongest result.

and Japan for US foreign aid do not approach statistical significance, although the results gradually move in the predicted direction as trade increases as a percentage of GDP. Exports do not discriminate as clearly between the US influence and G-5 influence hypotheses, because US exports and exports from the other G-5 countries are correlated ($r = 0.45$ for the set of program participants). However, the effects of US exports are substantially stronger and more significant. At high levels of vulnerability, total exports from Britain, France, Germany and Japan are estimated to have an effect that is in the same direction as the effect of US exports. The effect is only marginally significant, however, and the estimated effect of US exports is 4.6 times greater and highly significant.

In summary, these results support the hypothesis of US influence rather than the hypothesis of G-5 influence whenever the measures of national interests differentiate US interests from G-5 interests sufficiently clearly to permit a sharp test. For the analysis of the duration of program suspensions, the two measures of interests that allow a sharp comparative test of the hypothesis of US versus G-5 control, foreign aid and alliance portfolios, support the conclusion that the United States exercises disproportional informal influence over the duration of program suspensions. The results of replications using bank exposure and UN voting to measure interests are equally consistent with the interpretation that the G-5 exercise collective control over program suspensions and that the United States exercises sole control – the measures are simply too highly correlated to permit a comparative test of these hypotheses. The results for waivers follow a similar pattern. Replications replacing the two variables for which measures of US interests were found to have significant effects with parallel measures for G-5 countries – total aid and total exports from Britain, France, Germany and Japan – find much weaker effects of measures of G-5 interests. The results establish that US foreign aid is associated with the issuance of waivers, and foreign aid from other G-5 countries is not. G-5 exports had a marginally significant effect, but the substantive impact was much weaker than that of US exports. On balance, the evidence indicates that informal governance of the IMF is exercised by the United States, and that the role played by the other G-5 countries is marginal.

Cases: Russia and Argentina

Two cases serve to illustrate the mechanisms by which the United States exerts its informal influence over the enforcement of IMF programs, the ways in which US intervention depends upon the financial vulnerability of the borrowing country, and the diversity of motivations that the United States has for intervening on behalf of particular countries. The United States intervened extensively on behalf of both countries when they ran into difficulties with the IMF, but Russia and Argentina presented very different challenges to US policy makers. Russia played a critical role in the Clinton administration's foreign policy, as the most important former Communist country and the linchpin of a regional security strategy based on reassurance after the end of the Cold War. This is reflected in the fact that Russia was a substantial recipient of US foreign aid. At the height of its influence in Washington, in 1996, Russia received $416 million in US economic aid, or approximately two standard deviations more than the average country that participated in IMF programs during this period. Russia did not rate very highly on most of the other measures of US interests, however. Russia accounted for about 1 percent of foreign lending by US banks and $278 million in US exports, or about a quarter of a standard deviation above the mean on each variable, so economic interests provided only weak incentives for the United States to interfere in Russian relations with the IMF. Russia was about half of one standard deviation more supportive of US votes in the UN than average, and was half a standard deviation further from the United States' system of military alliances than the average country, so these strategic dimensions of US interests do not account for Russia's extraordinary treatment. Rather, Russia was important to US interests for the collection of strategic concerns that motivated US foreign aid, and this is captured in the statistical analysis.

On the other hand, Argentina has not been a substantial recipient of US foreign aid since the end of the Cold War, but has been a very important economic partner. Throughout the sample period, lending by US banks to Argentina averaged 4.5 percent of their total holdings of foreign assets, more than two standard deviations above the mean, and hovered between eight and nine percent of foreign assets between 1993 and 1996. Bank exposure declined from that high point but remained high relative to the sample, and Argentina became the most important emerging bond market by the year 2000. US exports to Argentina were consistently higher than to Russia, averaging $339 million per year, and reaching $417 million in 2001, or half a standard deviation above the mean. Argentina was more critical of US voting in the UN than Russia during most of the sample period, and was much more closely linked to the United States' network of military alliances – 1.7 standard deviations more closely than the average IMF program participant. Argentina's influence was based on its economic importance, particularly to US banks, on its close ties to other important US allies – particularly Brazil, Chile, Mexico, Spain and Italy – and on its skepticism towards US global leadership, which created an incentive for Washington to bolster sympathetic Argentine governments.

Russia

The failure to enforce conditionality in Russia has become emblematic of the broader IMF credibility problem. After the dissolution of the Soviet Union, Russia negotiated a Stand-By Agreement (SBA) in 1992, and no sooner was the ink dry on the agreement than the Central Bank of Russia tripled the money supply. Had Russia been an ordinary country, it would have been several years before the Fund tried to reengage – indeed, most of the mismanaged economies in the region, such as Ukraine and Bulgaria, had to wait – but the United States mobilized the G-7 to promote Russia's case, and the Executive Board created a new, low-conditionality facility, the Systemic Transformation Facility (STF), specifically designed to accommodate Russia. Russia received an STF in 1993 whose major condition was an inflation target of 7–9 percent per month. Despite the leniency of these conditions, which staff in the European II Department protested, Russia went off-track again, and the second disbursement of the STF was delayed; but again the United States pressed management for a waiver to allow the second disbursement to take place in 1994.[16] In the meantime, Russia's monetary policy had been tamed, but fiscal policy went off track, driven by weak tax collection and budgetary subsidies to enterprises.

After a collapse in the exchange rate in the fall of 1994, Russian policy makers forged a consensus around a new policy framework, which anchored monetary policy with an exchange rate band beginning in 1995. Russia and the IMF negotiated another SBA to accompany the new policy stance and incorporated the highly unusual precaution of requiring monthly monitoring of conditions.

[16] Interview with Hernandez-Cata, February 17, 1999, cited in Stone 2002.

For about nine months, Russia appeared to be implementing its conditions. Fiscal policy slipped out of control after the 1995 parliamentary elections, however, which President Yeltsin's supporters lost to representatives of the far left and far right of the political spectrum, and the budget deficit expanded rapidly during the presidential campaign in the spring of 1996. Meanwhile, Russia was negotiating with the IMF to replace its expiring stand-by with a three-year Extended Fund Facility (EFF), and President Clinton publicly urged that Russia's IMF support not be cut at the critical point.[17]

Looking backwards, it is hard to recapture the sense of crisis that reigned in the spring of 1996. The G-7 countries were convinced that Russia was at a turning point: if the Communist leader Gennadyi Zyuganov won the election, Russia's chances of consolidating democracy and market reform seemed lost. The dramatic fiscal expansion during the election campaign threatened a twin crisis on the exchange market and the market for government bonds (*Gosudarstvennye kratkosrochnye obligatsii*, or GKOs), and the Central Bank of Russia used hidden purchases of bonds and rubles to fend off the crisis. Under the circumstances, the Executive Board issued waivers covering Russian fiscal policy and debt, and the program was not suspended until the month after the election. Russian Central Bank officials believed that they had avoided a politically disastrous financial crisis by days in June and July 1996, while Yeltsin was hospitalized between the first and second rounds of the election.[18] There does not appear to have been any dissent within the G-7 about issuing these waivers; and although the board only learned later about the secret manipulation of Russian reserves that spring, it was fully aware that Russia was not abiding by the key conditions of its program. Nor was the IMF management unwilling to grant waivers in this case; even staff, which usually took a more orthodox stance on Russia than management, explained the decision in terms of geopolitics rather than macroeconomics.[19]

Had 1996 remained an exception, it might have been possible to avoid the financial crisis and partial default that occurred in August 1998. However, the program was suspended for only one month, and efforts to enforce conditionality throughout the rest of 1996 and 1997 were brief and inconsequential. In fact, although Russia's programs were suspended for non-compliance with key fiscal and monetary conditions once in 1995, three times in 1996, three times in 1997 and twice in 1998, these suspensions lasted only one or two months until the end of 1997. This accommodating stance prevented the IMF from exercising whatever leverage it had. Meanwhile, rapid capital inflows

17 *New York Times*. January 31, 1996: 1.
18 Interviews with Dubinin, Aleksashenko and Potemkin, cited in Stone 2002.
19 Interview with Horiguchi, November 8, 1999, cited in Stone 2002, 138–40.

temporarily reduced Russia's reliance on IMF financing and blunted the effects of program suspensions. Russia became a high-yield emerging market and conducted a rapid expansion of fiscal policy that was financed by capital inflows into the booming stock market and the market for GKOs. It was not until Russian markets felt the contagion effects of the Asian crisis at the end of 1997 that President Yeltsin began to understand the urgency of fiscal reform, by which time it was too late to avert the crisis. The IMF delayed one disbursement by three months in late 1997 and one by four months in early 1998, but rapidly reversed itself when the Russian bond market was seized by panic in May. The IMF rushed to negotiate a new package of reforms and financing, announcing that it would lend up to $11.2 billion to Russia in 1998 as part of a two-year package of support including the World Bank and bilateral lenders totaling $17.1 billion.

By the time the eleventh-hour rescue package was announced on July 20, 1998, however, market actors had drawn conclusions about the seriousness of Russian reform promises and the credibility of IMF conditionality in Russia. Although the package was unprecedented in size and contained a reform agenda of extraordinary breadth, it appeared to improve market conditions for only a few days. Key elements of the package, including budget cuts and tax increases, had to be pushed through by presidential decree because the Russian Duma refused to support them. Capital flight accelerated in early August in spite of frantic purchases of dollars by the Central Bank of Russia, and demand for government bonds vanished. Even at this late date, the IMF was prepared to consider another bail-out for Russia, and Stanley Fischer pitched the proposal in a conference call with the G-7 deputies. The origin of this proposal is unclear, but Fund insiders agree that it could not have been made without American support. The controversial July package had already strained the consensus in the G-7 to the breaking point, however, and the deputies, led by Germany, refused to be persuaded.[20]

On August 17 Russia ran out of funds, and the value of the ruble collapsed. Russian banks had taken advantage of interest rate differentials, borrowing heavily in dollars and lending in rubles, so the abandonment of the exchange rate band and the collapse of the bond market created a wave of insolvencies. The government and central bank declared a moratorium on debt service by private banks, and Yeltsin dismissed the government and the chairman of the central bank, ending Russia's last experiment with liberal politics.

[20] Interviews with IMF management and senior staff.

Argentina

Weak enforcement of conditionality was less obvious in the case of Argentina than in the case of Russia, but it was pervasive throughout Argentina's relationship with the IMF in the 1990s, and it laid the groundwork for the subsequent crisis.[21] Argentina's remarkably successful financial stabilization in the 1990s was based upon a currency board arrangement embodied in the Convertibility Law, which fixed the peso to the dollar at a one-to-one parity and obligated the Central Bank to hold reserves equal to base money. This was more rigid than Russia's exchange rate regime, but shared the same underlying weakness: fiscal deficits and expanding debt made the policy framework acutely vulnerable to shifts in market sentiment and unsustainable in the long run. Argentina consistently missed IMF targets for its fiscal deficit, and the debt grew from 29% of GDP in 1992 to 41% in 1998, and rose to 50% by 2000. Staff repeatedly voiced objections to the planned EFF for Argentina in 1996–8 because of its weak fiscal provisions, but management overruled these concerns, and the staff reports to the Executive Board did not disclose these objections.[22] Fund insiders regarded the level of Argentina's debt burden as barely sustainable even in the presence of the toughest economically feasible fiscal policy, and only as long as market perceptions remained favorable. It was high enough to lead to exploding debt dynamics – debt so high that debt service drives it steadily higher as a percentage of GDP – if market sentiment became unfavorable.[23]

Argentina failed to meet its targets under the EFF in 1997, and the program moved into a series of increasingly lengthy suspensions. However, continuing inflows of short-term capital financed Argentina's growing fiscal deficits and made it unnecessary for Argentina to draw on the IMF's resources – or to call on its shareholders to help unlock them. The burden of servicing the debt rapidly rose, from 4.9% of gross national income in 1996 to 9.9% in 2000, and this increased Argentina's vulnerability to sudden reversals of external financing. Market sentiment shifted in the fall of 2000, and it became clear that Argentina would be compelled to abandon its pegged exchange rate and would probably be forced into default if a major rescue package were not forthcoming. Argentina had been treating its IMF program as precautionary in 2000, but it turned to the Fund with a request to draw on the program and asked for a substantial augmentation in November. Argentina missed its target for the fiscal deficit in September, and would have missed the target for the December

21 Mussa 1998.

22 IEO 2004, 36. This assessment was confirmed in interviews with IMF officials involved in the negotiations.

23 Mussa 1998, 16–17.

review as well, had it not been modified. Staff was divided over whether it was advisable to expand the size of the loan facility under these circumstances, but management strongly supported the program at US urging. A key concern in 2000 was that a crisis in Argentina could easily spread to Brazil, perhaps leading to a repetition of the contagion effects recently experienced in the Asian crisis.[24] Nevertheless, the United States represented the lone voice strongly favoring the program in the G-7, and the other members deferred in spite of their reservations.[25]

Staff in the IMF's Western Hemisphere Department believed that this was Argentina's last chance. A substantial package of financial support was assembled and the conditions of the precautionary program were revised: fiscal conditions were loosened to accommodate the poor performance of the economy, but structural conditionality was increased in an effort to compensate. Staff believed that a failure to implement the program, and particularly to meet the fiscal conditions that had already been weakened, would make the crisis inevitable. The consensus view was that if the program went off-track after December 2000, the IMF should not extend itself further and Argentina should be allowed to fail.[26]

The program almost immediately went off-track. Two finance ministers and the central bank governor resigned in rapid succession, and Argentina missed its targets for the first quarter of 2001 for the federal fiscal deficit, the consolidated deficit of the public sector, the primary surplus, aggregate debt and short-term debt. The March review was delayed. At this point, the staff had serious misgivings, and the analysts closest to the front believed that the program should be suspended indefinitely. Short-term interest rates had jumped to 1,000 basis points above US Treasury bonds – to a level of about 14 percent – and the Argentine debt was no longer sustainable at those interest rates. In the context of a management decision to go forward, however, staff could not express a contrary view.[27] The staff report to the Executive Board for the May review used extraordinarily optimistic assumptions to build a case that the debt could still be sustainable, including growth rates that could not be attained at the current level of interest rates, primary surpluses (fiscal surpluses before debt service is included) that had not been reached even in the best years in the 1990s, and interest rates that were no longer being offered.[28] Misgivings

[24] There was no significant effect on Brazil when the crisis finally erupted a year later. However, it is possible that the breathing space of a year allowed enough creditors to unwind their positions to minimize the contagion effects.

[25] Blustein 2001, 101.

[26] Interviews with IMF staff members.

[27] IEO 2004.

[28] Mussa 1998, 77–81.

were raised in the Executive Board, particularly by the British alternate ED, but the decision to grant the waivers, further relax the conditions, and keep the program on track had been made informally at a higher level.[29]

The most controversial stage of the Argentine program came in August 2001, when the government requested an $8 billion augmentation (discussed in Chapter 7). At this point the program was effectively taken out of the IMF's hands by the US Treasury, which conducted negotiations with the Argentine government and won approval from skeptical members of the G-7.[30] Within the US government, Treasury was heavily lobbied by officials from the National Security Council and the Departments of State and Defense, who were in contact with their Argentine counterparts and emphasized that the collapse of the Argentine economy would have broader negative consequences for US policy in the region. The White House received calls from the presidents of Brazil, Chile and Mexico warning of the dire consequences for US influence in Latin America – and for the influence of the IMF – if Argentina did not receive emergency assistance. Argentina pulled out all the stops.

The most optimistic staff put the chance of success of the program at 20–30 percent at this point, and prominent voices including Kenneth Rogoff, the new head of the Research Department, were strongly opposed. However, none of this dissent was communicated to the Executive Board. A mission returned to Washington from Buenos Aires shortly before the proposal went to the board and brought back a pessimistic assessment of the unwillingness of provincial governors to go along with the new zero deficit law that was supposed to be the basis for meeting the program conditions in the fall. Although by September staff in the Western Hemisphere Department believed that the probability that the authorities would be able to implement the key fiscal target of the program was very low, they could not raise doubts of this nature without solid evidence. In communications with the Executive Board, the benefit of the doubt goes to the country authorities.[31] The Executive Board, meeting a week before September 11, 2001, passed the review of the Argentine program together with the augmentation, but the meeting was memorable for its unusual degree of open criticism and several pointed abstentions from the final vote.

In the case of Argentina, as in the case of Russia, the effect of a pattern of persistent non-enforcement of conditionality was that the sustainability of the foreign debt gradually deteriorated, and when the crisis came, the political

[29] Mr. Collins, the UK alternate ED, called for a "Plan B" in case the debt did not turn out to be sustainable and pointed out that "... the staff paper could have prepared a more in-depth analysis of the differences in the revised program from that agreed in January." Executive Board Minutes. EBM/01/53. May 21, 2001.

[30] Taylor 2007, 80–8; Blustein 2005, 145–51.

[31] Interviews with IMF staff.

system failed to respond. Far from tipping incentives in the direction of reform, the IMF weakened the incentives to come to grips with urgent problems. Argentina was no better able to reform its finances in September than it had been earlier in the year, and its policies failed to inspire confidence in the market. Capital flight accelerated in the fall; indeed, many observers inside and outside the Fund argued that IMF financing had simply provided a brief breathing space that allowed individuals and foreign financial institutions to withdraw their capital. The IMF had lost its credibility as an arbiter of sound policies, and as a predictable source of soft financing, it diluted market discipline. The collapse of the exchange rate, the banking system and the government followed in January, and Argentina went into default on its foreign debt. Riots forced the resignations of two presidents. The country moved into a deep recession, investors lost much of their wealth, and wages and employment dropped sharply.

Conclusions

Russia and Argentina are extreme cases because these were countries that were able to call on significant leverage with the United States and that found themselves in such dire circumstances that they were willing to cash in their influence. In short, they were textbook cases for the exercise of informal influence. They were not typical cases, but they provide ideal illustrations of the mechanisms and logical consequences of informal power. The IMF is subject to cross-pressures from its biggest shareholder that lead to inconsistent enforcement of conditionality and interfere with its mission as a guarantor of market stability. In extreme cases, the Fund has no credibility, conditionality becomes almost meaningless, and the IMF becomes no better than a captive – and at worst a facilitator – of the policies that run national economies into the ground. In both cases, the pressure to relax the enforcement of conditionality came unambiguously from the United States. US motivations were different in the two cases – in Russia primarily strategic, in Argentina primarily economic – but the logic of a coincidence of powerful US interests and intense interests in the borrowing country was the same.

Just as case studies are valuable for spelling out mechanisms and provide a weak basis for generalizing, statistical analysis is a powerful tool for generalizing and is poor at establishing causal mechanisms. The statistical analysis in this chapter demonstrates that the pattern of informal governance – the United States intervenes to relax enforcement in countries in which it has strong interests, but only when those countries perceive a strong interest in asking for US intervention – is consistent with the evidence of a global dataset. These tests are stronger than previous ones in the literature because the sample is global rather than regional, the data provide better measures of the key concepts, and the data contain controls for implementation and conditionality. The results are robust to alternative measures of US interests, alternative specifications, alternative methods, and two different dependent variables. The tests sharply discriminate the theoretical model of informal governance from alternative explanations, because the model predicts an interaction between US interests and borrower interests that is hard to account for with ad hoc explanations and that is unlikely to be due to omitted variables. US foreign aid, bank exposure, exports, UN voting and alliance patterns are all associated with weak enforcement of conditionality, but only when borrowing countries are vulnerable to sudden reversals of international financing.

Some of these tests also discriminate between the hypothesis of US influence and broader influence by the group of G-5 countries – including Japan, Germany, Great Britain and France as well as the United States – while others do not. Some of the variables measuring US interests, particularly UN voting and bank exposure, are highly correlated with measures for other G-5 countries, so it is impossible to distinguish effects of US interests from those of the other countries. Indeed, since some of these interests are common – the failure of a European bank affects the interests and stability of the US banking system, for example – it may be impossible in principle to determine where one country's interests end and another's begin. However, some of these tests, notably those involving US foreign aid and alliance patterns, strongly point to US influence and not to the influence of other leading members of the IMF Executive Board. When the statistical evidence is less clear, as in the case of economic interests, the historical record helps with interpretation. For example, several European countries had stronger economic interests than the United States in avoiding a default by Argentina, but it was the United States that pushed the IMF to continue lending when Argentina repeatedly missed its budget targets. Similarly, Germany was more highly exposed to default by Russia, but took a harder line on enforcing IMF conditions in Russia than the United States, particularly after 1996.

The evidence presented thus far indicates that informal influence is pervasive throughout the IMF product cycle, from decisions to provide access to Fund resources (Chapter 7) to the design of conditionality (Chapter 8) and on to the enforcement of conditionality reviewed in the present chapter. The statistical patterns at each stage are consistent with informal influence: countries that are important to US interests and vulnerable to reversals of external financing receive concessions from the IMF. Case studies illustrate the mechanisms by which the United States exercises influence at each stage, the motivations for doing so, and the consequences. Informal influence systematically weakens the incentives for the recipients of IMF financing to implement reform and prudent financial policies, and this imposes long-term costs because the United States has an interest in supporting the policies that the IMF promotes. The benefits to the United States of interfering in IMF governance are diverse, and are harder to measure than the costs, but appear to be compelling in the short term. The statistical evidence shows that the motivations involve foreign policy, economic interests and military security, and the case studies illustrate a wide range of reasons that operate in particular instances. The reasons are perhaps aptly described in the model as uniformly distributed temptations, however, because US foreign policy tends to be dominated by short-term objectives and election calendars rather than by long-term strategic planning.

10

Conclusions

This book began by setting out a theory of equilibrium institutions, which was organized around the concept of informal governance. Formal and informal governance represent alternative social choice mechanisms – the former based on voting and formal rules, the latter based on power and informal influence – and these two mechanisms coexist in international organizations. The choice of procedures that incentivize or delegitimate the use of informal power is a critical step in institutional design, and in equilibrium the mixture of these modes of governance in international organizations balances the power and interests of strong and weak states. Chapter 1 situated this argument in political theory, and Chapter 2 formalized it as a game-theoretic model.

The second part of the book explored the implications of this theory in three international organizations chosen for case studies: the IMF, the WTO and the EU. The cases demonstrated two propositions. The first proposition is that, in spite of the variety of issue areas, the varying memberships and the differing contexts in which these organizations operate, informal governance mechanisms play important roles in each. Formal rules are also important in each organization, but in each case, the functioning of the organization cannot adequately be understood without taking into account the many ways in which informal governance mechanisms modify or overrule the formal procedures. Scholars who study the EU and the WTO have devoted considerable attention to this phenomenon, but they have generally failed to connect the dots, because they have not appreciated that informal governance mechanisms exist primarily to serve the interests of powerful states, while formal rules are generally designed to protect the weak.

The second proposition to emerge from the case study chapters is that the balance between formal and informal governance varies substantially across international organizations in ways that are consistent with the expectations of the model. The model of informal governance generates comparative statics that relate the balance of formal and informal governance to the distribution of structural power (outside options and the externalities created by exit) and to the prevalence of temptations to override institutionally determined policy outcomes. When structural power is concentrated and temptations are infrequent, institutions that allow for substantial informal governance are chosen because they motivate the leading state to participate intensively, and the costs associated with informality are tolerable for the rest of the membership. Under these circumstances, institutions can be delegated substantial executive powers, and decision making can be consensual and non-transparent. On the other hand, as power becomes more dispersed or temptations become stronger, institutions must be formalized to reduce the abuse of power. Under these conditions, it is still possible for strong institutions to emerge in issue areas where cooperation is highly valuable, but they have to take relatively transparent, legalized forms. The locus of decision making shifts from the executive to the legislative arena, and the majority of delegated powers are judicial. If, on the other hand, cooperation is not valuable enough to induce powerful states to accept legal constraints, institutions will be weak when power is dispersed and temptations run high, and powerful countries will seek alternative means of accommodating their interests. These case studies are not intended as formal tests of the theory. Instead, their function is to determine how well the mechanism posited by the model fits empirical examples, to illustrate its usefulness in explaining important institutional variations, and to assess its applicability to organizations other than the IMF. The cases suggest that not only can the static differences between the IMF, the WTO and the EU be broadly explained by the model, but so can the ways in which various issues are handled within each organization and the broad shifts in the powers and competencies of each organization over time.

The third section of the book was more rigorous, and used a combination of quantitative analysis and qualitative research to test hypotheses drawn from the model in the context of IMF lending. According to the model, informal governance is exerted sporadically, when the interests of powerful countries are directly engaged, and it is used to make exceptions to formal rules. In the case of the IMF, exceptions to rules are generally beneficial to borrowers, rather than to creditors, and powerful countries are creditors. Waiving the rules can be beneficial to the United States, however, if this makes it possible to provide support for a valued ally, or if the borrowing country offers concessions to the United States in return. It is difficult to measure these concessions directly, but the theory implies that informal influence is exercised when US interests in a country and borrower interest in a loan are simultaneously intense.

The model does not specify why particular countries are important to US policy; in fact, it represents these motivations as a random variable, suggesting that they cannot be perfectly predicted. Consequently, this study uses five variables to proxy US interests that capture a wide range of possible motivations for the United States to exercise informal influence: US foreign aid, US bank exposure, US exports, affinity for US voting patterns in the UN General Assembly and alliance patterns. Similarly, although I cannot directly observe the urgency of the borrower's need for financing, it is possible to measure variables that make countries likely to need IMF assistance, and therefore more willing to make concessions in order to obtain it. This study employs three dimensions of vulnerability to sudden reversals of capital flows: trade openness, debt service as a percentage of exports and short-term debt as a percentage of total debt. Countries that have open economies, are highly leveraged, and depend upon continued access to capital markets to roll-over short-term credits are vulnerable to international financial shocks. The theory predicts that informal governance will be exercised, and the rules will be waived, when countries that are important to the United States have significant external vulnerabilities that make them willing to cooperate with US objectives.

Three chapters examine successive stages of the IMF product cycle and find remarkably robust evidence of informal governance. Chapter 7 investigates access to Fund resources and finds that two of the US interest variables, bank exposure and exports, are strongly associated with larger loans as a percentage of IMF quotas, but only when borrowers are unusually vulnerable. Chapter 8 uses IMF records of conditionality to construct a variable measuring the substantive scope of conditionality, and finds that all five interest variables are associated with reduced conditionality, but again these results obtain only in the presence of substantial vulnerability. Chapter 9 measures enforcement of IMF programs in two ways: the duration of program suspensions when programs go "off-track" because countries fail to comply with their conditions, and the number of waivers of conditionality the IMF grants when a program comes back into good standing after a suspension. The evidence shows that all five measures of US interests are associated with reductions in the rigor of program enforcement, but again these effects are conditional: they appear only when countries are unusually vulnerable to external financial shocks. Each of these chapters draws on country cases drawn from a set of particularly important recent crises to illustrate the mechanisms of informal governance.

The case studies – Mexico (1995), Korea (1997), Indonesia (1997), Russia (1998), and Argentina (2001) – were not discussed systematically, so before returning to the book's broader themes, this chapter briefly returns to a discussion of the five crisis cases and the reasons for the shortcomings of IMF performance. Each program had specific shortcomings, and problems arose at each stage of the IMF product cycle, but the underlying mechanism was the same. In each case, informal governance allowed the United States to insert its preferences into the process of program design and implementation, ultimately undermining the credibility of the IMF. Although the forms of intervention appear idiosyncratic in the context of the individual case studies, each type of US intervention that emerges in the case studies is consistent with a strong pattern of quantitative evidence presented in one of the previous chapters.

Five crises and IMF performance

A quarter century ago, Williamson summarized the charges of the IMF's critics as including a doctrinaire adherence to free markets, insensitivity to individual country conditions, and the overriding of national sovereignty.[1] The Fund continues to be criticized for ignoring borrowers' domestic political constraints and applying one-size-fits-all policy prescriptions without sensitivity to context.[2] Especially following the Asian crisis, the IMF was faulted for conditionality that sought to control too many policy variables, many of which extended beyond its traditional areas of competence;[3] moreover, it was claimed, such conditionality did not promote growth and may have damaged economic performance.[4] Sympathetic insiders and the Fund itself have conceded that conditionality may have been superficially implemented as a consequence, requiring a shift to greater "ownership" of reform by country authorities and "streamlining" of its content.[5] The analysis of this book suggests that these criticisms, although justified in some cases, fail to identify the central obstacle to improving IMF performance, which is informal power. The most serious concern posed by delegating powers to international organizations is not that they will pursue autonomous agendas, but that they will be captured by the most powerful state in the system. Likewise, the shortcomings of IMF programs are generally related to politically motivated inconsistencies in design and implementation.

The five crisis cases demonstrate some important common features as well

1 Williamson 1983.

2 Meltzer 2000; Easterly 2001; Stiglitz 2002.

3 Feldstein 1998; Hills *et al.* 1999; Goldstein 2001.

4 Feldstein 1998. An extreme example of the proliferation of conditions is the program introduced in Ukraine on the eve of its financial collapse in 1998, which contained 227 prior actions and performance criteria. Goldstein (2001) judged conditionality to have been excessively intrusive during the Asian crisis. Based on their conclusion that IMF-supported programs are associated with lower GDP growth rates, Przeworski and Vreeland (2000) inferred that lending is conditioned on inappropriate policy measures.

5 Khan and Sharma (2001) and Drazen (2002) call for greater ownership, and IMF (2005) introduced the initiative to streamline conditionality.

Table 10.1 *Summary of the five crisis cases.*

	Mexico 2/1/95	Indonesia 11/5/97	Korea 12/3/97	Russia 7/20/98	Argentina 3/10/00
Use of Fund Resources:					
Billion USD	$17.8	$10.0	$21.0	$13.8	$14.0
percent of quota	679	490	1938	425	800
Surveillance failures:					
Reserve levels	Gross reserves		Usable reserves	Gross reserves	
Banking Sector		Non-performing loans	Short-term foreign liabilities		
Conditionality:					
Fiscal balance (% GDP)	0.50	1.00	0.00	−5.70	−2.40
Structural benchmarks	14	63	15	82	30
Waivers:					
Previous program	0	NA	NA	19	1
Crisis program	7	7	1	2	5
Structural compliance	NA	73%	87%	NA	58%
External sector:					
Exchange rate regime	Managed float	Managed float	Managed float	Band	Currency board
Devaluation					
after one month	16.8%	27.5%	45.6%	26.7%	0.0%
after six months	8.1%	188.5%	1.9%	262.3%	295.0%

Source: IEO 2003, 2004; MONA; letters of intent; staff reports; PINs; IFS.

as significant variations. The United States, in particular, played different roles in the various cases that reflected different US interests. In addition, the way in which informal consultations took place evolved over time, in part in response to the crises themselves, and in part because of leadership changes at the Fund and in the US government. These variations highlight the fact that the Fund's informal governance is a moving target. Summary indicators of the five cases are presented in Table 10.1.

Ordinary IMF programs do not excite controversy, and each of these five cases did, but most of the action took place outside of the Executive Board. The Mexican case was unique in that EDs representing two G-7 countries abstained from the vote to approve the program, and in subsequent cases the management and the US Treasury were careful to avoid a repetition of this experience by engaging in prior consultations at a higher level. Conference calls including all of the G-7 deputy finance ministers (the "G-7 deputies") became an informal institution. Left out of the G-7, EDs representing small European countries were free to express critical opinions, and two abstained from the vote on the last-minute augmentation of the Argentine program in September 2001. Other EDs would have liked to do the same, but were instructed to vote in favor of the management proposal by their governments.[6] The Russian rescue in 1998 was a similar case in which several of the EDs were unenthusiastic, but in this case there were no abstentions. Focusing on variations in outcomes on the Executive Board, however, would both overstate the differences among the cases and understate the degree of disagreement that prevailed about all of them, because the Board was not the forum in which the real decisions were made.

An important element of variation across the five cases was the attitude taken by the United States: in several cases (Mexico, Russia, Argentina) the United States pushed the skeptical membership to extend Fund support, but in the Korean and Indonesian cases it put the brakes on a more ambitious bailout using bilateral contributions. The degree of US influence was not related to variations in how its preferences related to the formal voting rules, which is consistent with the argument that US influence does not depend upon threats to actually resort to a vote. In particular, US influence does not appear to have depended on whether the United States sought a bigger or smaller loan package, or whether it held a credible veto threat; it was decisive regardless.

Nevertheless, the style and modalities of US influence varied significantly. The partnership between Larry Summers at the US Treasury and Stanley Fischer as First Deputy Managing Director of the IMF worked very smoothly, indeed almost seamlessly during the Clinton administration. As a result, it was often difficult, even with the use of documents and participant interviews, to tell where US policy ended and management strategy began. In contrast, the IMF had a much less congenial relationship with the O'Neill Treasury in the early part of the George W. Bush administration. O'Neill and Taylor initially disengaged from the Fund and criticized it for engaging in ill-conceived bailouts, but then scrambled to take over the management of the Argentina program, and in places insisted on a strategy that the Fund regarded as incoherent.[7] Their policy towards the Fund was more similar to the Summers policy in substance than in style, however, and the difficulty of saying no to Argentina induced them to drop many of their early rhetorical differences. The Bush administration demonstrated that the United States was still powerful enough to exert substantial control over the IMF even without finesse and sophistication, but also that the effectiveness of informal governance depends on these qualities. The Clinton administration was no less guilty of abusing US power, but

[6] Interviews with former and present IMF EDs.

[7] Interviews with IMF staff, senior staff, and management.

it did so more subtly, because it understood much better that American power rests largely on consensus, and that the usefulness of international organizations as instruments depends on their legitimacy.

Although the substance of conditionality tends to be delegated to the Fund, there are variations across the cases, and particular G-7 governments became more intensely involved in some countries than in others. In each of the crisis cases, where US preferences clashed with those of other members – as in the case of structural conditionality in Indonesia and Korea, or in the case of supporting the Argentine currency board arrangement in 2001 – US preferences prevailed. In most cases, however, US preferences did not differ significantly from those of other G-7 countries or from the strategy preferred by the Fund, so the degree of influence that the United States exerted over outcomes is more difficult to ascertain. The variation in the breadth of structural conditionality across the crisis cases depended mainly upon the timing of the program – structural conditionality was at its height during 1997 and 1998 – and the conditions of the case at hand. Brazil and Argentina had straightforward fiscal and exchange rate problems, so far-reaching structural reforms did not seem to be called for. (Most of the structural conditionality in the Argentine program, for example, was related to taxation or expenditures.) On the other hand, particular conditions were routinely included in programs because they suited leading shareholders, and the country that exerted the overwhelming influence in the crisis cases was the United States.

Major rescue packages failed to reverse the erosion of market confidence in four of the five cases considered here. Only the program for Mexico succeeded in rapidly restoring confidence in the financial system. In part, this success was due to timing: a significant depreciation of the peso had already occurred before the program was initiated, while each of the other countries suffered dramatic devaluations while under IMF programs. In part the stabilization of the Mexican economy reflected the credibility of the bilateral US guarantee, however, which reflected a much deeper commitment than the United States was willing to make in any of the other cases. In three cases, Indonesia, Russia and Argentina, repeated rescue efforts failed, and financial markets did not respond to infusions of official support. In each case, it was clear to market participants that the government was not committed to a credible reform program with real prospects of success, and that the IMF lacked the credibility to enforce its conditionality. In Korea, the first program failed to restore confidence, leading to a dramatic collapse of the national currency and all of the damage that this can cause to the domestic financial system. It was only after the G-10 central banks adopted plans for coordinated rescheduling of commercial bank debt that the flight from the currency was stemmed. Similar approaches would not have been feasible in the other cases, however, because bank exposure represented less significant shares of indebtedness in the other countries. In the case of Mexico, sufficient financing was provided to meet short-term demands for foreign currency, and confidence returned; in the other cases, IMF lending was predicated on the assumption that it would catalyze private-sector participation. This assumption consistently proved to be false.

The fact that IMF lending to countries with systemic importance fails to generate catalytic effects that mobilize private capital flows is a symptom of the damage that informal influence does to IMF credibility. Catalytic effects could arise if market participants learned something new when they observed an IMF program. The new information might be about liquidity; but in these large crises, IMF rescue packages were anticipated and priced into the already depreciating value of assets, and provided no new information. Alternatively, catalytic effects might arise because IMF programs promised credible economic reforms; but credible reforms require credible enforcement of conditionality, and countries that are important to key shareholders are routinely able to circumvent arduous or politically risky conditionality. Whenever performance was poor in important countries, enforcement was weak. A growing body of research indicates that IMF lending generally does not have catalytic effects, and the governance of the Fund during crises may be an important element in the explanation.[8] Only bank lending responds strongly to IMF lending, and only when the G-7 countries coordinate efforts to coerce their banks to refinance their loans to support an IMF program.[9] The fact that catalytic effects do not follow major rescue packages undercuts the core of the IMF strategy for dealing with these crises.

The most consistent pattern across the five cases is the failure of surveillance, whether in the form of Article IV consultations or in the form of monitoring of conditionality, to identify risks of systemic crises in time to contain them, or to candidly assess the risks of proposed lending. Although the Fund has assimilated numerous lessons from the experiences of the five crises reviewed here, most of which have been articulated by outside observers – the emphases on better data standards, more transparency, streamlined conditionality, an exceptional access framework, contingent credit lines, and proposals for new frameworks for dealing with sovereign debt – it has not come to grips with the fundamental governance problems that make the Executive Board an

[8] This literature is reviewed in Steinwand and Stone 2008. See Bird and Rowlands 2002; Eichengreen *et al.* 2006; Jensen 2004. Bird and Rowlands find catalytic effects in middle-income countries but negative effects in their full sample; Mody and Saravia (2006) find lower bond spreads under a program for countries with mid-levels of reserves, but higher spreads for those with low- and high-reserve coverage.

[9] Gould 2006; Copelovitch 2010.

ineffective locus for surveillance. An important part of the problem is that the secrecy that surrounds IMF decision making makes it difficult to hold the institution or particular individuals inside or outside the Fund accountable for the roles they played during crisis management. The Fund has greatly increased the number of documents that it makes public in recent years, but information on the details of its decision making is not disclosed to the outside world or distributed within the organization, and this undermines its ability to learn from its own experience. This is not accidental; it is an essential feature of the informality and non-transparency of IMF governance.

The trade-off between autonomy and legitimacy dominates proposals to reform the IMF and to redistribute voting shares among its members, but the debate is inadequately informed by historical evidence and empirical data. The evidence suggests that the dangers of an autonomous IMF have been greatly overstated, and that the limitations on the Fund's autonomy are a more serious concern. The Fund typically exercises autonomy, but that autonomy can be revoked when the United States exercises its informal influence over the process of program design and implementation. This intervention distorts the application of conditionality and contributes to the IMF's credibility problems. The consequences of informal governance are a loss of credibility and transparency.

As one IMF insider told me, "If they ever succeed in reforming this institution, it will become irrelevant." The model of informal governance suggests that the balance of formal and informal governance is an equilibrium outcome, which reflects the distribution of power and interests among the membership. Under both Republican and Democratic administrations, the United States has found the IMF to be a remarkably valuable instrument of foreign policy, and it has not perceived a need for fundamental reforms that would make it less malleable. Attempts by the rest of the membership to carry out reform could reduce the willingness of the United States to invest authority in the IMF, making the institution less valuable to the broader membership. The degree of buy-in by the main shareholders is already a scarce resource, as the Korean crisis demonstrated in 1997. As a practical constraint, decision making must represent those who are able to provide official financing and who have access to the private financial institutions most likely to help resolve crises.

Legitimacy, crisis and change

The model of informal governance offers an explanation, then, for the puzzle of why the membership has refused for so long to reform IMF procedures to improve institutional performance, in spite of the fact that IMF insiders and officials representing the shareholders understand the ways in which informality undermines their common interests. However, the model also sets out the conditions under which meaningful reform can occur. The model suggested that power and legitimacy interact in precise ways, and traces out the implications of two kinds of change. First, a change in US interests can have far-reaching consequences that undermine the legitimacy of institutions. If the US temptation to intervene in an organization increases, this leads other countries to raise the barriers to informal influence by reforming internal procedures and increasing the transparency of decision making. The United States responds by exercising informal influence less frequently, because the cost of doing so publicly is prohibitive in all but the most urgent circumstances. In the long run, however, this causes the United States to reduce its commitment to the organization, and this may lead to institutional decline as other countries find the organization correspondingly less valuable.

This seems an apt description of the situation that prevailed on the eve of the global financial crisis of 2008, and in that sense the informal governance model offers an explanation for the crisis of legitimacy that the IMF was widely believed to face at the time. The United States had overplayed its hand over the previous fifteen years in a series of high-profile cases involving Mexico, Russia, Ukraine, Indonesia, Korea, Brazil, Argentina and Turkey. Many of these missteps took place in phases of IMF programs other than the design of conditionality – for example, in the cases of Mexico and Korea, the amount of access to IMF resources was critical. In the cases of Russia, Ukraine, Argentina and Turkey, US pressure led the IMF to relax the enforcement of conditionality, which provided temporary relief to unstable governments, but ultimately caused these countries' economic policies to fail. Meanwhile, although borrowing governments appreciated US help managing the Fund, resentment grew over the political and economic quid pro quos that the United States extracted in return. Furthermore, in the wake of the terrorist attacks of September 11, 2001, US foreign policy focused single-mindedly on the Middle East and put low priority on developments elsewhere. International institutions, including the IMF and the World Bank, were increasingly viewed as instruments of that policy, and the priority of defense policy overrode considerations of building long-term communities of interest. Under the administration of George W. Bush, unilateralism replaced multilateralism as a basic feature of US policy.

As a consequence of these developments, countries that were able to exit the IMF-sponsored insurance regime chose to do so, and self-insured against international financial risks by undervaluing their exchange rates and accumulating international reserves.[10] This was costly for these countries, tying up hundreds of billions of dollars that could have been used for investment in unproductive financial assets and transferring a substantial percentage of GDP to the United States in the form of seigniorage. In addition, this defensive strategy fueled the macroeconomic imbalances that helped to create the crisis that followed in the United States. Meanwhile, the Fund found itself virtually without customers, and since the interest it charges on its loans finances its operations, it announced plans in early 2008 to cut its payroll by 10 percent. For the United States, the consequence of the IMF's unpopularity was the loss of a convenient conduit of influence. The abuse of informal governance procedures tends to undermine the legitimacy of international institutions, and the exploitation of asymmetric interdependence tends to lead to its erosion. For the international system, the consequence of the IMF's legitimacy crisis was the weakening of a key advocate for open markets, economic reform and financial stability.

The perception of legitimacy problems within the Fund led to widespread calls for reform before the 2008 crisis. The Fund's public rhetoric acknowledged the legitimacy problem and for the first time adopted the view that the IMF itself had to be reformed, and the Executive Board adopted a number of documents designed to address these concerns. None of these has so far touched the fundamental issues of the role of the strong management and weak Executive Board, but they did lead to some procedural changes in the handling of confidential information and the publishing of letters of intent. In 2009, the Executive Board approved far-reaching changes in the treatment of secret documents, which may have the effect of finally increasing the transparency of IMF decision making. In addition, in order to shore up the legitimacy of the institution, formal vote shares and quotas were reapportioned in 2008. Table 10.2 summarizes the most significant changes. These changes do not correct the mismatch between the distribution of IMF quotas and the distribution of financial power in the world economy, although they move in that direction, but they do shift vote shares on the Executive Board away from the United States and its closest allies.

The second mechanism that the model identifies that can lead to reform of institutions is that change in the structural power of the United States affects the balance of formal and informal governance. For example, if outside options become less attractive to the United States, other countries will become less willing to accommodate US interests in order to induce US participation in multilateral institutions. As a result, barriers to informal influence will rise, which will cause the United States to exercise its influence over common

[10] Stone 2009c.

Table 10.2 *Changes in IMF quotas, 2008.*

Top Ten: Increasing Shares	Change	Quota	*Top Ten: Decreasing Shares*	Change	Quota
China	0.88	3.81	United Kingdom	−0.64	4.29
Korea	0.61	1.36	France	−0.64	4.29
India	0.42	2.34	Saudi Arabia	−0.41	2.80
Brazil	0.31	1.72	Canada	−0.37	2.56
Mexico	0.27	1.47	Russia	−0.35	2.39
Spain	0.22	1.63	Netherlands	−0.30	2.08
Singapore	0.18	0.59	United States	−0.29	16.73
Turkey	0.15	0.61	Belgium	−0.26	1.86
Ireland	0.13	0.53	Switzerland	−0.19	1.40
Japan	0.12	6.23	Australia	−0.18	1.31

Source: IMF website, www.imf.org. The table displays country quotas as percentages of total quotas.

policies less frequently. Conversely, as US power declines and the institutions become more formalized, the rest of the membership will find participation in common institutions more valuable.

Whether US structural power is in decline is a hotly debated subject, and answers will generally depend upon definitions that are normatively loaded. Certainly, political scientists and historians have been mistaken when they forecast imminent US decline in the past.[11] US global military preeminence at the beginning of the twenty-first century is without historical parallel. US influence in the former Soviet bloc and in areas that were contested spheres of influence during the Cold War has increased vastly, and the current overextension of the US military in two wars in the Middle East is a symptom of the fact that there is no longer a formidable rival that can deter US military adventures. US per capita income has not quite kept pace with America's closest rivals, increasing 43% since 1984, as compared to 45% in Europe and 47% in Japan, but US per capita income remains 1.4 times that of Europe and 1.3 times that of Japan. Record fiscal and trade deficits are troubling and unsustainable in the long run, as the crisis of 2008 demonstrated, but the ability of the United States to run these deficits for so long also demonstrated the extraordinary strength of the US economy.

For the purpose of understanding the effect of changing power on international governance, the definition of structural power provided by the model of informal governance may shed light on this debate. In this model, structural power consists of the attractiveness of exit options and the severity of the

[11] Kennedy 1987; Keohane 1984.

externalities that non-participation by the United States imposes on other countries. This definition is issue specific, and decline in these terms does not necessarily imply a decrease in the US standard of living or of US military capabilities. It is clear in these terms that US structural power has declined steadily in the trade arena since its high point after World War Two, when the United States accounted for the majority of world trade. The recovery of other developed countries and economic growth in the developing world, which have been so essential to American prosperity in the ensuing decades, guaranteed that other countries would obtain trade leverage of their own and challenge US domination of the trading system. This transition occurred decades ago with respect to Europe and Japan and led to a deepening of international cooperation, and the growing weight of developing countries since the conclusion of the Uruguay Round is likely to lead eventually to additional liberalization of trade in agriculture.

Gauging decline in the area of international finance is considerably more difficult. Certainly, US dominance of finance declined sharply in the 1950s as other major economies recovered, the dollar shortage eased, and demand emerged for other currencies. Japan emerged as a major financial power by the early 1980s, and China has become a significant financial force – albeit one without a fully convertible currency – in the new century. On one hand, record US current account deficits have made it possible for China and Japan to accumulate trillions of dollars in reserve assets, and on the other, their policies of buying large quantities of dollars in order to depress their currencies have produced and financed those deficits. These resources make them significant players in the international financial system, which has gradually been acknowledged, in each case after significant delays, in their shares of IMF quotas and vote shares. The rise of Asian countries has been matched by the relative decline in the economic weight of European countries, however, so the United States remains underrepresented in IMF quotas as a share of world trade or world GDP.

The financial crisis of 2008 has been widely hailed as a sign of the failure of the US economic model and as a harbinger – or perhaps a cause – of a precipitous US decline. Several considerations argue against such interpretations. First, the US economy remains the most innovative and flexible in the world, with unmatched human capital and deeper financial markets than any potential rival. The decline of any particular economic sector does not change this, and the shift of the US economy away from manufacturing and towards services is a sign of flexibility and adaptation to new opportunities rather than of underlying weakness. Second, the crisis itself revealed indications of significant US financial strength. As chaos descended on Wall Street, there was a sharp

Table 10.3 *Foreign exchange market turnover by currency pair.*

	2001			2004			2007		
	Amount	%	Cum.	Amount	%	Cum.	Amount	%	Cum.
US/euro	354	30	30	503	28	28	840	27	27
US/yen	231	20	50	298	17	45	397	13	40
US/sterling	125	11	61	248	14	59	361	12	52
US/Australian	47	4	65	98	5	64	175	6	58
US/Swiss	57	5	70	78	4	68	143	5	63
US/Canadian	50	4	74	71	4	72	115	4	67
US/Swedish			74			72	56	2	69
US/other	195	17	91	295	16	88	572	19	88
Euro/yen	30	3		51	3		70	2	
Euro/sterling	24	2		43	2		64	2	
Euro/Swiss	12	1		26	1		54	2	
Euro/other	21	2		39	2		112	4	
Other pairs	26	2		42	2		122	4	
All pairs	1,173	100		1,794	100		3,081	100	

Daily averages in April, in billions of US dollars and percentages. *Source*: Bank for International Settlements. *Triennial Central Bank Survey*. December 2007: 10, Table B.5, and author calculations.

increase in demand for US Treasury bills, as frightened foreign investors rushed to find safe investments. This, in turn, fueled a short-term rise in the nominal value of the dollar. The US Federal Reserve responded to the crisis not by limiting foreign lending, but by drastically expanding access to US dollars for other central banks, because it rightly calculated that the impact of any crisis in the United States would be more destabilizing to other countries' currencies than to its own. In any other country, a run on domestic financial institutions causes a run on government debt and a collapse of confidence in the currency. In the United States, the most serious crisis of confidence in the financial sector and the stock market since 1929 had the opposite effect, because the US dollar enjoys the status of the world's reserve currency.

The dollar has this special status for a variety of reasons, but the best indicator of the dollar's central role is its dominance in foreign currency transactions. The most recent comprehensive data come from the Bank for International Settlements, which conducts a multilateral data-collection exercise every three years. The pertinent data are displayed in Table 10.3.

If the dollar lost its role as the world reserve currency, this would lead to a precipitous decline in US financial importance and structural power. However, this could only occur if a more attractive alternative arose. The introduction of the euro in 1999 created the first challenger to the dollar's hegemonic position in international finance. The euro appears unlikely to displace the dollar, however, because of internal difficulties within Europe that create uncertainty and regulatory regimes that have prevented the emergence of a unified European financial market, or even of national markets with depth comparable to that of the United States. Uncertainty remains substantial because members of the euro zone retain independent fiscal authority, and the European Stability and Growth Pact is unenforceable (see Chapter 6). The emergence of a crisis of confidence in Greece in 2010, which quickly spread to Portugal, Spain and Italy, was a symptom of the underlying problem that threatened to tear the euro zone apart. The key conclusion to draw from the data in Table 10.3 is that as currency transactions dramatically rose in the first decade of the new century, the US dollar share of those transactions remained steady, and in fact gained relative to the euro. By 2007, transactions involving trades of dollars amounted to 88 percent of all currency transactions. This is significant both as a symptom of the centrality of the dollar to the international trade and finance systems, and as a cause of the dollar's continued stability due to network effects.[12] The dollar is at the center of a network of transactions, so currency traders can make transactions involving dollars more inexpensively than transactions involving other currencies. The dollar has a position in the network analogous to the hub of a wheel: it is involved in trades between the other currencies, and as a result retains the cost advantage that gives it a central position. Other factors reinforce this centrality, such as the US economy's role as a major import market, the depth of US financial markets that make dollars a desirable currency for investors, and the choices of central bankers around the world to hold dollars as a reserve currency.

As the crisis gathered steam and became truly global in 2008 and early 2009, it imparted a shock to the system of global financial governance. After several years of declining demand for IMF loans, countries across Eastern Europe scrambled for financial support. IMF resources had not kept pace with inflation over the previous several decades, and had steadily declined as a percentage of world trade or of global financial transactions, and concerns rose that the capacity of the IMF to lend might be insufficient to meet the demand, particularly if a major country needed support. The exogenous increase in the value of cooperation represented by a global crisis spurred the G-20 countries to agree in April 2009 to triple the size of IMF resources by expanding an IMF borrowing facility called the New Arrangements to Borrow (NAB) by 500 billion dollars (Table 10.4). The way in which this was done is significant. The alternative to

[12] Cohen 1998.

Table 10.4 *G-20 commitments to the New Arrangements to Borrow (NAB).*

	Amount	Commitment Date
Japan	100.0	2/13/2009
European Union	178.0	9/4/2009
Norway	4.5	3/28/2009
Canada	10.0	4/3/2009
Switzerland	10.0	4/8/2009
United States	100.0	6/18/2009
Korea	10.0	5/4/2009
Australia	5.7	5/12/2009
Russia	10.0	5/27/2009
China	50.0	6/9/2009
Brazil	10.0	6/10/2009
India	10.0	9/5/2009
Singapore	1.5	9/8/2009
Chile	1.6	9/24/2009
Total:	501.3	

Billion US dollars. *Source*: IMF website, www.imf.org.

lending money to the IMF was to expand IMF quotas, but expanding quotas in a way that was proportional to the new commitments to the NAB would have shifted voting power in the institution dramatically, giving substantially increased shares to Japan, China, Brazil, Korea and India. Instead, G-20 members expanded their credit lines to the IMF, but agreed to review quotas again by 2011.

After decades of resistance, the IMF seems to be headed towards significant reform, either because US misbehavior makes the status quo intolerable for the other powers or because the relative decline of US structural power makes them less inclined to defer to US interests. Whether the net effect is to weaken or strengthen the IMF, however, depends on the outcome of the race between US decline and US misbehavior. If the United States resists the temptation to abuse its informal power while US structural power declines, the effect will be to increase participation in the multilateral regime as it becomes more formalized. On the other hand, if unilateralism precedes structural decline, the net effect of reforming the IMF will be to cause the United States to disengage, leading to a general decline in participation in the institution.

Institutions and the legitimacy of cooperation

This book has set out a theory that contends that international organizations can best be understood as the product of the rational calculations of the leaders of states, which have conflicting interests and unequal power resources. Cooperation is generally possible if it is valuable enough to the participants, but the terms under which it takes place depend upon how power and interests are distributed. To the extent that the leading state has attractive outside options and its participation is important to the other states in the system, they will be compelled to defer to its preferences over institutional design. However, to the extent that other states have attractive alternatives, the leading state will have to accommodate their interests as well if it regards their participation as desirable. In principle, a variety of exchanges could be made that would balance the interests of strong and weak states, but the only credible trade-off is one that allows strong countries to deviate from cooperation when their interests are intense – because they cannot commit not to do so – and transfers an extra share of authority in ordinary times to the rest of the membership to compensate. Informal governance, then, is for the benefit of powerful countries, and it allows powerful countries to avoid outcomes that they could not commit to tolerating. Lesser powers give tacit consent to informal channels of influence because they find the formal rules of the institution advantageous enough that they benefit on average from participating as long as the informal mechanisms are not abused.

This account of international organization has three broad implications.

First, the theory explains the variety of international organizations. The fundamental intuition is that institutional design balances the participation constraints of strong and weak countries. As a consequence, the balance that is struck between formal and informal governance in any particular institution depends on the distribution of issue-specific power and the issue-specific temptations that arise to overrule common policies. Alternative explanations for institutional design that focus on transaction costs are less persuasive, because they fail to provide a role either for power or for conflict of interest. While transaction costs surely explain some elements of institutional design, institutions are not generally efficient or Pareto optimal. The evidence presented here suggests that the most important elements of institutional design are explained by the distribution of power.

Second, the theory provides an account of the normative aspects of international governance. International organizations are legitimate in the narrow sense that they are subject to the consent of self-interested states, or the elites that control them, and that these states would not participate if rational calculations did not indicate that they would benefit in expectation. States consent explicitly to institutional rules and implicitly to informal procedures, and the institutions of the international system constrain their behavior in important ways and provide the menu from which many of their strategies are drawn. States have identified extensive areas of common interest, and most of these issues are governed by international organizations. The international system is not, therefore, well characterized by conventional notions of anarchy. As is true of all institutions, however, international organizations internalize elements of anarchy, in the sense that outside options are reflected in the informal governance procedures that define how the formal rules function in practice. International cooperation is negotiated, and the bargaining depends on the resources and outside options that states bring to the table.

Third, the theory provides a systematic explanation for the characteristic dysfunctions of international organizations. Powerful states delegate authority to international institutions, but they do so in ways that allow them to retain substantial degrees of control. Influential states manipulate the rules, insist on privileged treatment for their own interests, and exploit their control of the agenda, and these strategies undermine the ability of institutions to provide effective international governance. The results are that international institutions suffer from credibility problems, that progress in forging new cooperative projects is slow, and that cooperation in many areas is blocked by the entrenched interests of founding members. These problems appear to be an inescapable consequence of the fact that international organizations exist in a system of states with unequal resources. However, there are important variations among institutions, and some of the major institutions of the international system have changed dramatically in recent decades, becoming more formalized as they have taken on new competencies. The evidence appears to support the theoretical prediction that international governance improves when the distribution of power becomes more egalitarian. This is a hopeful sign, from the vantage point of the early twenty-first century, as we anticipate the gradual decline of US power and the rise of numerous competing power centers.

Appendix: additional tables

Table A.7.1 *Effects of US influence on commitments of IMF resources.*

	US aid		Bank Exposure		Exports		UN Voting		Alliances	
	Coef. / *Std. Err.*	p	*Coef.* / *Std. Err.*	p	*Coef.* / *Std. Err.*	p	*Coef.* / *Std. Err.*	p	*Coef.* / *Std. Err.*	p
US Influence	−0.0011	0.14	−25.01	0.01	−0.0022	0.00	−0.0959	0.76	−0.3743	0.59
	0.0007		*9.52*		*0.0006*		*0.3099*		*0.6973*	
Interactions with:										
Trade/GDP	1.2×10^{-5}	0.29	2.6×10^{-1}	0.01	1.1×10^{-5}	0.08	−0.0028	0.40	−0.0094	0.21
	1.2×10^{-5}		1.0×10^{-1}		6.4×10^{-6}		*0.0033*		*0.0074*	
Debt Service/ Exports	-9.3×10^{-6}	0.31	2.6×10^{-1}	0.09	1.5×10^{-5}	0.04	0.0152	0.09	0.0230	0.02
	9.2×10^{-6}		1.5×10^{-1}		7.0×10^{-6}		*0.0089*		*0.0100*	
Short-term Debt	2.2×10^{-5}	0.57	7.2×10^{-1}	0.03	7.3×10^{-5}	0.00	−0.0018	0.87	0.0124	0.58
	3.8×10^{-5}		3.2×10^{-1}		1.2×10^{-5}		*0.0108*		*0.0225*	
Control variables:										
Trade/GDP	0.0006	0.63	0.0004	0.73	0.0003	0.77	0.0013	0.27	0.0047	0.17
	0.0012		*0.0011*		*0.0011*		*0.0012*		*0.0034*	
Debt Service/ Exports	0.0065	0.01	0.0063	0.00	0.0056	0.00	0.0092	0.00	−0.0050	0.33
	0.0023		*0.0020*		*0.0020*		*0.0029*		*0.0052*	
Short-term Debt	0.0007	0.85	−0.0015	0.65	−0.0024	0.47	0.0025	0.52	−0.0030	0.78
	0.0038		*0.0034*		*0.0034*		*0.0039*		*0.0111*	
Current Account	-1.5×10^{-5}	0.66	2.1×10^{-5}	0.67	-1.3×10^{-5}	0.80	-3.3×10^{-5}	0.33	1.2×10^{-5}	0.74
	3.4×10^{-5}		4.8×10^{-5}		5.3×10^{-5}		3.4×10^{-5}		3.7×10^{-5}	
Total Debt	1.4×10^{-5}	0.00	8.8×10^{-6}	0.00	1.2×10^{-5}	0.00	1.3×10^{-5}	0.00	1.2×10^{-5}	0.00
	1.9×10^{-6}		2.2×10^{-6}		2.2×10^{-6}		1.8×10^{-6}		1.8×10^{-6}	
⋮	⋮	⋮	⋮	⋮	⋮	⋮	⋮	⋮	⋮	⋮
Observations	351		351		351		350		351	
R^2	0.31		0.36		0.38		0.30		0.31	

Table A.7.1 *Effects of US influence on commitments of IMF resources (cont.).*

	US aid		Bank Exposure		Exports		UN Voting		Alliances	
	Coef. *Std. Err.*	p	*Coef.* *Std. Err.*	p	*Coef.* *Std. Err.*	p	*Coef.* *Std. Err.*	p	*Coef.* *Std. Err.*	p
⋮	⋮	⋮	⋮	⋮	⋮	⋮	⋮	⋮	⋮	⋮
Budget Balance/ GDP	−0.0278	0.01	−0.0358	0.00	−0.0347	0.00	−0.0279	0.01	−0.0315	0.00
	0.0103		*0.0098*		*0.0096*		*0.0104*		*0.0103*	
Time Under IMF Prog	−0.3527	0.00	−0.3286	0.00	−0.2935	0.01	−0.3989	0.00	−0.3798	0.00
	0.1155		*0.1104*		*0.1089*		*0.1156*		*0.1142*	
Foreign Debt/ GDP	-2.9×10^{-11}	0.87	-4.0×10^{-11}	0.81	-2.7×10^{-11}	0.87	-2.7×10^{-11}	0.88	-1.6×10^{-11}	0.93
	1.7×10^{-10}		1.6×10^{-10}		1.6×10^{-10}		1.7×10^{-10}		1.7×10^{-10}	
Reserves/GDP	0.0006	0.85	0.0010	0.77	0.0007	0.83	0.0006	0.86	0.0006	0.86
	0.0034		*0.0033*		*0.0032*		*0.0035*		*0.0035*	
GDP per capita	-2.1×10^{-6}	0.93	-6.6×10^{-6}	0.79	-2.0×10^{-5}	0.38	3.6×10^{-6}	0.89	1.2×10^{-6}	0.97
	2.5×10^{-5}		2.5×10^{-5}		2.3×10^{-5}		2.5×10^{-5}		2.7×10^{-5}	
Polity	−0.0217	0.00	−0.0191	0.00	−0.0186	0.00	−0.0205	0.00	−0.0174	0.02
	0.0064		*0.0062*		*0.0060*		*0.0065*		*0.0072*	
Devaluation	−0.0045	0.22	−0.0053	0.11	−0.0051	0.12	−0.0035	0.32	−0.0071	0.04
	0.0036		*0.0033*		*0.0032*		*0.0036*		*0.0035*	
Missing Data	−0.0039	0.99	0.2253	0.43	0.2124	0.45	0.1985	0.52	−0.0567	0.85
	0.2931		*0.2845*		*0.2782*		*0.3090*		*0.2943*	
Constant	−0.4036	0.00	−0.4118	0.00	−0.3871	0.00	−0.5314	0.00	−0.2500	0.44
	0.1322		*0.1204*		*0.1186*		*0.1308*		*0.3206*	
Observations	351		351		351		350		351	
R^2	0.31		0.36		0.38		0.30		0.31	

Note: The dependent variable is the natural logarithm of the ratio of IMF commitments to IMF quotas. OLS estimates. Standard errors in italics.

Table A.8.3 *US influence over the scope of conditionality.*

	Coef. *Std. Err.*	*p*	*Coef.* *Std. Err.*	*p*	*Coef.* *Std. Err.*	*p*	*Coef.* *Std. Err.*	*p*	*Coef.* *Std. Err.*	*p*
US aid	0.0009	0.00								
	0.0003									
U.S bank exposure			5.4161	0.04						
			2.6731							
US exports					0.0006	0.00				
					0.0002					
UN voting (S-US)							−0.2886	0.00		
							0.0979			
US alliance portfolio									0.4642	0.03
									0.2169	
Interactions with:										
Trade/GDP	-9.1×10^{-6}	0.01	−0.1040	0.00	-6.8×10^{-6}	0.00	0.0011	0.22	−0.0087	0.00
	3.5×10^{-6}		*0.0294*		2.0×10^{-6}		*0.0009*		*0.0021*	
Debt service/exports	-2.5×10^{-5}	0.00	−0.0821	0.01	-6.1×10^{-6}	0.00	0.0125	0.00	−0.0171	0.00
	8.3×10^{-6}		*0.0326*		1.7×10^{-6}		*0.0030*		*0.0032*	
Short-term debt	-3.6×10^{-5}	0.03	0.1586	0.12	-4.8×10^{-7}	0.88	0.0036	0.46	0.0150	0.04
	1.6×10^{-5}		*0.1016*		3.1×10^{-6}		*0.0048*		*0.0073*	
Control variables:										
Democracy	−0.0173	0.00	−0.0180	0.00	−0.0174	0.00	−0.0173	0.00	−0.0133	0.00
	0.0019		*0.0019*		*0.0019*		*0.0019*		*0.0021*	
Sub-Saharan Africa	−0.2430	0.00	−0.2259	0.00	−0.2164	0.00	−0.2225	0.00	−0.2473	0.00
	0.0242		*0.0239*		*0.0239*		*0.0240*		*0.0249*	
GDP per capita	-2.3×10^{-5}	0.00	-1.9×10^{-5}	0.01	-1.1×10^{-5}	0.12	-1.4×10^{-5}	0.04	-9.2×10^{-6}	0.16
	6.9×10^{-6}		7.1×10^{-6}		7.0×10^{-6}		6.7×10^{-6}		6.5×10^{-6}	
Missing scale	−0.1165	0.15	−0.1289	0.12	−0.1078	0.19	−0.0475	0.57	−0.1542	0.06
	0.0816		*0.0820*		*0.0819*		*0.0840*		*0.0819*	
Trade/GDP	−0.0001	0.69	0.0001	0.79	0.0002	0.59	−0.0003	0.34	0.0033	0.00
	0.0003		*0.0003*		*0.0003*		*0.0003*		*0.0010*	
Debt service/exports	−0.0003	0.67	−0.0003	0.73	−0.0002	0.79	0.0008	0.32	0.0081	0.00
	0.0007		*0.0008*		*0.0008*		*0.0008*		*0.0018*	
Short-term debt	−0.0038	0.12	−0.0061	0.01	−0.0058	0.01	−0.0049	0.07	−0.0129	0.00
	0.0025		*0.0024*		*0.0023*		*0.0027*		*0.0042*	
Short-term debt^2	0.0001	0.01	0.0001	0.00	0.0001	0.00	0.0001	0.06	0.0001	0.00
	3.9×10^{-5}		3.9×10^{-5}		3.9×10^{-5}		5.5×10^{-5}		3.9×10^{-5}	
⋮	⋮	⋮	⋮	⋮	⋮	⋮	⋮	⋮	⋮	⋮
$\ln(\alpha)$	−2.8484		−2.8386		−2.8351		−2.8608		−2.9089	
	0.1121		*0.1115*		*0.1112*		*0.1136*		*0.1174*	
α	0.0579		0.0585		0.0587		0.0572		0.0545	
	0.0065		*0.0065*		*0.0065*		*0.0065*		*0.0064*	
Observations	2823		2823		2823		2794		2823	

Table A.8.3 *US influence over the scope of conditionality (cont.).*

	Coef. *Std. Err.*	*p*	*Coef.* *Std. Err.*	*p*	*Coef.* *Std. Err.*	*p*	*Coef.* *Std. Err.*	*p*	*Coef.* *Std. Err.*	*p*
⋮	⋮	⋮	⋮	⋮	⋮	⋮	⋮	⋮	⋮	⋮
Left-Right Scale	0.0151	0.01	0.0108	0.06	0.0120	0.03	0.0133	0.02	0.0108	0.05
	0.0055		*0.0056*		*0.0056*		*0.0055*		*0.0056*	
Extended Program	0.1673	0.00	0.1105	0.00	0.1148	0.00	0.1269	0.00	0.0965	0.00
	0.0271		*0.0263*		*0.0259*		*0.0254*		*0.0256*	
Low Income Program	−0.0559	0.07	−0.0012	0.97	0.0075	0.80	−0.0041	0.89	0.0180	0.54
	0.0311		*0.0296*		*0.0294*		*0.0293*		*0.0291*	
Year	0.0193	0.00	0.0206	0.00	0.0196	0.00	0.0180	0.00	0.0194	0.00
	0.0046		*0.0046*		*0.0046*		*0.0047*		*0.0046*	
Number under	−0.0027	0.04	−0.0015	0.26	−0.0016	0.23	−0.0018	0.17	−0.0018	0.17
	0.0013		*0.0013*		*0.0013*		*0.0013*		*0.0013*	
Program duration	−0.0004	0.49	−0.0007	0.20	−0.0005	0.37	−0.0005	0.35	−0.0004	0.52
	0.0006		*0.0006*		*0.0005*		*0.0005*		*0.0006*	
Time to legis election	−0.0007	0.17	−0.0007	0.17	−0.0008	0.15	−0.0007	0.17	−0.0006	0.28
	0.0005		*0.0005*		*0.0005*		*0.0005*		*0.0005*	
Coalition members	−0.0248	0.00	−0.0219	0.00	−0.0212	0.00	−0.0216	0.00	−0.0272	0.00
	0.0047		*0.0047*		*0.0047*		*0.0047*		*0.0047*	
Presidential system	−0.0751	0.00	−0.0970	0.00	−0.0962	0.00	−0.0962	0.00	−0.0964	0.00
	0.0244		*0.0244*		*0.0243*		*0.0248*		*0.0250*	
Seats supporting gov't	0.0410	0.27	0.0273	0.46	0.0290	0.43	0.0259	0.49	0.0540	0.15
	0.0368		*0.0367*		*0.0367*		*0.0371*		*0.0370*	
Poor standing	−0.0383	0.29	−0.0361	0.33	−0.0426	0.24	−0.0506	0.17	−0.0590	0.10
	0.0365		*0.0370*		*0.0365*		*0.0366*		*0.0362*	
Constant	−36.3180	0.00	−38.9990	0.00	−36.8672	0.00	−33.7391	0.00	−36.6781	0.00
	9.1548		*9.2126*		*9.1782*		*9.2506*		*9.1083*	
$\ln(\alpha)$	−2.8484		−2.8386		−2.8351		−2.8608		−2.9089	
	0.1121		*0.1115*		*0.1112*		*0.1136*		*0.1174*	
α	0.0579		0.0585		0.0587		0.0572		0.0545	
	0.0065		*0.0065*		*0.0065*		*0.0065*		*0.0064*	
Observations	2823		2823		2823		2794		2823	

Negative binomial regression. Note: Standard errors in italics.

Table A.8.5 *Influence of other G-5 countries over the scope of conditionality.*

	Coef. *Std. Err.*	p	*Coef.* *Std. Err.*	p	*Coef.* *Std. Err.*	p
Total foreign aid	-4.6×10^{-5}	0.72				
	1.3×10^{-4}					
Average bank exposure			6.6001	0.11		
			4.1251			
Total exports					0.0001	0.61
					0.0001	
Interactions with:						
Trade/GDP	-3.1×10^{-6}	0.13	−0.2128	0.00	-2.4×10^{-6}	0.10
	2.1×10^{-6}		*0.0542*		1.4×10^{-6}	
Debt service/exports	1.6×10^{-5}	0.00	−0.0512	0.52	-2.7×10^{-6}	0.13
	5.0×10^{-6}		*0.0787*		1.8×10^{-6}	
Short-term debt	-3.9×10^{-6}	0.60	0.2863	0.07	1.3×10^{-6}	0.70
	7.5×10^{-6}		*0.1593*		3.3×10^{-6}	
Control variables:						
Democracy	−0.0166	0.00	−0.0183	0.00	−0.0174	0.00
	0.0019		*0.0019*		*0.0019*	
Sub-Saharan Africa	−0.2193	0.00	−0.2253	0.00	−0.2273	0.00
	0.0237		*0.0239*		*0.0240*	
GDP per capita	-1.1×10^{-5}	0.11	-1.3×10^{-5}	0.06	-1.8×10^{-6}	0.81
	6.6×10^{-6}		7.1×10^{-6}		7.2×10^{-6}	
Missing scale	−0.1198	0.14	−0.1467	0.07	−0.1364	0.09
	0.0816		*0.0816*		*0.0815*	
Trade/GDP	0.0001	0.87	4.6×10^{-5}	0.89	-4.8×10^{-5}	0.89
	0.0003		3.2×10^{-4}		3.3×10^{-4}	
Debt service/exports	−0.0021	0.01	−0.0009	0.25	−0.0004	0.67
	0.0008		*0.0008*		*0.0009*	
Short-term debt	−0.0049	0.05	−0.0050	0.04	−0.0042	0.07
	0.0025		*0.0024*		*0.0024*	
Short-term debt^2	1.1×10^{-4}	0.01	0.0001	0.01	9.4×10^{-5}	0.02
	4.0×10^{-5}		*0.0000*		3.9×10^{-5}	
⋮	⋮	⋮	⋮	⋮	⋮	⋮
$\ln(\alpha)$	−2.8459		−2.8480		−2.8531	
	0.1122		*0.1122*		*0.1126*	
α	0.0581		0.0580		0.0577	
	0.0065		*0.0065*		*0.0065*	
Observations	2823		2823		2823	

Table A.8.5 *Influence of other G-5 countries over the scope of conditionality (cont.).*

	Coef. *Std. Err.*	*p*	*Coef.* *Std. Err.*	*p*	*Coef.* *Std. Err.*	*p*
⋮	⋮	⋮	⋮	⋮	⋮	⋮
Left-Right Scale	0.0133	0.02	0.0121	0.03	0.0110	0.05
	0.0055		*0.0056*		*0.0056*	
Extended Program	0.1297	0.00	0.1222	0.00	0.1180	0.00
	0.0255		*0.0260*		*0.0259*	
Low Income Program	−0.0128	0.66	−0.0096	0.75	−0.0086	0.77
	0.0292		*0.0297*		*0.0301*	
Year	0.0182	0.00	0.0195	0.00	0.0212	0.00
	0.0046		*0.0046*		*0.0046*	
Number under	−0.0014	0.29	−0.0012	0.36	−0.0015	0.26
	0.0013		*0.0013*		*0.0013*	
Program duration	−0.0002	0.71	−0.0006	0.26	−0.0004	0.50
	0.0006		*0.0006*		*0.0005*	
Time to legis elections	−0.0008	0.13	−0.0009	0.10	−0.0008	0.13
	0.0005		*0.0005*		*0.0005*	
Coalition members	−0.0223	0.00	−0.0209	0.00	−0.0210	0.00
	0.0047		*0.0047*		*0.0047*	
Presidential system	−0.0752	0.00	−0.0963	0.00	−0.0970	0.00
	0.0250		*0.0240*		*0.0239*	
Seats supporting gov't	0.0326	0.38	0.0132	0.72	0.0144	0.70
	0.0367		*0.0367*		*0.0366*	
Poor standing	−0.0553	0.13	−0.0555	0.14	−0.0590	0.11
	0.0367		*0.0371*		*0.0365*	
Constant	−34.0766	0.00	−36.6271	0.00	−40.1586	0.00
	9.0673		*9.1563*		*9.2250*	
$\ln(\alpha)$	−2.8459		−2.8480		−2.8531	
	0.1122		*0.1122*		*0.1126*	
α	0.0581		0.0580		0.0577	
	0.0065		*0.0065*		*0.0065*	
Observations	2823		2823		2823	

Negative binomial regression. Note: Standard errors in italics.

Table A.8.7 *G-5 influence over conditionality – UN voting.*

	UK		France		Germany		Japan	
	Coef. *Std. Err.*	*p*	*Coef.* *Std. Err.*	*p*	*Coef.* *Std. Err.*	*p*	*Coef.* *Std. Err.*	*p*
UN voting	−0.1215	0.36	−0.1770	0.27	−0.1755	0.27	−0.0363	0.87
	0.1313		*0.1587*		*0.1597*		*0.2232*	
Interactions with:								
Trade/GDP	0.0020	0.11	0.0027	0.06	0.0046	0.00	0.0056	0.01
	0.0012		*0.0014*		*0.0015*		*0.0021*	
Debt service/exports	0.0056	0.11	0.0121	0.01	0.0127	0.00	0.0100	0.10
	0.0034		*0.0043*		*0.0042*		*0.0060*	
Short-term debt	−0.0087	0.09	−0.0082	0.17	−0.0129	0.03	−0.0274	0.01
	0.0051		*0.0060*		*0.0058*		*0.0098*	
Control variables:								
Democracy	−0.0173	0.00	−0.0177	0.00	−0.0182	0.00	−0.0179	0.00
	0.0019		*0.0019*		*0.0019*		*0.0020*	
Sub-Saharan Africa	−0.2072	0.00	−0.2076	0.00	−0.2032	0.00	−0.1989	0.00
	0.0240		*0.0241*		*0.0241*		*0.0240*	
GDP per capita	-1.2×10^{-5}	0.08	-1.6×10^{-5}	0.02	-2.0×10^{-5}	0.00	-1.4×10^{-5}	0.04
	6.9×10^{-6}		6.8×10^{-6}		6.8×10^{-6}		7.1×10^{-6}	
Missing scale	−0.0917	0.27	−0.0968	0.24	−0.1025	0.21	−0.1208	0.14
	0.0824		*0.0820*		*0.0814*		*0.0819*	
Trade/GDP	−0.0012	0.07	−0.0019	0.03	−0.0035	0.00	−0.0044	0.00
	0.0007		*0.0009*		*0.0010*		*0.0015*	
Debt service/exports	−0.0034	0.03	−0.0069	0.00	−0.0084	0.00	−0.0076	0.06
	0.0016		*0.0022*		*0.0026*		*0.0041*	
Short-term debt	−0.0026	0.35	−0.0013	0.71	0.0033	0.40	0.0125	0.04
	0.0028		*0.0034*		*0.0039*		*0.0062*	
Short-term debt^2	0.0002	0.00	0.0002	0.00	0.0002	0.00	0.0002	0.00
	0.0001		*0.0001*		*0.0000*		*0.0000*	
⋮	⋮	⋮	⋮	⋮	⋮	⋮	⋮	⋮
$\ln(\alpha)$	−2.8409		−2.8562		−2.8852		−2.8727	
	0.1120		*0.1132*		*0.1156*		*0.1146*	
α	0.0584		0.0575		0.0558		0.0565	
	0.0065		*0.0065*		*0.0065*		*0.0065*	
Observations	2794		2794		2794		2794	

Table A.8.7 *G-5 influence over conditionality – UN voting (cont.).*

	UK		France		Germany		Japan	
	Coef. *Std. Err.*	p	*Coef.* *Std. Err.*	p	*Coef.* *Std. Err.*	p	*Coef.* *Std. Err.*	p
⋮	⋮	⋮	⋮	⋮	⋮	⋮	⋮	⋮
Left-Right Scale	0.0137	0.01	0.0131	0.02	0.0138	0.01	0.0133	0.02
	0.0056		*0.0056*		*0.0055*		*0.0055*	
Extended Program	0.1284	0.00	0.1308	0.00	0.1342	0.00	0.1302	0.00
	0.0256		*0.0255*		*0.0254*		*0.0255*	
Low Income Program	0.0033	0.91	0.0012	0.97	0.0003	0.99	0.0025	0.93
	0.0295		*0.0294*		*0.0292*		*0.0296*	
Year	0.0164	0.00	0.0158	0.00	0.0172	0.00	0.0153	0.00
	0.0047		*0.0046*		*0.0046*		*0.0046*	
Number under	−0.0015	0.27	−0.0018	0.17	−0.0022	0.10	−0.0017	0.21
	0.0013		*0.0013*		*0.0013*		*0.0013*	
Program duration	−0.0004	0.43	−0.0004	0.42	−0.0003	0.54	−0.0004	0.48
	0.0006		*0.0006*		*0.0005*		*0.0005*	
Time to legislative election	−0.0006	0.27	−0.0006	0.25	−0.0005	0.33	−0.0005	0.33
	0.0005		*0.0005*		*0.0005*		*0.0005*	
No. coalition members	−0.0235	0.00	−0.0232	0.00	−0.0238	0.00	−0.0260	0.00
	0.0047		*0.0047*		*0.0047*		*0.0047*	
Presidential system	−0.0969	0.00	−0.0809	0.00	−0.0647	0.01	−0.0881	0.00
	0.0255		*0.0256*		*0.0260*		*0.0249*	
Seats supporting gov't	0.0158	0.68	0.0277	0.47	0.0429	0.26	0.0407	0.29
	0.0379		*0.0379*		*0.0377*		*0.0382*	
Poor standing	−0.0462	0.21	−0.0484	0.19	−0.0556	0.13	−0.0495	0.18
	0.0369		*0.0368*		*0.0366*		*0.0366*	
Constant	−30.4354	0.00	−29.2057	0.00	−31.9019	0.00	−28.2937	0.00
	9.4217		*9.1822*		*9.1688*		*9.2275*	
$\ln(\alpha)$	−2.8409		−2.8562		−2.8852		−2.8727	
	0.1120		*0.1132*		*0.1156*		*0.1146*	
α	0.0584		0.0575		0.0558		0.0565	
	0.0065		*0.0065*		*0.0065*		*0.0065*	
Observations	2794		2794		2794		2794	

Negative binomial regression. Note: Standard errors in italics.

Table A.8.8 *G-5 influence over conditionality – alliances.*

	UK		France		Germany		Japan	
	Coef. *Std. Err.*	*p*	*Coef.* *Std. Err.*	*p*	*Coef.* *Std. Err.*	*p*	*Coef.* *Std. Err.*	*p*
Alliances	−0.5458 *0.3027*	0.07	−0.5387 *0.3025*	0.08	−0.5507 *0.3030*	0.07	−0.8589 *0.2980*	0.00
Interactions with:								
Trade/GDP	0.0026 *0.0029*	0.36	0.0027 *0.0029*	0.35	0.0026 *0.0029*	0.36	0.0056 *0.0028*	0.04
Debt service/exports	0.0313 *0.0049*	0.00	0.0312 *0.0049*	0.00	0.0311 *0.0049*	0.00	0.0350 *0.0051*	0.00
Short-term debt	−0.0331 *0.0092*	0.00	−0.0336 *0.0092*	0.00	−0.0326 *0.0092*	0.00	−0.0177 *0.0091*	0.05
Control variables:								
Democracy	−0.0186 *0.0020*	0.00	−0.0186 *0.0020*	0.00	−0.0186 *0.0020*	0.00	−0.0180 *0.0020*	0.00
Sub-Saharan Africa	−0.2228 *0.0242*	0.00	−0.2228 *0.0242*	0.00	−0.2224 *0.0242*	0.00	−0.2344 *0.0245*	0.00
GDP per capita	-6.2×10^{-6} 6.7×10^{-6}	0.36	-6.2×10^{-6} 6.7×10^{-6}	0.36	-6.2×10^{-6} 6.7×10^{-6}	0.36	-5.6×10^{-6} 6.6×10^{-6}	0.40
Missing scale	−0.0818 *0.0808*	0.31	−0.0816 *0.0807*	0.31	−0.0822 *0.0808*	0.31	−0.0699 *0.0809*	0.39
Trade/GDP	−0.0017 *0.0021*	0.41	−0.0017 *0.0021*	0.41	−0.0017 *0.0021*	0.42	−0.0050 *0.0025*	0.05
Debt service/exports	−0.0209 *0.0032*	0.00	−0.0204 *0.0032*	0.00	−0.0208 *0.0032*	0.00	−0.0286 *0.0042*	0.00
Short-term debt	0.0133 *0.0066*	0.04	0.0131 *0.0065*	0.04	0.0129 *0.0066*	0.05	0.0061 *0.0078*	0.44
Short-term debt^2	0.0002 *0.0000*	0.00	0.0002 *0.0000*	0.00	0.0002 *0.0000*	0.00	0.0002 *0.0000*	0.00
⋮	⋮	⋮	⋮	⋮	⋮	⋮	⋮	⋮
$\ln(\alpha)$	−2.9007 *0.1169*		−2.9007 *0.1169*		−2.8992 *0.1168*		−2.9001 *0.1170*	
α	0.0550 *0.0064*		0.0550 *0.0064*		0.0551 *0.0064*		0.0550 *0.0064*	
Observations	2823		2823		2823		2823	

Table A.8.8 *G-5 influence over conditionality – alliances (cont.).*

	UK		France		Germany		Japan	
	Coef. *Std. Err.*	p	*Coef.* *Std. Err.*	p	*Coef.* *Std. Err.*	p	*Coef.* *Std. Err.*	p
⋮	⋮	⋮	⋮	⋮	⋮	⋮	⋮	⋮
Left-Right Scale	0.0099	0.07	0.0099	0.07	0.0099	0.07	0.0098	0.08
	0.0055		*0.0055*		*0.0055*		*0.0056*	
Extended Program	0.1208	0.00	0.1206	0.00	0.1208	0.00	0.1201	0.00
	0.0254		*0.0253*		*0.0254*		*0.0253*	
Low Income Program	0.0081	0.78	0.0080	0.78	0.0079	0.79	0.0116	0.69
	0.0290		*0.0290*		*0.0290*		*0.0290*	
Year	0.0185	0.00	0.0185	0.00	0.0185	0.00	0.0188	0.00
	0.0046		*0.0046*		*0.0046*		*0.0046*	
Number under	−0.0017	0.19	−0.0017	0.19	−0.0017	0.19	−0.0017	0.19
	0.0013		*0.0013*		*0.0013*		*0.0013*	
Program duration	0.0002	0.77	0.0002	0.77	0.0002	0.77	0.0001	0.82
	0.0006		*0.0006*		*0.0006*		*0.0006*	
Time to legislative election	−0.0008	0.16	−0.0008	0.16	−0.0008	0.16	−0.0007	0.17
	0.0005		*0.0005*		*0.0005*		*0.0005*	
No. coalition members	−0.0213	0.00	−0.0213	0.00	−0.0213	0.00	−0.0226	0.00
	0.0046		*0.0046*		*0.0046*		*0.0047*	
Presidential system	−0.1153	0.00	−0.1154	0.00	−0.1161	0.00	−0.0975	0.00
	0.0279		*0.0278*		*0.0279*		*0.0272*	
Seats supporting gov't	0.0135	0.72	0.0126	0.73	0.0134	0.72	0.0298	0.42
	0.0369		*0.0369*		*0.0369*		*0.0372*	
Poor standing	−0.0774	0.03	−0.0780	0.03	−0.0772	0.03	−0.0734	0.04
	0.0365		*0.0365*		*0.0365*		*0.0364*	
Constant	−34.3452	0.00	−34.3600	0.00	−34.3350	0.00	−34.4591	0.00
	9.0654		*9.0644*		*9.0674*		*9.0962*	
$\ln(\alpha)$	−2.9007		−2.9007		−2.8992		−2.9001	
	0.1169		*0.1169*		*0.1168*		*0.1170*	
α	0.0550		0.0550		0.0551		0.0550	
	0.0064		*0.0064*		*0.0064*		*0.0064*	
Observations	2823		2823		2823		2823	

Negative binomial regression. Note: Standard errors in italics.

Table A.9.1 *Duration of program interruptions.*

	Haz. Ratio	*p*	*Haz. Ratio*	*p*	*Haz. Ratio*	*p*	*Haz. Ratio*	*p*	*Haz. Ratio*	*p*
Unmet conditions	0.77494	0.00	0.77633	0.00	0.77646	0.00	0.78396	0.00	0.78067	0.00
	0.01980		*0.02003*		*0.02010*		*0.02025*		*0.02039*	
Scope of conditions	1.07802	0.00	1.08183	0.00	1.08345	0.00	1.07880	0.00	1.08477	0.00
	0.01598		*0.01611*		*0.01618*		*0.01616*		*0.01662*	
US aid	0.99522	0.00								
	0.00167									
U.S bank exposure			3.6×10^5	0.29						
			4.4×10^6							
US exports					0.99880	0.18				
					0.00089					
UN voting (S-US)							3.90066	0.00		
							1.75808			
US alliance portfolio									1.24201	0.85
									1.45390	
Interactions with:										
Trade/GDP	1.00002	0.30	1.14447	0.35	1.00001	0.27	0.99054	0.04	0.99733	0.80
	0.00002		*0.16593*		*0.00001*		*0.00458*		*0.01049*	
Debt service/exports	1.00009	0.11	1.04745	0.73	1.00002	0.05	0.95270	0.00	1.02286	0.15
	0.00006		*0.13796*		*0.00001*		*0.01338*		*0.01611*	
Short-term debt	1.00020	0.02	0.53971	0.24	1.00000	0.96	0.96763	0.20	1.06691	0.11
	0.00008		*0.28187*		*0.00002*		*0.02496*		*0.04261*	
Control variables:										
⋮	⋮	⋮	⋮	⋮	⋮	⋮	⋮	⋮	⋮	⋮
$\ln(\rho)$	0.38294	0.00	0.37105	0.00	0.36929	0.00	0.37607	0.00	0.37292	0.00
	0.02471		*0.02441*		*0.02448*		*0.02466*		*0.02466*	
Observations	3401		3401		3401		3401		3401	

Table A.9.1 *Duration of program interruptions (cont.).*

	Haz. Ratio	*p*	*Haz. Ratio*	*p*	*Haz. Ratio*	*p*	*Haz. Ratio*	*p*	*Haz. Ratio*	*p*
⋮	⋮	⋮	⋮	⋮	⋮	⋮	⋮	⋮	⋮	⋮
Control variables:										
GDP per capita	1.00006	0.03	1.00003	0.36	1.00005	0.16	1.00006	0.03	1.00003	0.35
	0.00003		*0.00003*		*0.00003*		*0.00003*		*0.00003*	
Democracy	0.98676	0.14	0.99072	0.31	0.98992	0.28	0.99248	0.42	0.98959	0.27
	0.00898		*0.00916*		*0.00921*		*0.00929*		*0.00938*	
Missing scale	1.16062	0.70	1.64416	0.19	1.47503	0.31	1.61328	0.23	1.43665	0.35
	0.45038		*0.62440*		*0.56595*		*0.64101*		*0.55647*	
Reserves/imports	0.99163	0.33	0.98638	0.14	0.98655	0.15	0.98912	0.36	0.98615	0.15
	0.00856		*0.00921*		*0.00916*		*0.01177*		*0.00961*	
Trade/GDP	0.99525	0.01	0.99689	0.07	0.99571	0.02	0.99670	0.05	0.99822	0.71
	0.00181		*0.00171*		*0.00175*		*0.00170*		*0.00479*	
Debt service/	1.00019	0.96	1.00070	0.87	0.99756	0.58	0.99601	0.33	0.98947	0.29
exports	*0.00369*		*0.00428*		*0.00444*		*0.00405*		*0.00984*	
Short-term debt	0.98447	0.25	0.99231	0.54	0.99511	0.69	0.97824	0.15	0.96236	0.09
	0.01327		*0.01245*		*0.01233*		*0.01477*		*0.02198*	
Short-term debt^2	1.00015	0.48	1.00011	0.60	1.00004	0.84	1.00041	0.17	1.00011	0.58
	0.00021		*0.00020*		*0.00020*		*0.00030*		*0.00020*	
$\ln(\rho)$	0.38294	0.00	0.37105	0.00	0.36929	0.00	0.37607	0.00	0.37292	0.00
	0.02471		*0.02441*		*0.02448*		*0.02466*		*0.02466*	
Observations	3401		3401		3401		3401		3401	

Weibull regression – proportional hazard metric. Note: Standard errors in italics. Hazard ratios presented in the proportional hazards metric (hazard ratios greater than one reduce the expected duration). Regional fixed effects not reported.

Table A.9.3 *Frequency of waivers.*

	Coef. *Std. Err.*	*p*	*Coef.* *Std. Err.*	*p*	*Coef.* *Std. Err.*	*p*	*Coef.* *Std. Err.*	*p*	*Coef.* *Std. Err.*	*p*
Unmet conditions	0.27	0.00	0.26	0.00	0.26	0.00	0.27	0.00	0.25	0.00
	0.04		*0.04*		*0.04*		*0.04*		*0.03*	
Scope of conditions	0.17	0.00	0.15	0.00	0.16	0.00	0.16	0.00	0.15	0.00
	0.03		*0.02*		*0.03*		*0.03*		*0.02*	
US aid	1.3×10^{-3}	0.58								
	2.4×10^{-3}									
U.S bank exposure			1.0×10^{2}	0.00						
			2.7×10^{1}							
US exports					6.4×10^{-3}	0.01				
					2.4×10^{-3}					
UN voting (S-US)							−1.39	0.08		
							0.80			
US alliance portfolio									3.52	0.06
									1.88	
Interactions with:										
Trade/GDP	4.8×10^{-5}	0.07	−1.25	0.00	-6.8×10^{-5}	0.01	-4.5×10^{-3}	0.50	−0.04	0.02
	2.6×10^{-5}		*0.35*		2.5×10^{-5}		6.7×10^{-3}		*0.02*	
Debt service/exports	-2.2×10^{-4}	0.11	−2.24	0.03	-1.8×10^{-4}	0.01	0.07	0.01	−0.01	0.70
	1.4×10^{-4}		*1.04*		6.2×10^{-5}		*0.03*		*0.03*	
Short-term debt	-9.4×10^{-5}	0.41	2.02	0.07	1.3×10^{-4}	0.03	0.10	0.04	−0.27	0.00
	1.1×10^{-4}		*1.12*		5.7×10^{-5}		*0.05*		*0.09*	
Control variables:										
⋮	⋮	⋮	⋮	⋮	⋮	⋮	⋮	⋮	⋮	⋮
$\ln(\alpha)$	−0.32		−0.46		−0.38		−0.34		−0.41	
	0.19		*0.20*		*0.20*		*0.19*		*0.20*	
α	0.73		0.63		0.68		0.71		0.66	
	0.14		*0.13*		*0.14*		*0.14*		*0.13*	
Observations	608		608		608		602		608	
LR $\chi^2(17)$	221.72		243.96		228.68		223.28		233.12	
Prob > χ^2	0.00		0.00		0.00		0.00		0.00	
Pseudo R^2	0.15		0.16		0.15		0.15		0.16	
Log likelihood	−635.36		−624.24		−631.88		−628.59		−629.66	

Table A.9.3 *Frequency of waivers (cont.).*

	Coef. *Std. Err.*	p	*Coef.* *Std. Err.*	p	*Coef.* *Std. Err.*	p	*Coef.* *Std. Err.*	p	*Coef.* *Std. Err.*	p
⋮	⋮	⋮	⋮	⋮	⋮	⋮	⋮	⋮	⋮	⋮
Control variables:										
GDP per capita	-1.1×10^{-4}	0.07	-3.6×10^{-4}	0.00	-1.6×10^{-4}	0.01	-1.3×10^{-4}	0.04	-6.4×10^{-5}	0.29
	$\mathit{6.3 \times 10^{-5}}$		$\mathit{9.5 \times 10^{-5}}$		$\mathit{6.3 \times 10^{-5}}$		$\mathit{6.3 \times 10^{-5}}$		$\mathit{6.1 \times 10^{-5}}$	
Democracy	−0.01	0.28	−0.01	0.47	−0.01	0.52	−0.01	0.44	0.00	0.85
	0.01		*0.01*		*0.01*		*0.01*		*0.01*	
Missing scale	0.98	0.05	0.86	0.07	1.08	0.03	1.16	0.03	0.86	0.08
	0.50		*0.48*		*0.48*		*0.52*		*0.49*	
Reserves/imports	−0.01	0.44	−0.02	0.27	−0.02	0.20	−0.01	0.51	−0.03	0.17
	0.02		*0.02*		*0.02*		*0.02*		*0.02*	
Trade/GDP	−0.01	0.01	0.00	0.35	0.00	0.19	−0.01	0.01	0.01	0.29
	0.00		*0.00*		*0.00*		*0.00*		*0.01*	
Debt service/exports	−0.01	0.04	−0.01	0.07	−0.01	0.25	−0.01	0.35	−0.01	0.38
	0.01		*0.01*		*0.01*		*0.01*		*0.02*	
Short-term debt	-1.6×10^{-3}	0.94	4.0×10^{-3}	0.84	-1.8×10^{-2}	0.34	3.3×10^{-2}	0.18	1.0×10^{-1}	0.01
	$\mathit{2.0 \times 10^{-2}}$		$\mathit{1.9 \times 10^{-2}}$		$\mathit{1.9 \times 10^{-2}}$		$\mathit{2.5 \times 10^{-2}}$		$\mathit{3.8 \times 10^{-2}}$	
Short-term debt^2	-8.9×10^{-5}	0.80	-1.7×10^{-4}	0.61	1.1×10^{-4}	0.74	-1.0×10^{-3}	0.06	1.1×10^{-4}	0.74
	$\mathit{3.4 \times 10^{-4}}$		$\mathit{3.3 \times 10^{-4}}$		$\mathit{3.3 \times 10^{-4}}$		$\mathit{5.6 \times 10^{-4}}$		$\mathit{3.3 \times 10^{-4}}$	
Constant	−1.41	0.00	−1.27	0.00	−1.48	0.00	−1.65	0.00	−2.48	0.00
	0.37		*0.35*		*0.36*		*0.37*		*0.82*	
$\ln(\alpha)$	−0.32		−0.46		−0.38		−0.34		−0.41	
	0.19		*0.20*		*0.20*		*0.19*		*0.20*	
α	0.73		0.63		0.68		0.71		0.66	
	0.14		*0.13*		*0.14*		*0.14*		*0.13*	
Observations	608		608		608		602		608	
LR $\chi^2(17)$	221.72		243.96		228.68		223.28		233.12	
Prob > χ^2	0.00		0.00		0.00		0.00		0.00	
Pseudo R^2	0.15		0.16		0.15		0.15		0.16	
Log likelihood	−635.36		−624.24		−631.88		−628.59		−629.66	

Negative binomial regression. Note: Standard errors in italics. Regional fixed effects not reported.

References

Abbott, Kenneth W. and Snidal, Duncan. 2000. Hard and Soft Law in International Governance. *International Organization*, 54(Summer), 421–456.

Abdelal, Rawi. 2007. *Capital Rules: The Construction of Global Finance*. Cambridge, MA: Harvard University Press.

Acemoglu, Daron and Robinson, James A. 2005. *Economic Origins of Dictatorship and Democracy*. Cambridge University Press.

Achen, Christopher H. 2006. Institutional Realism and Bargaining Models. In: Thomson, Robert, Stokman, Frans N., Achen, Christopher H. and König, Thomas (eds), *The European Union Decides*. Cambridge University Press.

Alesina, Alberto, Angeloni, Ignazio and Shuknecht, Ludger. 2005. What Does the European Union Do? *Public Choice*, 123(June), 275–319.

Alter, Karen. 2006. Private Litigants and the New International Courts. *Comparative Political Studies*, 39, 22–49.

Bagwell, Kyle and Staiger, Robert W. 2002. *The Economics of the World Trading System*. Cambridge, MA: MIT Press.

Banks, Jeffrey and Weingast, Barry R. 1992. The Political Control of Bureaucracies under Asymmetric Information. *American Journal of Political Science*, 36(May), 509–524.

Barnett, Michael and Finnemore, Martha. 2004. *Rules for the World: International Organizations in Global Politics*. Ithaca: Cornell University Press.

Barro, Robert J. and Lee, Jong-Wha. 2005. IMF programs: Who is Chosen and what are the Effects? *Journal of Monetary Economics*, 52(7), 1245–1269.

Barton, John H., Goldstein, Judith L., Jostling, Timothy E. and Steinberg, Richard H. 2006. *The Evolution of the Trade Regime: Politics, Law, and Economics of the GATT and the WTO*. Princeton University Press.

Bayard, Thomas O. and Elliott, Kimberly Ann. 1994. *Reciprocity and Retaliation in U.S. Trade Policy*. Washington, DC: Institute for International Economics.

Bayne, Nicholas and Putnam, Robert. 1984. *Hanging Together: Cooperation and Conflict in the Seven-Power Summits*. Cambridge, MA: Harvard University Press.

Bird, Graham and Rowlands, Dane. 2002. Do IMF Programmes Have a Catalytic Effect on Other International Capital Flows? *Oxford Development Studies*, 30(3), 229–249.

Blustein, Paul. 2001. *The Chastening: Inside the Crisis that Rocked the Global Financial System and Humbled the IMF*. New York: Public Affairs.

Blustein, Paul. 2005. *And the Money Kept Rolling In (and Out): Wall Street, the IMF, and the Bankrupting of Argentina*. New York: Public Affairs.

Borchardt, Klaus-Dieter. 2000. *The ABC of Community Law*. Luxembourg: Office for Official Publications of the European Communities.

Boughton, James M. 2001. *Silent Revolution: The International Monetary Fund, 1979–1989*. Washington, DC: International Monetary Fund.

Bown, Chad P. 2004. On the Economic Success of GATT/WTO Dispute Settlement. *Review of Economics and Statistics*, 86(3), 811–823.

Bown, Chad P. 2005. Participation in WTO Dispute Settlement: Complainants, Interested Parties and Free Riders. *World Bank Economic Review*, 19(2), 287–310.

Braumoeller, Bear F. 2004. Hypothesis Testing and Multiplicative Interaction Terms. *International Organization*, 58(4), 807–820.

Broz, J. Lawrence and Hawes, Michael Brewster. 2006. U.S. Domestic Politics and International Monetary Fund Policy. In: Hawkins *et al.* (2006).

Buchanan, Allen and Keohane, Robert O. 2004. The Preventive Use of Force: A Cosmopolitan Institutional Proposal. *Ethics and International Affairs*, 18, 1–22.

Bull, Hedley. 1977. *The Anarchical Society: A Study of Order in World Politics*. New York: Columbia University Press.

Burnside, Craig and Dollar, David. 2000. Aid, Policies, and Growth. *American Economic Review*, 90(4), 847–868.

Busch, Marc L. and Reinhardt, Eric. 2000. Bargaining in the Shadow of the Law: Early Settlement in GATT/WTO Disputes. *Fordham International Law Journal*, 24(1–2), 158–172.

Busch, Marc L. and Reinhardt, Eric. 2002. Testing International Trade Law: Empirical Studies of GATT/WTO Dispute Settlement. In: Kennedy, Daniel M. and Southwick, James D. (eds), *The Political Economy of International Trade Law: Essays in Honor of Robert Hudec*. New York: Cambridge University Press.

Busch, Marc L. and Reinhardt, Eric. 2003. Developing Countries and the GATT/WTO Dispute Settlement. *Journal of World Trade*, 37(4), 719–735.

Busch, Marc L., Reinhardt, Eric and Shaffer, Gregory. 2010. Does Legal Capacity Matter: A Survey of WTO Members. *World Trade Review*, forthcoming.

Calvert, Randall L. 2001. The Rational Choice Theory of Social Institutions: Cooperation, Coordination, and Communication. In: Banks, Jeffrey and Hanushek, Eric (eds), *Modern Political Economy: Old Topics, New Directions*. Cambridge University Press.

Calvert, Randall L., McCubbins, Mathew D. and Weingast, Barry R. 1989. A Theory of Political Control and Agency Discretion. *American Journal of Political Science*, 33(August), 588–611.

Carrubba, Clifford J. 2005. Courts and Compliance in International Regulatory Regimes. *Journal of Politics*, 67(3), 669–689.

Carrubba, Clifford J., Gabel, Matthew and Hankla, Charles R. 2008. Judicial Behavior under Political Constraints: Evidence from the European Court of Justice. *American Political Science Review*, 102, 435–452.

Chwieroth, Jeffrey M. 2009. *Capital Ideas: The IMF and the Rise of Financial Liberalization*. Princeton University Press.

Coase, Ronald. 1960. The Problem of Social Cost. *Journal of Law and Economics*, 3(October), 1–44.

Cohen, Benjamin J. 1986. *In Whose Interest? International Banking and American Foreign Policy*. New Haven: Yale University Press.

Cohen, Benjamin J. 1998. *The Geography of Money*. Ithaca: Cornell University Press.

Copelovitch, Mark S. 2004. *Private Debt Composition and the Political Economy of IMF Lending*. Paper 04–05. Weatherhead Center for International Affairs, Harvard University, Cambridge, MA.

Copelovitch, Mark S. 2005. *Global Governance in Changing Markets: Private Debt and the Politics of International Monetary Fund Lending*. Ph.D. thesis, Department of Government, Harvard University.

Copelovitch, Mark S. 2010. *The International Monetary Fund in the Global Economy: Banks, Bonds, and Bailouts*. Cambridge University Press.

Crombez, Christophe. 2003. The Democratic Deficit in the European Union. *European Union Politics*, 4, 101–120.

Cukierman, Alex and Tommasi, Mariano. 1998. When Does It Take a Nixon to Go to China? *American Economic Review*, 88(March), 180–197.

Davis, Christina L. 2003. *Food Fights Over Free Trade: How International Institutions Promote Agricultural Trade Liberalization*. Princeton University Press.

Davis, Christina L. 2010. *Why adjudicate? Enforcing Trade Rules*. Manuscript. Princeton University.

De Gregorio, José, Eichengreen, Barry, Ito, Takatoshi and Wyplosz, Charles. 1999. *An Independent and Accountable IMF*. Geneva Reports on the World Economy, no. 1. London: Centre for Economic Policy Research.

Diebold, William, Jr. 1952. *The End of the ITO*. Essays in International Finance, vol. XVI. Princeton, NJ: International Finance Section, Department of Economics and Social Institutions, Princeton University.

Dollar, David and Pritchett, Lant. 1998. *Assessing Aid. What Works, What Doesn't and Why*. New York: Oxford University Press.

Downs, George W., Rocke, David M. and Barsoom, Peter N. 1996. Is the Good News about Compliance Good News for Cooperation? *International Organization*, 50, 379–406.

Downs, George W., Rocke, David M. and Barsoom, Peter N. 1998. Managing the Evolution of Multilateralism. *International Organization*, 52(Spring), 397–419.

Drazen, Allan. 2002. *Conditionality and Ownership in IMF Lending: A Political Economy Approach*. Discussion Paper 3562. Center for Economic Policy Research.

Dreher, Axel. 2004. The Influence of IMF Programs on the Reelection of Debtor Governments. *Economics and Politics*, 16, 53–75.

Dreher, Axel and Jensen, Nathan M. 2007. Independent Actor or Agent? An Empirical Analysis of the Impact of US Interests on IMF Conditions. *Journal of Law and Economics*, 50, 105–124.

Dreher, Axel and Vaubel, Roland. 2004. The Causes and Consequences of IMF Conditionality. *Emerging Markets Finance and Trade*, 40, 26–54.

Dreher, Axel, Marchesi, Silvia and Vreeland, James Raymond. 2008. The political economy of IMF forecasts. *Public Choice*, 137(1), 145–171.

Easterly, William. 2001. *The Elusive Quest for Growth: Economists Adventures and Misadventures in the Tropics*. Cambridge and London: MIT Press.

Edwards, Sebastian. 2005 (March). *Capital Controls, Sudden Stops and Current Account Reversals*. Working Paper 11170. NBER.

Eichengreen, Barry J., Gupta, Poonam and Mody, Ashoka. 2006 (April). *Sudden Reversals and IMF-Supported Programs*. Working Paper 06/101. IMF.

Fang, Songying. 2005. *International Institutions and Bargaining*. Ph.D. thesis, Department of Political Science, University of Rochester.

Farrell, Henry and Hèritier, Adrienne. 2003. Formal and Informal Institutions under Codecision: Continuous Constitution-Building in Europe. *Governance*, 16(4), 577–600.

Farrell, Henry and Hèritier, Adrienne. 2004. Interorganizational Cooperation and Intraorganizational Power: Early Agreements under Codecision and Their Impact on the Parliament and the Council. *Comparative Political Studies*, 37(10), 1184–1212.

Feldstein, Martin. 1998. Refocusing the IMF. *Foreign Affairs*, 77(March/April), 20–33.

Franchino, Fabio. 2007. *The Powers of the Union: Delegation in the EU*. Cambridge University Press.

Fratzscher, Marcel and Reynaud, Julien. 2007. *Is IMF Surveillance Even-handed?* Mimeo. European Central Bank.

Gardner, Richard. 1980. *Sterling-Dollar Diplomacy in Current Perspective: The Origins and the Prospects of Our International Economic Order*. 3rd edn. New York: Columbia University Press.

Garrett, Geoffrey and Smith, James McCall. 2002. *The Politics of WTO Dispute Settlement*. Manuscript. UCLA.

Garrett, Geoffrey and Weingast, Barry R. 1993. Ideas, Interests, and Institutions: Constructing the European Community's Internal Market. In: Goldstein, Judith, and Keohane, Robert O. (eds), *Ideas and Foreign Policy: Beliefs, Institutions, and Political Change*. Ithaca: Cornell University Press.

Gartzke, Erik, Jo, Dong-Joon and Tucker, Richard. 1999. *The Similarity of UN Policy Positions, 1946–96*. 2.5 edn. www.vanderbilt.edu/˜rtucker/data/a_˜nity/un/similar.

Gilpin, Robert. 1981. *War and Change in World Politics*. Cambridge University Press.

Gold, Joseph. 1972. *Voting and Decision in the International Monetary Fund: An Essay on the Law and Practice of the Fund*. Washington, DC: International Monetary Fund.

Goldstein, Morris. 2001. *IMF Structural Conditionality: How Much Is Too Much?* Working Paper 01–04. Institute for International Economics, Washington.

Gould, Erica R. 2003. Money Talks: Supplementary Financiers and International Monetary Fund Conditionality. *International Organization*, 57(Summer), 551–586.

Gould, Erica R. 2006. *Money Talks: The International Monetary Fund, Conditionality, and Supplementary Financiers*. Stanford University Press.

Grieco, Joseph M. 1990. *Cooperation Among Nations: Europe, America, and Non-tariff Barriers to Trade*. Ithaca: Cornell University Press.

Guzman, Andrew T. and Simmons, Beth A. 2005. Power Plays and Capacity Constraints: The Selection of Defendants in WTO Disputes. *Journal of Legal Studies*, 34, 557–598.

Hawkins, Darren G., Lake, David A., Nielson, Daniel L. and Tierney, Michael J. (eds). 2006. *Delegation and Agency in International Organizations*. New York: Cambridge University Press.

Hayes-Renshaw, Fiona and Wallace, Helen. 1997. *The Council of Ministers*. New York: St. Martin's Press.

Heckman, James. 1979. Sample Selection Bias as a Specification Error. *Econometrica*, 47(1), 153–161.

Helleiner, Eric. 1994. *States and the Reemergence of Global Finance: From Bretton Woods to the 1990s*. Ithaca: Cornell University Press.

Henning, C. Randall. 1998. Systemic Conflict and Regional Monetary Integration: The Case of Europe. *International Organization*, 52, 537–573.

Hills, Carla A., Peterson, Peter G. and Goldstein, Morris. 1999. *Safeguarding Prosperity in a Global Financial System: The Future International Financial Architecture*. Report. Council on Foreign Relations and Institute for International Economics, Washington, DC.

Hirschman, Albert O. 1970. *Exit, Voice, and Loyalty: Responses to Decline in Firms, Organizations, and States*. Cambridge, MA: Harvard University Press.

Hoekman, Bernard M., Mattoo, Aaditya and English, Philip (eds). 2002. *Development, Trade, and the WTO: A Handbook*. Washington, DC: World Bank.

Horn, Henrik, Mavroidis, Petros C. and Nordström, Hakan. 1999 (December). *Is the Use of the WTO Dispute Settlement System Biased?* Discussion Paper 2859. CEPR, London.

Hudec, Robert E. 1993. *Enforcing International Trade Law: The Evolution of the Modern GATT Legal System*. Salem, NH: Butterworth Legal Publishers.

Independent Evaluation Office. 2003. *The IMF and Recent Capital Account Crises: Indonesia, Korea, Brazil*. Report. International Monetary Fund, Washington, DC.

Independent Evaluation Office. 2004. *The IMF and Argentina, 1991–2001*. Report. International Monetary Fund, Washington, DC.

Independent Evaluation Office. 2009. *IMF Performance in the Run-Up to the Current Financial and Economic Crisis: An Issues Paper*. Report. International Monetary Fund, Washington, DC.

International Monetary Fund. 2005. *Review of the 2002 Conditionality Guidelines*. Washington, DC.

Ivanova, Anna, Mayer, Wolfgang, Mourmouras, Alex and Anayiotos, George. 2003. *What Determines The Implementation of IMF-Supported Programs?* Working Paper 03–8. International Monetary Fund.

Jensen, Nathan M. 2004. Crisis, Conditions, and Capital: The Effects of International Monetary Fund Agreements on Foreign Direct Investment Inflows. *Journal of Conflict Resolution*, 48(2), 194–210.

Kahler, Miles. 1990. The United States and the International Monetary Fund: Declining Influence or Declining Interest? Pages 91–114 of: Karns, Margaret and Mingst, Karen (eds), *The United States and Multilateral Institutions: Patterns of Changing Instrumentality and Influence*. Boston: Unwin Hyman.

Kalandrakis, Tasos. 2006. Proposal Rights and Political Power. *American Journal of Political Science*, 50(April), 441–448.

Kennedy, Paul. 1987. *The Rise and Fall of the Great Powers: Economic Change and Military Conflict from 1500 to 2000*. New York: Random House.

Keohane, Robert O. 1984. *After Hegemony: Cooperation and Discord in the World Political Economy*. Princeton University Press.

Keohane, Robert O. and Nye, Joseph S. 1977. *Power and Interdependence: World Politics in Transition*. Boston: Little, Brown and Co.

Keohane, Robert O., Moravcsik, Andrew and Slaughter, Anne-Marie. 2000. Legalized Dispute Resolution: Interstate and Transnational. *International Organization*, 54(3), 457–488.

Khan, Mohsin S. and Sharma, Sunil. 2001. *IMF Conditionality and Country Ownership of Programs*. Working Paper 01/142. International Monetary Fund.

Kirshner, Jonathan. 1995. *Currency and Coercion: The Political Economy of International Monetary Power*. Princeton University Press.

Knack, Stephen. 2001. Aid Dependence and the Quality of Governance: Cross-Country Empirical Tests. *Southern Economic Journal*, 68(2), 310–329.

König, Thomas, Luetgert, Brooke and Dannwolf, Tanja. 2006. Quantifying European Legislative Research: Using CELEX and PreLex in EU Legislative Studies. *European Union Politics*, 7(4), 553–574.

Koremenos, Barbara. 2006. Contracting around International Uncertainty. *American Political Science Review*, 99(November), 549–565.

Koremenos, Barbara, Lipson, Charles and Snidal, Duncan. 2001. The Rational Design of International Institutions. *International Organization*, 55(Autumn), 761–800.

Kraft, Christian. 2007. *Joining the WTO: The Impact of Trade, Competition and Redistributive Conflicts on China's Accession to the World Trade Organization*. Frankfurt am Main: Peter Lang.

Krasner, Stephen D. (ed.). 1983. *International Regimes*. Ithaca: Cornell University Press.

Krasner, Stephen D. 1985. *Structural Conflict: The Third World against Global Liberalism*. Berkeley: University of California Press.

Krasner, Stephen D. 1999. *Sovereignty: Organized Hypocrisy*. Princeton University Press.

Kreps, David M. 1990. *Game Theory and Economic Modeling*. Oxford University Press.

Krugman, Paul. 1997. What Should Trade Negotiators Negotiate About? *Journal of Economic Literature*, 35, 113–120.

Kucik, Jeffrey and Reinhardt, Eric. 2008. Does Flexibility Promote Cooperation? An Application to the Global Trade Regime. *International Organization*, 62(3), 477–505.

Kuziemko, Ilyana and Werker, Eric. 2006. How Much Is a Seat on the Security Council Worth? Foreign Aid and Bribery at the United Nations. *Journal of Political Economy*, 114, 905–930.

Kydland, Finn E. and Prescott, Edward C. 1977. Rules Rather than Discretion: The Inconsistency of Optimal Plans. *Journal of Political Economy*, 85, 437–491.

Maggi, Giovanni. 1999. The role of multilateral institutions in international trade cooperation. *American Economic Review*, 89(1), 190–214.

Mansfield, Edward D. and Reinhardt, Eric. 2003. The Multilateral Determinants of Regionalism: The Effects of the GATT/WTO on the Formation of Preferential Trading Arrangements. *International Organization*, 57(4), 826–862.

Mansfield, Edward D., Milner, Helen V. and Rosendorff, B. Peter. 2000. Free to Trade: Democracies, Autocracies, and International Trade. *American Political Science Review*, 94(June), 305–321.

Martin, Lisa L. 2000. *Democratic Commitments: Legislatures and International Cooperation*. Princeton University Press.

Martin, Lisa L. 2006. Distribution, information, and delegation to international organizations: the case of IMF conditionality. In: Hawkins *et al.* (2006).

Mattilla, Mikko and Lane, Jan-Erik. 2001. Why Unanimity in the Council? A Roll Call Analysis of Council Voting. *European Union Politics*, 2(1), 31–52.

McCubbins, Mathew D. and Schwarz, Thomas. 1984. Congressional Oversight Overlooked: Police Patrols versus Fire Alarms. *American Journal of Political Science*, 28(February), 165–179.

McKelvey, Richard D. 1976. Intransitivities in Multidimensional Voting Models and Some Implications for Agenda Control. *Journal of Economic Theory*, 12, 472–482.

McKelvey, Richard D. 1979. General conditions for global intransitivities in formal voting models. *Econometrica*, 47, 1085–1112.

Mearsheimer, John J. 2001. *The Tragedy of Great Power Politics*. New York: Norton.

Meltzer, Allan H. 2000 (March). *Final Report*. Report. International Financial Institution Advisory Commission (Meltzer Commission).

Meunier, Sophie. 2005. *Trading Voices: The European Union in International Commercial Negotiations*. Princeton University Press.

Mikesell, Raymond Frech. 1994. *The Bretton Woods Debates*. Essays in International Finance, vol. 192. International Finance Section, Department of Economics, Princeton University.

Milesi-Ferretti, Gian Maria. 1995. The Disadvantage of Tying Their Hands: On the Political Economy of Policy Commitments. *Economic Journal*, 105(433), 1381–1402.

Milgrom, Paul and Roberts, John. 1992. *Economics, Organization and Management*. Englewood Cliffs, NJ: Prentice Hall.

Miller, Gary J. 1992. *Managerial Dilemmas: The Political Economy of Hierarchy*. Cambridge University Press.

Milner, Helen V. 1997. *Interests, Institutions, and Information: Domestic Politics and International Relations*. Princeton University Press.

Milner, Helen V. and Moravcsik, Andrew (eds). 2009. *Power, Interdependence and Non-State Actors in World Politics: Research Frontiers*. Princeton University Press.

Mody, Ashoka and Saravia, Diego. 2006. Catalysing Private Capital Flows: Do IMF Programmes Work as Commitment Devices? *Economic Journal*, 843–867.

Moe, Terry M. 1990. Political Institutions: The Neglected Side of the Story. *Journal of Law, Economics, and Organization*, 6, 213–254.

Moore, Michael O. 2002. Commerce Department Antidumping Sunset Reviews: A First Assessment. *Journal of World Trade*, 36(2), 675–698.

Moore, Michael O. 2005. "Facts Available" Dumping Allegations: When Will Foreign Firms Cooperate in Antidumping Petitions? *European Journal of Political Economy*, 21(1), 185–204.

Moravcsik, Andrew. 1998. *The Choice for Europe: Social Purpose and State Power from Messina to Maastricht*. Ithaca: Cornell University Press.

Mundell, Robert. 1960. The Monetary Dynamics of International Adjustment under Fixed and Flexible Exchange Rates. *Quarterly Journal of Economics*, 74, 227–257.

Mussa, Michael. 1998. *Argentina and the Fund: From Triumph to Tragedy*. Washington, DC: Institute for International Economics.

Mussa, Michael and Savastano, Miguel. 1999. The IMF Approach to Economic Stabilization. *NBER Macroeconomics Annual*, 14.

Nielson, Daniel L. and Tierney, Michael J. 2003. Delegation to International Organizations: Agency Theory and World Bank Environmental Reform. *International Organization*, 57(Spring), 241–276.

North, Douglass C. and Weingast, Barry R. 1989. Constitutions and Commitment: The Evolution of Institutions Governing Public Choice in Seventeenth-Century England. *Journal of Economic History*, 69, 803–832.

Oatley, Thomas and Yackee, Jason. 2000. *Political Determinants of IMF Balance of Payments Lending: The Curse of Carabosse?* Mimeo. University of North Carolina at Chapel Hill.

Odell, John. 2000. *Negotiating the World Economy*. Ithaca: Cornell University Press.

Oye, Kenneth. 1992. *Economic Discrimination and Political Exchange: World Political Economy in the 1930s and 1980s*. Princeton University Press.

Pauly, Louis W. 1997. *Who Elected the Bankers? Surveillance and Control in the World Economy*. Ithaca: Cornell University Press.

Polak, Jacques J. 1991. *The Changing Nature of IMF Conditionality*. Essays in International Finance, vol. 184. Department of Economics, Princeton University.

Pollack, Mark A. 2003. *The Engines of Integration: Delegation, Agency and Agenda Setting in the European Union*. New York: Oxford University Press.

Pollack, Mark A. 2006. Delegation and Discretion in the European Union. In: Hawkins *et al*. (2006).

Pop-Eleches, Grigore. 2009. *From Economic Crisis to Reform: IMF Programs in Latin America and Eastern Europe*. Princeton University Press.

Powell, Robert. 1991. Absolute and Relative Gains in International Relations Theory. *American Political Science Review*, 85(4), 1303–1320.

Powell, Robert. 1999. *In the Shadow of Power: States and Strategies in International Politics*. Princeton University Press.

Prusa, Thomas and Skeath, Susan. 2002. The Economic and Strategic Motives for Antidumping Filings. *Weltwirtschaftliche Archiv*, 138(3), 389–413.

Przeworski, Adam. 1991. *Democracy and the Market; Political and Economic Reforms in Eastern Europe and Latin America*. New York: Cambridge University Press.

Przeworski, Adam and Vreeland, James Raymond. 2000. The effect of IMF programs on economic growth. *Journal of Development Economics*, 62, 385–421.

Przeworski, Adam and Vreeland, James Raymond. 2002. A Statistical Model of Bilateral Cooperation. *Political Analysis*, 10, 101–112.

Przeworski, Adam, Alvarez, Michael E., Cheibub, Jose Antonio and Limongi, Fernando. 2000. *Democracy and Development: Political Institutions and Well-Being in the World, 1950–1990*. Cambridge Studies in the Theory of Democracy. CCambridge University Press.

Putnam, Robert D. 1988. Diplomacy and Domestic Politics. *International Organization*, 42(Summer), 427–461.

Reinhardt, Eric. 2001. Adjudication without Enforcement in GATT Disputes. *Journal of Conflict Resolution*, 45(April), 174–195.

Rosendorff, B. Peter and Milner, Helen V. 2001. The Optimal Design of International Trade Institutions: Uncertainty and Escape. *International Organization*, 55(Autumn), 829–858.

Ruggie, John G. 1993. Multilateralism: The Anatomy of an Institution. In: Ruggie, John G. (ed.), *Multilateralism Matters: The Theory and Praxis of an Institutional Form*. New York: Columbia University Press.

Schelling, Thomas C. 1960. *The Strategy of Conflict*. Cambridge, MA: Harvard University Press.

Schneider, Christina J. 2009. *Conflict, Negotiation and European Union Enlargement*. Cambridge University Press.

Schneider, Gerald and Cederman, Lars-Erik. 1994. The Change of Tide in Political Cooperation: A Limited Information Model of European Integration. *International Organization*, 48(Autumn), 633–662.

Shaffer, Gregory. 2005. Can WTO Technical Assistance and Capacity Building Serve Developing Countries? *Wisconsin International Law Journal*, 23.

Shaffer, Gregory. 2009. Developing Country Use of the WTO Dispute Settlement System: Why It Matters, the Barriers Posed, and Its Impact on Bargaining. In: Hartigan, James (ed.), *Trade Disputes and the Dispute Settlement Understanding of the WTO: An Interdisciplinary Assessment*. Bingley: Emerald.

Shepsle, Kenneth A. 1979. Institutional Arrangements and Equilibrium in Multidimensional Voting Models. *American Journal of Political Science*, 23, 23–57.

Signorino, Curtis S. and Ritter, Jeffrey M. 1999. Tau-b or Not Tau-b: Measuring the Similarity of Foreign Policy Positions. *International Studies Quarterly*, 43(1), 115–144.

Silberston, Aubrey. 2003. Anti-dumping Rules – Time for Change? *Journal of World Trade*, 37(6), 1063–1081.

Snidal, Duncan. 1991. Relative Gains and the Pattern of International Cooperation. *American Political Science Review*, 85(3), 701–726.

Stasavage, David. 1997. The CFA Franc Zone and Fiscal Discipline. *Journal of African Economies*, 6(1), 132–167.

Stasavage, David. 2003. *The Political Economy of a Common Currency: The CFA Franc Zone Since 1945*. Burlington, VT: Ashgate.

Steinberg, Richard. 2002. In the Shadow of Law or Power? Consensus-Based Bargaining and Outcomes in the GATT/WTO. *International Organization*, 56(2), 339–374.

Steinberg, Richard. 2004. Judicial Law-Making at the WTO: Discursive, Constitutional, and Political Constraints. *American Journal of International Law*, 98.

Steinwand, Martin C. and Stone, Randall W. 2008. The International Monetary Fund: A Review of the Recent Evidence. *Review of International Organizations*, 3(June), 123–149.

Steunenberg, Bernard. 2001. Enlargement and Institutional Reform in the European Union: Separate or Connected Issues? *Constitutional Political Economy*, 12, 349–368.

Steunenberg, Bernard and Selck, Torsten J. 2006. Testing Procedural Models of EU Legislative Decision-Making. In: Thomson, Robert, Stokman, Frans N., Achen, Christopher H. and König, Thomas (eds), *The European Union Decides*. Cambridge University Press.

Stiglitz, Joseph E. 2002. *Globalization and Its Discontents*. New York: W. W. Norton.

Stone, Randall W. 1996. *Satellites and Commissars: Strategy and Conflict in the Politics of Soviet-Bloc Trade*. Princeton University Press.

Stone, Randall W. 2002. *Lending Credibility: The International Monetary Fund and the Post-Communist Transition*. Princeton University Press.

Stone, Randall W. 2004. The Political Economy of IMF Lending in Africa. *American Political Science Review*, 98, 577–591.

Stone, Randall W. 2008. The Scope of IMF Conditionality. *International Organization*, 62(Fall), 589–620.

Stone, Randall W. 2009a. IMF Governance and Financial Crises with Systemic Importance. Pages 369–74 of: Lamdany, Ruben and Martinez-Diaz, Leonardo (eds), *Studies of IMF Governance: A Compendium*. Washington, DC: Independent Evaluation Office of the IMF.

Stone, Randall W. 2009b. Institutions, Power and Interdependence. In: Milner, Helen, and Moravcsik, Andrew (eds), *Power, Interdependence and Non-State Actors in World Politics: Research Frontiers*. Princeton University Press.

Stone, Randall W. 2009c. Risk in International Politics. *Global Environmental Politics*, 9(3), 40–60.

Strange, Susan. 1988. *States and Markets*. London: Pinter.

Tallberg, Jonas. 2003. The Agenda-Shaping Powers of the EU Council Presidency. *Journal of European Public Policy*, 10, 1–19.

Taylor, John B. 2007. *Global Financial Warriors: The Untold Story of International Finance in the Post-9/11 World*. New York: W. W. Norton.

Thacker, Strom C. 1999. The High Politics of IMF Lending. *World Politics*, 52(October), 38–75.

Tsebelis, George. 1994. The Power of the European Parliament as a Conditional Agenda-Setter. *American Political Science Review*, 88(March), 128–142.

Tsebelis, George and Garrett, Geoffrey. 2000. Legislative Politics in the European Union. *European Union Politics*, 1(February), 9–36.

Tsebelis, George and Garrett, Geoffrey. 2001. The Institutional Foundations of Interngovernmentalism and Supranationalism in the European Union. *International Organization*, 55, 357–390.

Vaubel, Roland. 1986. A Public Choice Approach to International Organization. *Public Choice*, 51, 39–57.

Voeten, Erik. 2001. Outside Options and the Logic of Security Council Action. *American Political Science Review*, 95(December), 845–858.

Voeten, Erik. 2005. The Political Origins of the Legitimacy of the United Nations Security Council. *International Organization*, 59(Fall), 527–557.

Voeten, Erik. 2008. The Impartiality of International Judges: Evidence from the European Court of Human Rights. *American Political Science Review*, 102(4), 417–433.

Vreeland, James Raymond. 2003. *The IMF and Economic Development*. Cambridge: Cambridge University Press.

Waltz, Kenneth N. 1979. *Theory of International Politics*. New York: McGraw-Hill.

Weber, Max. 1946. Politics as Vocation [Politik als Beruf]. In: Gerth, H.H., and Mills, C. Wright (eds), *From Max Weber: Essays in Sociology*. New York: Oxford University Press. Originally published by Duncker and Humblodt, Munich (1919).

Whittome, L. Alan. 1995. Report on Fund Surveillance of Mexico, 1993–94. IMF: Executive Board Staff Report (March 23).

Williamson, John. 1983. *IMF Conditionality*. Washington: Institute for International Economics.

Williamson, Oliver E. 1985. *The Economic Institutions of Capitalism: Firms, Markets, Relational Contracting*. New York: Free Press.

Woods, Ngaire. 2006. *The Globalizers, The IMF, The World Bank and their Borrowers*. Ithaca: Cornell University Press.

Index